I0474281

First Job,
Great Job

AMERICA'S HOTTEST BUSINESS
LEADERS SHARE THEIR SECRETS

Authors Choice Press

San Jose New York Lincoln Shanghai

First Job, Great Job
America's Hottest Business Leaders Share Their Secrets

All Rights Reserved © 1996, 2000 by Jason R.Rich

No part of this book may be reproduced or transmitted in any form or by any means, graphic, electronic, or mechanical, including photocopying, recording, taping, or by any information storage or retrieval system, without the permission in writing from the publisher.

Authors Choice Press
an imprint of iUniverse.com, Inc.

For information address:
iUniverse.com, Inc.
620 North 48th Street, Suite 201
Lincoln, NE 68504-3467
www.iuniverse.com

Originally published by Macmillan Spectrum

ISBN: 0-595-13131-X

Printed in the United States of America

Table of Contents

INTRODUCTION v

1. **DEBBI FIELDS** Founder & President, Mrs. Fields Cookies **1**

2. **HOWARD LINCOLN** Chairman, Nintendo of America, Inc. **11**

3. **NICK VALENTI** President & CEO, Restaurant Associates Corp. **19**

4. **ANTHONY P. CONZA** President, Founder & CEO, Blimpie International **25**

5. **STEPHANIE SONNABEND** President, Sonesta Hotels **33**

6. **LOREN J. HULBER** President & CEO, Day-Timers, Inc. **39**

7. **NICOLE MILLER** President, Founder & Designer, Nicole Miller, Inc.
   BUD KONHEIM CEO, Nicole Miller, Inc. **51**

8. **BILL DeVRIES** President & CEO, Foot Locker **59**

9. **NATASHA ESCH** President, Wilhelmina Models **65**

10. **SIDNEY SWARTZ** Chairman, CEO & President, The Timberland Company **73**

11. **JOHN J. McDONALD** President, Casio, Inc. **81**

12. **JACK CHADSEY** President & CEO, Sunglass Hut International, Inc. **89**

13. **RUSSELL A. BOSS** President & CEO, A.T. Cross Company **97**

14. **JIM McCANN** President & CEO, 1-800 FLOWERS **103**

15. **DR. AMAR BOSE** Founder, Chairman & Technical Director, Bose Corporation **111**

16. **JERRY YANG** Co-Founder & Chief Yahoo, Yahoo! Inc.
TIM KOOGLE President & CEO, Yahoo! Inc. **117**

17. **JEFF TAYLOR** Founder, CEO Interactive Division,
The Monster Board (TMP Worldwide) **129**

18. **MICHAEL DAVIS** President & CEO, Motown Animation **137**

19. **JERI TAYLOR** Creator/Executive Producer, Star Trek: Voyager **143**

20. **SARINA SIMON** President, Philips Media Home and
Family Entertainment **151**

21. **MICHAEL D. ZISMAN** Executive Vice President & CEO,
Lotus Development Corp. **159**

22. **JANE COOPER** President, Paramount Parks **167**

23. **DOUG LOGAN** Commissioner, Major League Soccer **175**

24. **SCOTT FLANDERS** President, Macmillan Publishing USA **181**

25. **TOM JACKSON** Founder, The Career Development Team, Inc.,
Chairman, Equinox Corporation **189**

THE TOP 10 THINGS YOU JUST GOTTA DO 195

INDEX 205

INTRODUCTION

When I started working on this book, I really didn't know where it was going to lead or exactly what information would be included within it. My goal was to provide a reliable source of information to people, like you, who are about to graduate from college or grad school, and are starting to look for a job or launch a career. The obvious thing to do when you're in this situation is to start sending out résumés, just like everyone else, and hope for the best. Being armed with the right information, however, before starting this process will mean the difference between getting yourself just any old job that may lead nowhere and finding your ultimate dream job that will allow you to pursue a productive, successful, and extremely enjoyable career. *First Job, Great Job* gives you the insider secrets from some of the top business leaders in America who have been very successful in a variety of fields.

I know from firsthand experience that the job search can be a very confusing, frustrating, and intimidating time in someone's life. After all, you're going from the structured and sheltered environment of school, and probably for the first time in your life, you're being forced to make decisions that will impact the rest of your life. Now that's pretty intimidating, especially if you have absolutely no clue about what type of career you want to pursue. Despite what you've been told by educators, your parents, your friends, and others, if you're thinking that you have to "find yourself" before choosing a career, that's pretty normal. Very few people graduate from school with a passion and a career path already laid out. With little or no experience in the business world, how are you supposed to make the right career decisions that will impact the rest of your professional life? The answer: Proceed with caution and don't make hasty decisions—make educated decisions. This book will teach you how to do this. Let the advice offered by the business leaders within this book act as a compass to help you find direction and set your career goals.

First Job, Great Job: America's Hottest Business Leaders Share Their Secrets isn't going to be like all of those other "get a job" books on the market, because what this one offers is a direct link to some extremely successful people, all of whom at one point in their lives were in exactly the same boat as you are in today. These people not only discovered how to get their first job, but they've mastered what it takes to reach the top.

This book provides you with a unique opportunity—to learn directly from the people who are leading some of America's most popular and successful companies into the next millennium. Even if your parents are "well connected" and are friendly with many successful business people, chances are you won't have the opportunity to sit down with too many of them in-person and get some serious career advice. From this book, you'll get answers to some of your job search-related questions, and at the same time, you'll receive extremely practical and useful advice from people in the know. These are the people actually doing the hiring in today's job market.

What this book offers to you is direct access to these business leaders' thoughts, ideas, and personal experiences. Who better to offer career advice than people who have already reached a high level of success? No matter what type of career you're interested (or think you're interested) in pursuing, by reading *First Job, Great Job* you'll obtain information that's based on decades' worth of real-world, firsthand experience in the workplace—and that's a resource that no single career guidance counselor, educator, parent, friend, or relative can offer to you.

Unfortunately, there are neither easy answers nor an exact series of steps that you can follow in order to get yourself a job and launch your career. Every single person has a totally different job search experience. What you'll get from this book is information

about what you can expect at each step in the job search process, and you'll read tips and suggestions from business leaders about what they think you should and shouldn't do as your quest for a job begins.

Let's face it, not everyone is cut out to be a President, CEO, or founder of a multi-million-dollar company. Even if you don't have aspirations to be a top-level executive, you're probably going to find that the information in this book will help to inform and inspire you toward success, in whatever it is that you choose to pursue.

When you begin your job search, your goal is to get yourself a job and to begin your career (duh). The key word here is *your* career. One piece of advice without exception every single business leader interviewed for this book offered was that if you're going to be successful in whatever it is that you choose to do, it has got to be something that you want to do, and that you really love. Don't settle for just any job offer that comes along, and don't let anyone force you into accepting a job that you don't think you'll be happy and productive in. This may mean going against the advice of people you love and respect, but in the end, it's your life, and you have to make decisions that will allow you to lead your own life, make your own mistakes, and achieve your own success.

What's the difference between the people interviewed in this book and every other human on the planet? That's easy. The people who are today's business leaders have discovered what it takes to follow their dreams and make them come true. Other than that, everyone in this book is just like you and me. Do you have to be a genius or come from a wealthy family to be successful?

Absolutely not! I hope, by reading this book, you'll begin to believe that if you can dream it, you can do it—through **hard work, dedication, patience,** and **persistence**. It's very simple. Just because you have a college diploma, even if it's from a top-notch Ivy League school, nobody owes you anything. If you're not willing to put forth the effort to get yourself a great job and then succeed in that position, then it's nobody's fault but your own if you wind up in a boring, dead-end job. Sorry, but that's how the real world operates, and if you go into the real world understanding this, you've got a much better chance for success. Whatever you do, never give up and don't settle.

To get yourself a great job, you've got to be informed, persistent, dedicated, and have a passion for whatever it is that you want to do. Sure, an education is critical, and previous work experience (internships, summer jobs, part-time jobs, etc.) will be helpful, but there are many very well educated people who wind up in dead-end jobs. This book provides you with the knowledge you'll need to help you avoid falling into a career path that leads to misery.

If you have access to the Internet's World Wide Web, then you have an opportunity to discover a lot more information about many of the companies featured in this book.

To access the Information Superhighway (a.k.a. the Net), you'll need a computer that's equipped with a modem. Next, you'll need access to the Internet. Internet access is available via any of the major on-line services, such as America Online, The Microsoft Network, and CompuServe. You can also obtain access to the Internet from a local Internet service provider in your city

(any computer store will be able to provide you with the phone number of a service provider in your area). Often you can pay a flat, low monthly fee for unlimited Internet access from a local service provider. If you don't own a personal computer, try visiting your college's computer center or library, or the public library in your town.

Now, as you read this book, you're going to learn about the thoughts and opinions of many different types of people, from many different backgrounds, all of whom work in very different industries and occupations. To get the most out of what this book offers, I suggest you read **all** of the interviews and keep an open mind. Then, as you begin your job search, reread the interviews that pertained to you or interested you, and apply the advice that fits your personality and the occupation you hope to pursue.

Everyone (yes, you too)—no matter what race, religion, sex, or type of background you have—can achieve success and land a great job. It might not happen overnight, in a week, or even in a month, but if you're persistent and you open your eyes to the opportunities around you, then you can and you will ultimately achieve your goals! It all starts with a dream, a set of goals, and a plan.

Finally, many people have asked me how I chose the people interviewed within this book. Well, I began with the goal of finding the Presidents, CEOs, and founders of companies I thought were exciting and interesting. I looked at what company's products I use, and then I asked a bunch of friends, who are also in their mid and late 20s, what companies they'd be interested in reading about in this type of book. (Yes, I wear Timberland shoes and boots. I wear Nicole Miller ties. I use a

Day-Timer Planner to keep my life organized, and I have Lotus 1-2-3 on my computer's hard disk. I'm a fan of the *Star Trek: Voyager* TV series, and when I'm using the Internet, I often connect to Yahoo! to help me navigate the Web. I bought my sunglasses at Sunglass Hut, and I've ordered flowers from 1-800-FLOWERS—and the people I've sent them to have always loved 'em. I play Nintendo video games, and when I've needed new sneakers, the place I go to at the mall is Foot Locker. Get the picture?)

My goal was to offer a selection of business leaders, all with different backgrounds and who work in different industries, in order to provide you with the broadest range of experience and advice to draw upon. I believe that I've achieved my objective in finding a group of extremely interesting people. I know I've learned a lot from interviewing each of them, and I'm sure

you'll learn a lot and be inspired by reading what each person had to say.

I have interviewed dozens of top business leaders. I've taken dozens of hours' worth of interviews, and have compiled this information into a format that's easy to read. Now all you have to do is read it and follow at least some of the advice that's offered. If you happen to find one of the interviews, or a specific piece of advice, to be exceptionally useful as you begin your job search, please drop me a note via e-mail, and let me know what information was particularly helpful. Send your comments, via the Internet, to me at the following e-mail address:

jr7777@aol.com

Good luck, and may all of your goals and dreams come true!

Here's a listing of Web site addresses
you might be interested in visiting

First Job, Great Job	http://www.firstjob.com
Nintendo of America	http://www.nintendo.com
Day-Timers	http://www.daytimer.com
Nicole Miller	http://www.nicolemiller.com
Wilhelmina Models	http://www.wilhelmina.com
Casio	http://www.casio-usa.com
1-800-FLOWERS	http://www.1800flowers.com
Yahoo!	http://www.yahoo.com
The Monster Board	http://www.monster.com
Star Trek: Voyager	http://www.paramount.com
Sonesta Hotels	http://www.travelfair.com/sonesta.htm
Blimpie	http://www.blimpie.com
Sunglass Hut International	http://www.sunglasshut.com
Restaurant Associates	http://www.restaurant-assoc.com
Philips Media Home and Family Entertainment	http://www.media.philips.com
Lotus Development	http://www.lotus.com
Paramount Parks (Canada's Wonderland)	http://canada.ibm.net:80/wonderland
Paramount Parks (Great America)	http://www.rollercoaster.com/pga
Paramount Parks (Kings Island)	http://www.pki.com
Major League Soccer	http://www.infortel.com/mls/index.htm
Macmillan Publishing	http://www.mcp.com
JobTrack	http://www.jobtrak.com
CareerMosaic	http://www.careermosaic.com

DEBBI FIELDS

FOUNDER & PRESIDENT
Mrs. Fields Cookies

COMPANY BACKGROUND

Debbi Fields founded Mrs. Fields Cookies in 1977 with no money, no college degree, and no experience. "I set out to re-create the cookies that I had made at home, but I wanted to offer them to everyone who wanted fresh, warm chocolate chip cookies that were made from the very best ingredients available. That was my dream." Today, Mrs. Fields Cookies has over 700 locations and continues to grow. Mrs. Fields Cookies operates company-owned locations, plus has franchises throughout America and in other countries including Saudi Arabia, Singapore, the Philippines, and Hong Kong. "This business started out in my kitchen at home. My dream was to do something that I loved."

PERSONAL HISTORY

Debbi Fields has turned her passion for baking cookies into a multimillion-dollar business. Her drive and determination have allowed her to succeed against all odds. Unlike many of the business leaders featured in this book, she didn't come from a wealthy family, have a top-notch

Mrs. Fields ®

"If you really believe you can do something, you'll somehow find a way. You will overcome all obstacles and challenges."

education, work her way up the corporate ladder in a corporate environment, or enter into an already established family business. Debbi's company started with a dream and succeeded because of her positive attitude and hard work.

"I am the youngest of five sisters. My father was a welder, and what I learned from him is that whatever I do, I have to love it, and be the best at it as I possibly can. Growing up, I loved making cookies. It was my hobby. I was always the kid with the cookies. I went through two years of college trying to decide what I wanted to do, and during that time I decided that I wanted to do what I really loved, and that was making cookies and sharing them."

TOPICS COVERED IN THIS INTERVIEW

☞ **How the right attitude can lead to success**

☞ **Setting career goals**

☞ **The questions you should ask during a job interview**

☞ **Landing the job you interview for**

☞ **Creating a résumé that works**

☞ **Advice for working women**

Back in 1977, you began to transform a dream into an international business. Is this still possible today if someone has a unique idea?

"I think anything is possible. It's all based on your attitude. I don't believe that ability is the most important possession that someone can have. There are a lot of people who are very smart and well educated, but they don't succeed. What allows people to move mountains and make dreams come true is their attitude. If you really believe you can do something, you'll somehow find a way. You will overcome all obstacles and challenges. If you want to start your own business, I recommend that you first take a job working in the industry you want to get into. Learn about other companies' procedures and systems, so you can pick up the tricks of the trade, then take that information and later go out on your own."

When did you launch your career, and what did you learn from that experience?

"I was never a gifted student in school. I used to daydream a lot, and was bored by school. The best advice I can give someone who is still in school is that they should be the best that they can be, and get everything out of it that they possibly can. An education is something that you can take with you. It's something that nobody can ever take away. Apply yourself, challenge yourself, and be the best student you can be. You don't have to be an A student, as long as you're doing your best, and you know inside that you've given it everything you've got. Some of us weren't destined to be geniuses in physics, but we may be great at English or another subject.

"I began working at the age of 13. I worked for the Oakland A's baseball team, and was the first female foul line ball catcher, third base side. I was absolutely awful at catching the balls, but I really tried hard. From this experience, I became very comfortable being in front of large groups of people. At the time, I also shared my cookies with everyone on the team and with the people who worked at the stadium. One benefit of this job was that I got to spend time with a lot of very famous people, like Reggie Jackson. What I learned from this was that there was no difference between famous people and nonfamous people, except that the famous people had a talent to do something extremely well. As a result of this job, I got to travel a lot at a young age, plus do things that I would not have otherwise had the opportunity to do.

"When I was 15, I got my second job, working at a major department store. I worked after school and evenings. I started out as a clerk, and after a while, I was promoted to being in charge of the entire boys' department. I approached that job the same way I approached my view of life. That boys' department became my own personal department. I remember how important it was for me to make people feel welcome. I wanted them to feel special when they came into my department. I took a lot of pride in my work, and kept all of the displays looking organized and perfect. My department not only represented the department store, but it represented me personally. This was something that management took notice of. When someone gets their first job, don't set out to be average. Be spectacular! Management always notices those people who go the extra mile. If you want to move up, get a promotion, obtain more responsibility, and make more money, all you have to do is exceed expectations. Be on time. Be kind. Be honest, and give more than people expect you to give. Follow this philosophy and amazing things will happen!"

What advice can you offer young people setting career goals?

"Take baby steps. Take on small tasks and accomplish lots of small things that allow you to work closer to achieving your ultimate goals. Don't take on everything at once. When I interview someone applying for a job

"When someone gets their first job, don't set out to be average. Be spectacular! Management always notices those people who go the extra mile."

"If you want to move up, get a promotion, obtain more responsibility, and make more money, all you have to do is exceed expectations. Be on time. Be kind. Be honest, and give more than people expect you to give. Follow this philosophy and amazing things will happen!"

at my company, I always ask the applicant, 'What are your goals?' I am always looking for people who have goals. I don't care what their goals are, as long as they have them. They may want a job to earn enough money to buy a car and pay for their car insurance. That's a goal. A goal can be materially based. If I know the applicants have a goal for themselves, I know that, eventually, they're going to achieve it. If someone responds that he or she has no goals, it means that person doesn't have any reason to go to work in the morning. I am a firm believer that goals give someone a reason to wake up in the morning. Your goals should make you happy and they should be achievable.

"I started working when I was 13 because my parents didn't have enough money to send me on a ski trip with my friends. I wanted the best ski gear, the best outfit, and more than anything, I wanted to go on that trip. My first reason for getting a job was to earn enough money so I could go on that school ski trip. Later, my goal for working was to buy myself a car when I turned 16. As soon as I turned 16, I paid cash for my orange Volkswagen bug. Looking back, these were small things to work toward, but at the time, they were very important to me, and achieving these goals gave me incredible confidence in myself and my abilities. Money is not the most important thing, but

having the goal of earning enough money to go on that ski trip and, later, to buy a car were stepping stones for building my confidence and teaching me to set bigger goals.

"Another time early in my life when I set goals for myself was when I was in school and achieving poor grades. I attended a junior college with one goal in mind. I wanted to get one A. I knew that if I could earn an A, others would follow. Through hard work and determination, I earned that first A, and then additional As followed."

What tips can you offer on finding a job that you'll love?

"Examine what you love to do, and analyze your personality. Don't just apply for any job that comes along. Find job opportunities that have something to do with what you really love doing. That way, you'll be really excited about your job. If you love fashion, for example, then work in a store that sells fashion, or find a job in the fashion industry. After analyzing your personality, if you determine that you don't like to be around people, then target your job search to opportunities that place you in more of an office environment. Don't set yourself up for doing things you know you don't like. Don't settle. Most importantly, challenge yourself to constantly learn on the job, and to be the best at what you do."

What types of questions should the applicant ask during an interview?

"During an interview, find out about the work schedule. You want to know if the schedule is flexible. Inquire about what the expectations are for the job. Are there uniforms involved? Who pays and cares for the uniforms? What kind of on-the-job training is available? What opportunities are there to move upwards within the company? How often do employees receive performance reviews? How does the employer rate employees? What does the employer look for (dependability, salesmanship, etc.)? Also, find out how long it will take to get your first promotion.

"Before accepting a position, you want to determine how far up you'll be able to go within that company. There's a restaurant chain, called Outback Steakhouse, that starts you off in an entry-level position as a waiter/waitress, but you work your way up the system. Ultimately, based on your performance, capabilities, and your attitude, you can become a managing partner and have an ownership in the business, which allows you to do really well financially. Those types of opportunities exist. I started out as a mini-

mum wage worker. The whole concept behind minimum wage is to start you off in an entry-level position. You shouldn't ever be willing to stop there. Once you take an entry-level position, start working toward where you'll go next."

Once you find job opportunities, how do you land the job?

"It all comes down to attitude. You want to make sure that you show up for an interview on time. Even if you're dropping by a potential employer's office just to pick up a job application and schedule an interview, look the part and dress professionally. Always put your best self forward. If you have to fill out an application, fill it out neatly. Ask up front if a company has the types of job openings that you're looking for, and if they do, find out from the company what the best approach to take is in order to submit your résumé and obtain an interview.

"Select the places that you want to work for. The places that look like they're going to be the most fun are the places you want to apply to. When you actually go for your interview, show up early, and look spectacular. You don't need to wear expensive clothes, but you have to look neat, clean, and pressed. If you're not willing to put forth your best efforts, you're going to wind up with an average job that you won't like. During the actual interview, be open and honest with the employer. Tell them why you want to work at their company, and why it's important for them to hire you."

"Select the places that you want to work for. The places that look like they're going to be the most fun are the places you want to apply to."

What advice can you share about putting together a résumé?

"Think of your résumé as being an extension of yourself. You want your résumé to represent you in the most positive light. What I like to see on a résumé is a listing of work-related experiences, including how long an applicant remained at each job, and what positions they held. As an employer, when you hire someone, you want them to stay with your company for a long time, because you're going to put the time and effort into training them. As a result, when I see from someone's résumé that they've jumped from job to job, I immediately want to know why. Having excellent references is also important, but your urge to grow and to be challenged is most important. What it comes down to, however, is that your attitude is everything.

"The best references come from your ex-bosses. It's important never to burn a bridge, because the people you used to work for make excellent references. Your co-workers and work record should also speak well of you. Your willingness to work hard and your integrity are traits that employers definitely look at. Remember, working hard and being taken advantage of on the job are two separate issues."

What are the worst mistakes you've seen people make when applying for a job?

"They don't take their job search seriously. They come into an interview and don't seem to care. If someone brings to an interview an attitude that they don't care whether or not they get a job, then they're blowing it for themselves. I fully understand that most people don't have a lot of money, especially when they first get out of school, so I don't

care what they wear as long as they are clean. Take a shower and iron your clothes before an interview so that you look your best. A lot of people arrive late for their interview or show up totally unprepared. That's not acceptable."

To be successful, what skills must you have that you may not have been taught in school?

"You have to learn about risk taking, and how to build up your self-esteem and self-confidence. The best things you can do to help boost your confidence and self-esteem are to do things that challenge you. Participating in organized team sports is great for learning how to work as a team and for building up confidence. When it comes to self-esteem, never lose sight of your own personal abilities and gifts. Always remember that giving up is the easiest thing that you can do. If, for example, your grades are suffering in school, work on improving one subject at a time and focus your efforts. One of the things young people have to learn is that they don't have to give in to peer pressure. It's okay for you to be special and unique and not follow the crowd."

How can someone overcome nervousness during a job interview?

"Being nervous is okay. It's a human emotion and it's normal. My recommendation for young people is to get involved in drama.

Participating in drama classes, for example, forces you to perform in front of a group and helps to improve your presentation skills and overcome stage fright. Participating in a debating class or on a debate team is also extremely useful for learning to present yourself and your thoughts in front of other people." Many cities in America also have clubs known as Toast Masters. These groups are designed to help people develop the skills necessary to communicate well with others. Groups like Toast Masters help people feel more comfortable speaking in front of people, plus offer excellent networking opportunities.

"In an actual job interview situation, it's okay to say, 'I am so excited about this job. I really want it, and it's very important to me, but I'm very nervous. Please forgive my nervousness.' Once you tell people that, not only will they try to help you through it, you'll also be less nervous."

Other than having a positive attitude, what other qualities do you possess that have allowed you to succeed?

"I won't take no for an answer. I won't give up. I know what my limitations are, but at the same time, I never know if I'll succeed at something unless I try. My greatest failure is to not try. I'd rather say to myself that I did the best that I could, but this isn't working, than to never have tried at all. Too many people make a decision about what they can and can't do, without actually trying. That's a big mistake. I think everyone possesses the potential to be great, but they have to be willing to try.

"At one of the Mrs. Fields Cookies locations, I was told by management that they were going to fire the entire staff

because sales were way down. I was told that the employees had no enthusiasm or spirit. I walked into the store and the product was perfect, plus the store was so meticulously clean, you could eat off the floor. Immediately, I saw that these people had a lot of pride in their work, and that they really cared. If people care, they can do anything. Obviously, the problem was that they couldn't sell because they didn't know how to. When I walked into the store, everyone was so quiet. I asked one of the employees if she thought that she could sell a cookie if the store offered a buy one, get one free special to the customer. That employee looked at me and said, 'Yeah, I think so.' I said, 'Let me try it first. If I succeed, then you can give it a try.' When I made this offer to a customer, that customer was very excited and bought the cookie. I then sent the employee to assist the next customer. She timidly explained the special offer to the customer, and that customer also accepted it. I knew all along that all of the customers who came into the store and walked up to the counter were going to buy a cookie whether or not we had a special offer, but I wanted to boost the confidence of the employees and encourage them to take a risk and try selling. Selling is one of the hardest things that someone can do. It's an art. Many people are afraid of being rejected.

"I wound up spending the day at that store, doing various things to boost the confidence of the employees, and at the same time, raising the stakes of what they had to accomplish. I was giving away lots of product, but I was teaching them how to sell, and they were learning. In the end, these people had a record-breaking day. During a

typical day, that location didn't earn more than $700. I told them that if by the end of the day, they reached sales of $2,000, I'd take them all out to dinner at the restaurant of their choice. By that night, they surpassed this goal using their newly acquired selling skills. In one day, I taught the staff how to sell, and that Mrs. Fields Cookies location became very successful. As long as people care, they can do anything. Sometimes, they just have to be shown how to succeed."

What advice do you have for women entering the workplace?

"For me, it was difficult because people didn't take me seriously. I never let being a woman limit myself. Just because I was a woman who didn't have a good education or a lot of money, I wasn't going to let these things stop me from going into the cookie business. When I was trying to secure financing, banks rejected me constantly, but that didn't mean I was going to stop asking. I was determined. Determination is the most important thing. If you're about to start looking for a job, you have to wake up in the morning and say to yourself, 'I'm going to find a job in a profession that I'm good at,

where I can continue to learn and grow! When I get the job, I am going to be one of the company's best employees…period.' Someone's sex or race doesn't matter. If you set yourself up to succeed, you will, and it's all based on your attitude. Don't let people not take you seriously. If you accidentally take a job where your talents aren't appreciated, find a different job where you are appreciated. Don't give up. I run into too many people who say that they hate their job. I tell them not to settle. Find a job that they enjoy."

You come from a big family, and now have several children of your own. What advice can you give to women about managing their career and their family life?

"First of all, I have always believed that Mrs. Fields Cookies is an extension of my family. It was very important for me to have my children, but I also love working. If you're going to be successful at work and manage a family, you have to be prepared to plan. There are so many responsibilities that you're going to face. I worry about the kids, what's for dinner, the house, and other family-related issues, plus I worry about work. I figure that anyone who can be a mom can do anything. Being a mom is about endless love, challenging yourself, and organization. Those same skills are needed to be successful in business. If you're a mom and a business person, don't be afraid to ask for help. Have your kids help out around the house. My 14-year-old daughter is skilled at helping with the laundry. One of my other daughters is responsible for feeding the pets. I feel that it's

"If you set yourself up to succeed, you will, and it's all based on your attitude."

"I feel that it's important to involve the family in managing the daily responsibilities of the family."

important to involve the family in managing the daily responsibilities of the family.

"If you're very career-minded, but you fall in love and want to start a family, don't limit yourself. Make sure that your family is on track, then pursue your career. If you don't take care of your family, your career suffers. If there are problems at home, or your kids are sick, your body may be at work, but your mind will still be at home. It's really important to have a support system. Find people you trust who you can call upon to watch your kids if they have to stay home from school because they're sick, or work it out in advance with your employer, so that you can work from home on days when you have to be with your children. If I'm not taking care of my family, then my business suffers too."

LAST WORD

"I won't take no for an answer. I won't give up. I know what my limitations are, but at the same time, I never know if I'll succeed at something unless I try. My greatest failure is to not try."

HOWARD LINCOLN CHAIRMAN
Nintendo of America, Inc.

COMPANY BACKGROUND

For many prospective employees, Nintendo represents a dream company. Whether someone is working in customer service, finance, marketing, or the legal department of Nintendo, everyone working for the company has one thing in common---they love playing video games!

America's first exposure to Nintendo home video games took place in 1985, when the 8-bit Nintendo Entertainment System (NES) was released. This gaming system found its way into over 30 million U.S. homes. The NES is now considered an antique, having been replaced by technology that's far more advanced and powerful. Nintendo

now offers the hand-held Game Boy, the 16-bit Super Nintendo Entertainment System (Super NES), and the Virtual Boy 3-D gaming system. Most recently, in fall 1996, Nintendo launched the 64-bit Nintendo 64 video game system.

Nintendo of America, Inc.'s current video game systems, along with games and accessories for these systems, are sold in more than 20,000 retail locations across America. The company also publishes a monthly magazine, called *Nintendo Power*, and operates one of the most popular on-line

forums on America Online (Keyword: Nintendo).

Nintendo of America is based in Redmond, Washington. Its parent company, Nintendo Co. Ltd., is based in Japan.

PERSONAL HISTORY

While growing up in Oakland, California, Howard Lincoln was involved with the Boy Scouts and his local church group. He

Nintendo®

11

> ## "My parents always encouraged me to be the best at whatever it was that I set out to do."

attended the University of California at Berkeley as an undergraduate, and went on to graduate from UC Berkeley's law school. Howard admits, however, that in his early college years he wasn't a very good student. In fact, in his early college years he flunked out of school, but was later readmitted.

After graduating from law school, Howard spent just under four years in the military, as an officer in the Judge Advocate General's Corps of the Navy. He strongly believes that his military experience represents the best education he has ever received.

Upon leaving the military, Howard went to work for a Seattle-based law firm. Within five years, in 1976, he was made a partner in that firm. Howard had become a successful lawyer but, by 1981, he found that his work lacked challenge and had become boring. It was around this time that he first met Mr. Minoru Arakawa, Nintendo of America's President.

As a lawyer, Howard believed that job referrals could come from any existing or past clients, so he treated all of his clients as if they were his biggest. "I always believed that if I did the very best work possible for all of my clients, I never knew where it would lead. Thus, I did first-class law work for my large and small clients. One of my clients in the early 1980s was a small trucking company that got itself involved in importing Nintendo arcade games. My client referred me to Nintendo, which was opening a

division in America and needed legal work done. From that referral, I began working for Nintendo as a lawyer, starting in 1982. Nintendo had about 30 employees and was not at all known in America. Since I was somewhat bored with my current legal work, I was prepared to take a risk and join Nintendo as an executive vice president. This was in 1983, and at the time, I was the managing partner at my law firm, and the other people at the firm thought I was totally nuts for leaving in order to work at a small company in a very risky industry."

In 1985, when Nintendo launched its first home video game system in America, it quickly become extremely successful, and Nintendo became a household name. In 1994, Howard was appointed chairman of Nintendo of America and placed on the board of directors of Nintendo Co. Ltd. in Japan.

As if running Nintendo wasn't the ultimate dream job, in 1992, when Nintendo chose to invest heavily in the purchase of the Seattle Mariners baseball team, Howard was put in charge of the acquisition, which Howard considers to be one of the true highlights of his career.

"I thrive on working in environments that are fast-moving and constantly changing. Every time Nintendo launches a new home video game system, such as the Nintendo 64, we bank the future success of the entire company on that launch."

**TOPICS COVERED
IN THIS INTERVIEW**

☞ **Setting career-related goals**

☞ **How early failures can lead to
success**

☞ **The importance of the education
that is taught in the military**

☞ **What qualities employers look for
in applicants**

☞ **Tips for making the best impression during the interview process**

☞ **Questions you should ask the
employer during the interview**

When did you begin setting career goals for yourself?

"I don't know that I ever really set goals and then measured my success based on the goals that I accomplished. I don't think that setting long-term goals led to my success. I have always been very competitive. I came from a family with a very modest financial back-ground. Nobody in my family had ever graduated from a university, so early on my goals were partially set by my parents, who did everything in their power so that I would have the opportunity to attend college. My parents always encouraged me to be the best at whatever it was that I set out to do.

"After college, I went on to law school, because I wasn't sure what I really wanted to do. I thought I might want to be an engineer, but I didn't have the mathematical back-ground. In college, I decided I'd become a lawyer, because I figured it was better than graduating from college and having a degree with no career goal or direction.

"While in school, I discovered the true secrets to success, which are hard work, concentration, and focus. It didn't take a rocket scientist to determine that to get into a good law school, I needed straight As in my junior and senior years in college. I also figured out that the people who did really well in law school would wind up with the best jobs, so I set out to achieve excellent grades in school. Once I figured this out I became goal-oriented, in that I knew I had to do well in college and in law school, so I guess that was my goal."

What lessons did you learn from your parents that led to your success?

"One piece of advice that my father told me, and I have since passed it along to my own son, is that in junior high and high school you might not be the most popular kid, but often it's the cool kids in school that wind up in a dead-end job, like pumping gas or flipping hamburgers. America needs people to pump gas, but my father told me that I didn't have to be one of those people. To have a career that would be more challenging and more enjoyable, I was told to concen-trate on working really hard. Being pushed to earn good grades in school helped to teach me that hard work leads to something worthwhile."

> *"When I flunked out, my father got me a job working at a gas station, and that was a revelation for me. I have nothing against people who work at gas stations, but it was when I held this job that I learned about the endless drudgery that most people experience in their lives."*

Howard's biggest lesson that ultimately helped him to achieve the level of success that he has today was flunking out of college. "When I flunked out, my father got me a job working at a gas station, and that was a revelation for me. I have nothing against people who work at gas stations, but it was when I held this job that I learned about the endless drudgery that most people experience in their lives. Once I experienced that defeat and was exposed to what the real world could be like, I returned to college, and I really focused myself by working hard."

Based on your early experiences, what do you think it takes to succeed?

"The secret to success is to work hard all of the time, and always do the best work that you can. These days, I work very long hours, and there is no substitute for that. You always have to be on the lookout for opportunities and take advantage of them. The final thing you need for success is luck. I am a very lucky person. Growing up, I had no idea that I would wind up working for a company that would become a household name or that I would have the opportunity to buy a Major League Baseball team. You can't just sit around waiting to get lucky. There's a saying, 'You have to make your own luck,' and I really believe this to be true. You can make your own luck by seizing opportunities and working hard."

Would you recommend that college graduates who don't have a clear direction for their future follow in your footsteps and join the military?

Howard is a firm believer in the education people acquire when they join the military. "I came from a generation where most employees worked for companies being run by people who fought in World War II, so those employers had a high respect for people coming out of the military. I strongly believe that the military is a great maturer of people. You learn self-discipline and leadership skills in a way that you never forget. For most people, including the ones who get shot at, the military becomes a very important and positive part of their life. When you come out of the military, and you're applying for jobs at companies being run by people who were also in the military, you will have an advantage, because the employers with the military experience know what qualities the military teaches, and most employers want these qualities in their employees."

How can college graduates find the best job opportunities available?

"The world is becoming a lot more competitive, and far fewer entry-level positions are available. Employers are seeing a lot of college graduates who are being forced to take jobs that are either outside of their areas of interest or that don't take full advantage of the level of education they have. The best advice I can give to recent graduates is that they must understand we're living in a tough and cruel world, but it is a world where people who work hard will achieve success. I think young people today don't understand how much flexibility they have in their lives. If they can't immediately get a job doing whatever it is they ultimately want to do, they should be willing to accept a job in a related field with the goal of either doing well in this new field or gaining the experience necessary that will allow them to obtain the job that they originally wanted."

As an employer, what qualities do you look for in applicants?

"I know when we hire people at Nintendo, we look for people who love our products, who have a good education, and who have good communication skills. We also look for people who are well mannered and enthusiastic. Dressing appropriately for a job interview is also critical. At Nintendo, our dress code is more casual than at some other companies, and I personally don't wear a tie, but I fully expect an applicant to come dressed in business attire for an interview.

"We look at many résumés. Everyone seems to have good grades, a good education, and some work experience, so what we concentrate on is what sets applicants apart, such as their personality and motivation. Young people have to understand that there is nothing wrong with looking a potential employer right in the eye. When you shake hands, use a firm grip. Showing respect, with

responses like 'Yes, sir' or 'No, sir,' also goes a long way in terms of separating yourself from the competition. If someone comes in for an interview, looks me in the eye, and enthusiastically says that they really want to work for Nintendo, and then they give specific reasons for wanting to work here, that person is going to be considered a much better candidate than someone who can't look me in the eye or muster up enough confidence to tell me why he or she should be hired. We look for people who are good video game players, since that's what we do. Someone who is a good player, plus has the skills and qualities that I've mentioned, will start in an entry-level position at Nintendo, but they won't remain there for too long, since we often promote people from within."

What type of information do you think is important to show on a résumé?

"I personally don't like goofy résumés. There is a fine line between a résumé that states facts fairly and tries to draw my eyes to it and a résumé that makes me think that the applicant is totally nuts. I don't hire anyone

"Young people have to understand that there is nothing wrong with looking a potential employer right in the eye. When you shake hands, use a firm grip."

"You can't just sit around waiting to get lucky. There's a saying, 'You have to make your own luck,' and I really believe this to be true."

based on their résumé. Generally, all résumés reflect a very positive image of the applicant, and they all pretty much look alike. What I look for on a résumé is information about the applicant's outside activities, and for things that make them stand out. If someone is going from one job to another, I am extremely interested in why the applicant is changing jobs. I want to know why they left their previous position. I don't like seeing big gaps on people's résumés, nor do I like finding out that they didn't include jobs on their résumé that didn't work out."

What do you expect from an applicant during the interview process?

Since Howard places less importance on résumés, he puts more emphasis on how people perform during the interview process. "In the interview, I really try to see if the chemistry is there, and if the applicant will fit well within the company. I have already used the résumé to choose the most qualified applicants, so now that I've narrowed down the search, I look at each applicant's personality, their strengths, and their weaknesses. I study an applicant's mannerisms as much as what they say. I watch the applicant's hands to determine now nervous they are, and I look at how much eye contact the applicant establishes. I also think a good sense of humor is important, and I like applicants to

answer the questions that are posed to them. Someone's personality and manners are what actually come out during an interview, and it's these traits that set people apart from one another. As I said before, most résumés from people applying for a specific job look alike, and all applicants come into an interview dressed pretty much the same way, so I look for what sets people apart in a positive way. Most of these things are intangible."

What questions should the applicant ask the employer during the interview?

"I think it's important for applicants to ask relevant questions about the company they're applying to. Ask intelligent questions. If I see someone who goes though their notes during an interview and has to choose what predetermined question they should ask next, I'm not as impressed as I am with someone who comes up with a few good questions off the top of their head during our conversation. I like to hear applicants say things like, 'I've been reading about your company and I'm fascinated by (*insert topic*). Can you explain it?' This shows that you're interested in the company, and you've done research. Now, you must demonstrate some interest in the answer. Also, ask questions about the people you'll be working with. Determine if you will enjoy working with these people. Before the interview and during it, try to learn as much about the company's strengths and weak-

"What I look for on a résumé is information about the applicant's outside activities, and for things that make them stand out."

"The biggest mistake someone can make is not having a good answer when I ask them why they want to work for my company. If they don't know why I should hire them, how am I supposed to know?"

nesses as you can. Is the company downsizing? Are sales for the company down in recent quarters? Learn about the company's recent performance, what the future of the company holds, and what risks are associated with working for the company. Is the company you're applying to part of a fast-moving and very risky industry that could fall apart quickly? Are you prepared to take that risk? Finding out as much as you can about a company will go a long way toward helping you determine if you'll ultimately enjoy the job before you accept it. This knowledge will also prepare you for what to expect once you begin working for the company."

Do you ever use trick questions during an interview in order to test an applicant?

"No. I don't think that's fair. Asking trick questions is like kicking an animal, and I find it offensive. I want the applicant to leave the interview thinking that I was gracious, perhaps probing, but very fair. Good leaders

are people who treat their employees decently, and I treat applicants how I treat all of my employees, and that's with respect." If an employer asks unfair or trick questions, that should give you, the applicant, some insight about how that company treats its employees, and that's something you want to know about before accepting a job.

If someone doesn't have a personal connection to someone at a company, to whom should a résumé be sent?

"Begin by sending a résumé to the human resources department at a company. This is where networking comes in handy. If I receive a résumé cold, without a personal referral, it almost automatically gets forwarded to human resources without getting any personal attention from me. I simply don't have time to read unsolicited résumés and respond to them. If the résumé comes with a personal referral from someone I know, however, then it has a much better chance of getting personal attention."

LAST WORD

"While in school, I discovered the true secrets to success, which are hard work, concentration, and focus." You have to also be willing to take risks in order to pursue your dreams and have a career that you enjoy. "You can make your own luck by seizing opportunities and working hard."

NICK VALENTI
PRESIDENT & CEO
Restaurant Associates Corp.

COMPANY BACKGROUND

Restaurant Associates Corp. is a New York-based company that owns and operates 125 restaurants. The company is divided into three divisions, two of which are chain restaurant operations--including 45 Mexican restaurants in California that operate under the name Acolpoco and 30 restaurants in New Jersey that operate under the name Charlie Brown's. The third division operates 50 individual, one-of-a-kind restaurants.

PERSONAL HISTORY

Having grown up in a family that owned and operated restaurants, Nick grew up knowing that he to wanted to be in the hospitality business. Throughout high school, he worked at a restaurant owned by his older brother. "I was always interested in the hospitality business, specifically the restaurant side of it. I liked the idea of having personal contact with the customers." Over 26 years ago, while attending New York City Community College, Nick went to work for Restaurant Associates Corp. "In spite of being told to get a variety of different work experiences at different companies, I have remained at Restaurant Associates for my entire career. I began my career in the management training program, which resulted in me being placed in a steward's position. I was responsible for buying and receiving products for the restaurant." From there, Nick went on to hold various managerial positions until he became the general manager of one of

RestaurantAssociates

TOPICS COVERED
IN THIS INTERVIEW

☞ What it takes to be successful in the restaurant (hospitality) industry

☞ The importance of job training programs

☞ Working for a restaurant chain versus an individual restaurant

☞ What applicants should look for when applying for a job at a restaurant

☞ Setting career-related goals

☞ Making the best impression with your résumé and during the job interview process

Restaurant Associates' restaurants. "From the time I began the training program until I became the general manager of a restaurant it took approximately 30 months. At the time, this restaurant generated about $1 million in revenue per year. Normally, a general manager holds that position for a year or two before being promoted. However, I took a different path and stayed at that restaurant for seven years, building its revenue to $6.5 million per year. This experience allowed me to learn the restaurant business backwards and forwards. Because the restaurant I was managing kept growing, the job kept my interest. My responsibilities kept changing and expanding."

Eventually, Nick took on a position as a multiunit supervisor, where he oversaw the operations of multiple restaurants owned by Restaurant Associates. That led him to a position where he began developing operations for the company. Soon after that, he became President of the company's restaurant division. He held this position for 12 years. Since 1994, Nick has held the position of CEO and President of the entire company.

What does it take for someone to be successful in the restaurant industry?

"First of all, you should have done well in school. That may sound simplistic, but restaurant employers want to see that you have demonstrated a strong commitment to your education. Secondly, in our industry, it is important that applicants obtain some practical experience while in school, for example, by working at a restaurant during their summer vacations. This is a difficult

"Good managers have to be able to work well with employees, plus have the ability to develop positive relationships with their customers."

> *"If you intend to be working for an organization or an individual, look at the opportunity from a long-term perspective."*

industry to work in. It is physically demanding and can often require long hours. We look for applicants who are capable of handling this challenge and are really interested in this industry."

In terms of personality traits, Nick believes that the most successful managers in his industry are those who are comfortable working with other people. "Good managers have to be able to work well with employees, plus have the ability to develop positive relationships with their customers. Someone working in this industry has to be able to convey a sense of hospitality and warmth, and they must have the urge to please their customers."

How important is a restaurant's training program for someone interested in this type of career?

"Training should not be rushed. I would recommend to anyone coming out of school that they should obtain as much specialized training as the company they're working for will provide. This training will serve you well for the rest of your career."

Nick believes that someone's first job can be working for either a restaurant chain or an individual restaurant. "At the entry level, someone is going to get a general exposure to the restaurant business no matter where they begin working. If at all possible, I would suggest experiencing more than one operation during your first few years in the industry. At Restaurant Associates, during my training program I was exposed to several

different types of operations, because the company owned both chains and individual restaurants. Had I joined a chain, like The Olive Garden, for example, the only exposure I would have gotten is how that chain operates."

In terms of ultimate success, is it better to launch your career working for a large restaurant chain or an individual restaurant?

"The industry has changed over the years. Now, someone who is a qualified manager can be extremely successful working for either a large chain or an individual restaurant. The chain industry has come up with some very innovative compensation programs, many of which allow managers to earn some form of equity involvement in the company they're working for. Independent restaurants have the ability to be more creative in terms of their compensation plans. If you intend to work for an organization or an individual, look at the opportunity from a long-term perspective. If you plan on spending your entire career in this industry and working your way up, you might ultimately have more potential for success working for a large organization where more types of opportunities will become available to you. If you're committed to going into your own restaurant business, you can also be extremely successful, but that requires a whole different set of skills and commitments."

> *"A company that trains its employees well almost always does well. For someone first entering this industry, the training aspect is paramount."*

What should the applicant look for when applying for a job in the restaurant industry?

"Begin by examining each company's history to determine if there's longevity there. An organization that turns over their restaurants and reconceptualizes them every few years, or opens up a number of locations but then closes a number of locations that's close to the number that were opened, is a situation you want to avoid. You want to look at the company's track record. Make sure that they've been in business for a while and that their concepts are able to withstand the test of time. You don't want to work for a restaurant that does a booming business for a year or two and then closes because the concept gets old. For someone looking for a entry-level position, you want to look for a company with stability and consistency."

The biggest thing applicants should look at when evaluating a job opportunity in the restaurant industry is the training program that will be available to them. "A company that trains its employees well almost always does well. For someone first entering this industry, the training aspect is paramount. There are a number of companies that will hire you out of school, but they'll throw you into a position and expect you to fend for yourself. That's not the type of business you want to work for."

How should someone go about setting realistic career-related goals when they're first starting a career in the restaurant industry?

"I would recommend talking to as many people who are already working in the industry as you can. Talk to people you know, and then visit some restaurants and strike up a conversation with the managers at those restaurants. You want to learn as much about what the industry is all about as you can, then set your goals based on the experiences you expect to have. When setting your goals, don't set a strict timeline for achieving those goals, because there are a lot of factors in this industry that can't be controlled."

Nick believes that once you've set your career-related goals, the best way to find the best job opportunities available is through networking. "Any time you can get a personal recommendation or introduction into a business, that's the best way to discover the best job opportunities available. I'd also recommend talking to people who are currently working in the type of job you want. If your initial goal is to become a general manager of a restaurant within a chain, you should make an effort to informally talk to a few of the managers who currently work for the chain you think you want to work for. Very often, those people will give you valuable advice and insight into the company."

Are there specific types of classes that can help someone interested in working within your industry get a head start?

"Aside from the technical courses that are offered at some schools relating to food and restaurant management, I think that courses that focus on practical experience or improving the student's interpersonal skills will prove to be useful. Courses that stress human resources and labor relations are also important. I would also recommend that if someone

"You want to learn the business as thoroughly as you can, because you'll be relating back to that early training experience a lot more often than you might think throughout your entire career."

has an opportunity to spend a semester abroad, they should take advantage of it."

What types of information should be incorporated into someone's résumé if they want to enter into the restaurant industry?

"The most important thing employers look for on a résumé is previous experience at successful restaurants or chains. We want to see that people have worked at successful operations and that they've made meaningful contributions. For someone coming out of school, this still applies when listing after-school, part-time, or summer jobs that they've held."

How can someone make the best impression during a job interview?

"Be sincere, be yourself, and don't make promises that you can't keep. Never treat a job interview like your entire life is riding on doing well in that interview. Also, don't try to be someone that you're not. It is important to go into an interview knowing what type of job you're interested in, but you must be flexible. Advise the interviewer that you have an interest in a specific job, but that you understand that the job might not be

available, so you'll be flexible. You want to show flexibility, but you want to make it clear where your ultimate interests lie."

The biggest mistake Nick has seen applicants make is overrepresenting their work experience. "On your résumé, and during the interview, you want to highlight your work experience, but you don't want to exaggerate your experiences or skills so that you won't be able to deliver."

What are the qualities that you possess that have allowed you to succeed?

"Commitment and loyalty. I accepted whatever work assignments I was given, and once I was given those assignments, I did my very best to get the job done. I feel that commitment and loyalty are two of the most important traits that someone can demonstrate. It's also important to show that you really enjoy what you're doing. If you enjoy your work, you will be much more successful."

One reason why getting restaurant-related experience while you're still in school is so important is because this industry isn't for everyone. You want to determine if this industry is right for you before you graduate and have to begin your career.

LAST WORD

"Once you enter into an industry, be fair to yourself and take the time to participate in whatever training programs are offered. You want to learn the business as thoroughly as you can, because you'll be relating back to that early training experience a lot more often than you might think throughout your entire career."

ANTHONY P. CONZA

PRESIDENT, FOUNDER & CEO
Blimpie International

COMPANY BACKGROUND

Blimpie International, Inc. was founded in 1984, when Tony Conza and two high-school buddies created and sold their first BLIMPIE submarine sandwich behind a store counter in Hoboken, New Jersey. Within a year, the first BLIMPIE franchise was sold. BLIMPIE now has over 1,300 franchised outlets in 44 states and around the world. In 1995, the company was ranked number 25 on *Forbes* magazine's list of the 200 Best Small Companies in America.

The company is also active in various charitable programs, including the Boys & Girls Clubs of America, donating food to children's events at the local level, and contributing over $250,000 to the organization's National Violence Prevention Program. BLIMPIE International was also the first major user or supplier to sell tuna that is caught in a way that does not endanger the lives of dolphins.

BLIMPIE outlets are opening at a rate of approximately 40 new locations per month. The chain is also expanding in Europe and Latin America. Corporate headquarters are in New York City and BLIMPIE International, Inc. trades on the NASDAQ National Market System under the symbol BMPE.

PERSONAL HISTORY

Anthony P. Conza established the first BLIMPIE sandwich shop with two of his high-school pals. Today, the company is the second largest sandwich shop chain in America. Tony has become a principal contributor to the internationally acclaimed Jose Limon Dance Company, and serves as Chairman of the Board of this New York-based dance company. He's also a member of the Institute of American Entrepreneurs, the Hall of Fame at Frank Hawkins Institute of Private Enterprise, the National Restaurant Association, the New York State Restaurant Association, the National Italian American Association, and the International Franchise Association. Through BLIMPIE International, Tony is extremely involved with the Boys & Girls Clubs of America on a personal level. He serves as chairman of the group's national marketing committee, and sits on the organization's Board of Governors.

"My father worked on Wall Street for years, and before my friends and I opened the first BLIMPIE location, I had no background in business. The jobs I had up till then were as an order clerk on Wall Street. My friends and I wanted to sell a certain type of sandwich we discovered on the Jersey Shore, where we used to go on weekends and during summer vacations. We decided to open a sandwich shop that would specialize in this type of sandwich. Of course, none of us had any money to start this business, but we found a friend who loaned us $2,000, and shortly after that, we opened the first BLIMPIE store."

TOPICS COVERED IN THIS INTERVIEW

- ☞ **How a positive attitude creates success**
- ☞ **Finding the best jobs available**
- ☞ **The importance of a résumé and cover letter**
- ☞ **The "A.C.T." success philosophy**

What have you learned from starting your own business?

"Back when we started the business, we had no training, no experience, and no money, which is not the best advice I would offer to anyone interested in starting their own business. Just about everything we did was through trial and error, which is probably the riskiest and most expensive way that you can go into business. It seemed that as we got started, we had to do everything wrong once, before we could do it right. About seven years ago, BLIMPIE International experienced what I call its rebirth. In the 1980s, we tried to diversify, and as a result we lost our focus and a lot of money. The ultimate result was that the BLIMPIE chain stopped expanding. When we finally woke up, we decided to refocus on the ideas we had when we first started the company. This is when we sat

"Anyone who is looking for a job or wants to keep their job or expand their career must have a totally positive attitude. Approach your future with a passion."

down and really got ourselves organized. We began by making a list of everything we wanted to accomplish. We started with big goals, and worked our way down to the smallest details. We called this list '101 Small Improvements.' Next, we determined that we starting a company, the first thing you do is determine what the company stands for. What's its positioning? I think a person looking for a job has to do the same thing. You have to determine who you are, and what you stand for. The worst thing that

> "The worst thing that someone can do is decide to go out and find a job by picking up a newspaper and blindly sending out résumés to every company that has a 'Help Wanted' ad."

had to totally eliminate any negative attitudes that existed within the organization. Anyone who is looking for a job or wants to keep their job or expand their career must have a totally positive attitude. Approach your future with a passion. The one thing, more than anything, that allowed our company to experience a rebirth was the fact that we developed a passion for making it happen, and everyone involved developed a positive attitude. That's the best advice I can share."

Can you elaborate more on what you discovered during the rebirth of your company?

"Success is about more than simply making money. It is about accomplishing something. People who think that they can develop a passion for something by desiring money are often doomed to failure. If you have a true passion for something, the money will eventually follow, if you work hard."

How is launching a career like starting a business?

"To get your career off the ground, there are several things you have to do. If you're

someone can do is decide to go out and find a job by picking up a newspaper and blindly sending out résumés to every company that has a 'Help Wanted' ad. As a person, you have to determine what type of job you're interested in, and then what kind of environment you want to work in. If someone doesn't enjoy being in a highly structured organization, then a finance-related job at a banking company is not the right job for them. Figure out who you are and what you stand for. You need a focus. Just like a brand or a product can't be all things to all people, neither can a person applying for a job. Once you figure out who you are and where you want to go, you must determine how you're going to get there. First seek out an industry, and then specific companies within that industry that you'd like to be employed by. Planning in advance is important. Do research and explore what different industries are all about. Read magazines and newspapers, like *Forbes, Inc., Business Week,* and the *Wall Street Journal.* Even the Business section of *USA Today* will be helpful and informative. Learn as much as you can about the companies and the industry that interests you. The more you

> *"The best thing you can do to help ensure that your résumé gets read is to include a personalized and custom-written cover letter with your résumé. The cover letter gives you an opportunity to stand out from the dozens or maybe hundreds of other people who are applying for the same position as you are."*

know, the better off you'll be when you start applying for jobs and going out for interviews."

Once you know what you want to do, how can you find the best jobs?

"I would try to find companies that appeal to what you want to do."

How important is the résumé as a tool for obtaining a job?

"As an employer, I use the résumé to make sure that the applicant hasn't been job jumping, and that he or she has some experience for the position I need to fill. I think too many résumés look like they've been written by a résumé company or copied out of a résumé book. They say little about the applicant as a person, and as a result, they wind up in the garbage. There aren't too many things you can do to make the résumé itself stand out. The best thing you can do to help ensure that your résumé gets read is to include a personalized and custom-written cover letter with your résumé. The cover letter gives you an opportunity to stand out from the dozens or maybe hundreds of other

people who are applying for the same position as you are. Thus, your cover letter should not be filled with the stereotypical statements that every applicant uses. What will impress a manager or someone in the position to hire you is a cover letter that is well thought out and includes information about how your personal and professional goals fit in with the company's overall goals. I would never write a cover letter to a manager or top-level executive that says, 'My goal is to have your job,' but there are ways to show that you're interested in working your way up the ladder."

If you don't have a contact within a company, how can you get a foot in the door?

"Send a personal letter to one of the top-level people within that company. When doing your research about a company, try to pinpoint a person within the company that you can approach, and then send a letter or make a phone call to that person."

How can someone make the best impression during an interview?

"Think of yourself as an actor going out on an audition. You want to go into an interview having developed intelligent, well thought out opinions. Have a good understanding of the company you're interviewing with. If the company you're applying to is a public company, read its annual report before the interview. Within the annual report is the company's mission statement, which is a company's way of explaining where it's going and what its values are. During an interview, if you can show an understanding of the company's goals and objectives, it shows you're a thinker and that the job you're applying for is important enough to you that you spent some time doing research. I personally prefer to conduct an interview in a more conversational style, rather than to treat it as a question and answer period. Be prepared for this approach when you go for an interview. The interviewee should be professional at all times, and be able to hold a conversation."

What is your personal philosophy toward success? What does it take?

"I use the A.C.T. guideline when evaluating if a potential employee will be successful within our company. The A in 'A.C.T.' stands for *attitude*. One of the biggest reasons why businesses fail is because of negative attitudes among the employees. Approach a job with a positive attitude and a passion. The one factor which differentiates outstanding performers from good performers is passion. Part of your passion for something should involve not letting other people tell you what you can and can't do.

"For example, a few years back, I decided that I was going to run in the New York City marathon. About two months before the

The A.C.T. philosophy =
Attitude + Communication + Tolerance/Think.

As part of the conversation between an employer and an applicant, what types of questions should the applicant ask?

"If during the course of the interview, the employer demonstrates an obvious interest in you, then you can bring up topics such as a starting date, salary, and benefits. These topics should not be brought up early in the interview, but I think that during the interview an employer knows that these topics are of interest to the applicant, especially if the interview is going well. At BLIMPIE, we offer employees stock options, which I think is a benefit that's definitely worth asking about."

actual marathon, I broke my big toe. The doctor told me to forget about running. I went home depressed, but the next morning, I began thinking to myself that this doctor was overweight and probably never ran a block in his life. I continued training by riding a bicycle for two hours at a time, and after a while I began running again. Ultimately, I wound up running the marathon. Another example of this is when we opened our first BLIMPIE location. During a conversation I had with a friend who owned a coffee shop, he told me that there was no way I'd be successful if all we sold were sandwiches. Obviously, he was wrong. As a

"The people you'll be working with is an important factor when it comes to determining how happy you'll be working for a company, and how successful you'll ultimately become."

result of these experiences, I have learned not to let other people tell me what I can and can't do.

"The C in the word 'A.C.T.' stands for *communication*. For someone first entering the workplace, the word *communication* means the ability to express ideas with other people. Learn how to speak in public. Being able to address large and small groups is critical in today's business world. Being a good communicator helps people build up their trust in you. Take an interest in other people, and from that, you'll get a much better insight into how to deal with them.

"Finally, the T in 'A.C.T.' stands for *tolerance*. Treat everyone with respect, no matter who they are. Put yourself in other people's shoes. Understand that you're not always going to get your way. There always has to be room for compromise in every situation. The T in 'A.C.T.' also stands for *think*. As the President and CEO of BLIMPIE International, I can excuse incorrect decisions by subordinates, but I can't excuse someone who doesn't think when it comes to solving a problem or dealing with a situation. If you have to make an important decision, spend some time and think about the possible solutions. Then, go to your boss or supervisor, tell them about the solutions you've come up with, and, if necessary, ask what they think or solicit their advice. Don't simply go to them with a problem and ask them to come up with a solution. Don't say, 'Here's the problem. What do you plan to do about it?' Also, never make decisions based on incorrect or incomplete facts."

What other advice do you have for someone who wants to be successful at their new job?

"Using the metaphor of an actor, be prepared to be the understudy for your boss or supervisor. Spend time learning about their job and responsibilities, so if anything ever happens to your boss—maybe they get sick, promoted, or leave the company—you can take over their responsibilities because you already have the knowledge. No matter what type of career you choose to pursue, always strive for excellence. If you discover later that it's the wrong place for you, you can always leave and go somewhere else. If you go into a job thinking to yourself that this is a long-term career decision, then the chances of your success within that company become much better, because your attitude will be better. Even if the job eventually doesn't work out, by getting the most out of your job, you'll be that much more qualified and prepared for the next one that comes along."

How can someone determine if they'll be happy at a job, before they accept a job offer?

"One of the easiest things you can do is ask to meet some of the people who work for the company, outside of the person or people who you interviewed with. Ask to meet the people you'll be working with on a day-to-day basis. The people you'll be working with is an important factor when it comes to determining how happy you'll be working for a company, and how successful you'll ultimately become. If your personality matches the personalities of the other people within the company, then you have a major advantage. If you like the people, then you have a much better chance of liking your job."

What's the biggest obstacle you've had to overcome in your career, and how have you done it?

"I started in business with a lack of training, experience, and money. How can someone in this position overcome these obstacles? Well, in respect to training and experience, work for a company that offers a detailed and established training program, and take advantage of that program to improve your skills. Here at BLIMPIE we have a BLIMPIE Business School, which all of our new employees and franchise owners are put through. We combine instruction with on-the-job training."

On a day-to-day basis, what keeps you motivated?

"It's not money. Sure, money is important. It becomes like a score card, but I do what I do because it's exciting and fun. I spend more time with my work than I do with any other single thing in my life, so if it isn't fun, then there is no reason for me to continue. If you ever get into a job that you're not happy with, it might be because you have expectations instead of goals. Having expectations implies that someone else has to do something, and that's where people get frustrated. You can't always change other people. When you set goals, these are objectives that you personally set out to accomplish. For me, I have to be happy doing whatever it is that I'm doing, and I think being happy goes a long way toward keeping me motivated. I also like to feel like I'm continuously growing. Part of my job is to keep the other people in the organization happy and motivated."

Growing up, did you have any mentors?

"Actually, yes. My father always wanted to own his own home. He worked for the New York Stock Exchange, but never made enough money to go out and buy a house, so he decided to build one himself. He worked a second job to accumulate enough money to buy building materials, then over the course of three years he got the help of family and friends, and he built his own home. This made me realize early on that if you really want to accomplish something, it's possible if you're willing to put in the effort."

LAST WORD

"If you're an aggressive person who wants to get out into the world and grow, then you want a company that has a similar attitude and corporate philosophy. Discovering these companies will require research. If you read an article about a company that really piques your interest, then make contact with that company. Companies, like BLIMPIE International, that are aggressive are always looking for people who are aggressive, sincere, and want to pursue success."

STEPHANIE SONNABEND
PRESIDENT
Sonesta Hotels

COMPANY HISTORY

Operating a hotel chain requires hundreds of employees with many different skills and specialties in each hotel. Sonesta Hotels was started by Stephanie's grandfather in the 1940s. "He was never really involved in the management of the hotels. He was more of an entrepreneur who bought and sold the properties. My father and his two brothers actually ran the business for many years."

Currently the Sonesta Hotels chain includes 18 hotels and resorts around the world.

PERSONAL HISTORY

Stephanie's career in the hotel business began in high school, when she started working after school and during vacations in various positions at the hotels her family owned. "I worked in many different jobs over the years. I did everything from being a waitress to working on the computer systems. I also held several jobs that were outside of my family's hotel business, because I wanted other types of experiences."

As she got older, Stephanie doesn't recall being pressed by her family to join Sonesta Hotels. In fact, she says that it wasn't until after she graduated from business school that her father started recruiting her to accept a

Sonesta Hotels & Resorts

> *"If you accept a job that lets you learn specific skills that are marketable elsewhere, or that will help you move up within the organization, then that job is a starting point for your career."*

position within the company. "He was very persuasive. Eventually, I was given the opportunity to take over the company as its President."

Among her responsibilities as President of Sonesta Hotels is hiring corporate division heads and general managers for each of the chain's hotels. "I don't get involved with the hiring of lower-level employees at each of our hotels, but I certainly know how all of the hiring and recruiting is done."

TOPICS DISCUSSED IN THIS INTERVIEW

☞ **What makes a good résumé?**

☞ **Making a good first impression during an interview**

☞ **Do you have the right type of personality to excel in a service business?**

What's the difference between getting a job and launching a career?

"When you get a job, if it is something that can and will lead to something else, then I would say that you've launched a career. In the hotel business, you can accept a job in a specific area, or you can choose a position that will lead to promotions and allow you to expand your career within the hotel industry. It all has to do with your attitude. If you accept a job that lets you learn specific skills that are marketable elsewhere, or that will help you move up within the organization, then that job is a starting point for your career."

What type of experience does someone need to break into the hotel/resort business?

"Practically none. The wonderful thing about this industry is that you can begin with an entry-level position that requires no special skills or previous experience, and over time, you can work your way up to a management position or a corporate-level position. The hotel industry offers many different types of entry-level positions, ranging from secretarial jobs, working in the kitchen/stewarding department, front desk clerks, and bellmen. If someone is coming out of grad school with no hotel management experience, they're not going to find a position working for a hotel chain because their salary demands will be too high for an entry-level position." If, while you're still in school, you develop an interest in hotel or restaurant management, this is something that you can study in school, so upon graduation, you'll be able to apply for jobs that are above entry-level positions.

If someone's long-term goal is to manage a hotel or resort, what is the best career track for them?

"Find a discipline within the hotel business that you really enjoy. Most of our hotel managers begin by working their way up in the food and beverage, sales and marketing, or rooms division within a hotel. Start in one of these areas and put yourself on a track that allows you to learn not only about the division you're working in, but also about how other divisions within the hotel operate. The more general knowledge you acquire as you specialize in one area of hotel operations, the better off you'll be. Once you start within a specific division, you'll want to work your way toward becoming the manager of that division as your first career goal. Before applying for a job, spend some time thinking about what it is that you really like and want to do. You might want to make lists of things that you enjoy and don't enjoy. Do you like being around people all the time? Do you like doing detailed work? If you have a clear understanding about yourself, you'll be much better off when you begin looking for a job, because you'll have a better grip on what you're actually looking for. If you don't immediately get the job that you want, try applying for similar jobs that will allow you to develop the necessary skill set that will help you eventually get the job you want."

Working at a hotel or resort requires a certain type of personality. What traits does someone need to be successful in this field?

"In many ways, the hotel business is a lot like theater, because when you're working, you're always on stage. You always need to present yourself in a professional manner and be cheerful. You must be willing to do whatever it takes to help the guest, even if they're yelling at you. People who are outgoing, enjoy working with people, and are friendly have the most potential for success within a service-oriented business. The training you'll receive when you begin most service-related jobs will help to perfect the interpersonal skills you'll need, but you really need to enter the job already having the right type of personality."

How can someone find the best positions at various hotels and resorts?

"Begin by contacting the human resources department of the organization you want to work for. What's nice about this industry is that the skills you learn in entry-level positions are often transferable to other jobs within this industry and to other industries. When you work at a hotel, you develop a skill set that becomes marketable. Most hotels and resorts are seasonal businesses, which means that during the busier times of year, they tend to hire many more people. The best time to apply for a job at a hotel or resort is two or three months before that hotel's busy season begins."

"You always need to present yourself in a professional manner and be cheerful."

"I believe networking is one of the most powerful tools young people have for finding the best jobs available."

Does Sonesta get many applications from recent graduates interested in summer positions as interim jobs before starting their real career?

"We certainly get some of that, especially in our resort locations. There's a big difference between taking an interim job for the summer after you graduate and going from job to job for several years upon graduation. You don't want to develop a reputation for not being able to hold down a job. However, taking a summer job while you're in school, or right after you graduate, is an excellent way to get your feet wet and get exposure to various opportunities available within a company."

How important is networking within your business?

"Extremely important. Most jobs are found by networking. It's much less of a gamble for an employer to hire someone that comes highly recommended by a current employee. I would certainly be more likely to hire someone who comes recommended by someone I know than I would be to hire someone coming off the street. I believe networking is one of the most powerful tools young people have for finding the best jobs available. To take full advantage of the power of networking, people first beginning their career should talk to their parents' friends and with everyone they know, including people they've worked with in the past during summer jobs. The referrals that carry the most weight with an employer are the ones where the person recommending you knows you very well. I often get calls from people asking if I can help a friend of a friend by recommending them for a job. My personal belief is that I can't really help that person because I don't know them. Thus, I'm not willing to go to bat for them and put my name behind them. If I know the person, however, I'm more than happy to pass their résumé along to other business leaders who might be able to offer them a position."

In your opinion, what makes a good résumé?

"I like systematic résumés. The résumés that drive me nuts are the ones that talk about skill sets without referring specifically to the jobs someone has held. When I review a résumé, I want to see what specific jobs the applicant has had, and what level of responsibility they've held. For someone coming out of school who has limited experience, their résumé should not be more than a single page. I don't need to see a lot of letters of recommendation or lots of extra paperwork attached to the résumé, except for a well-written cover letter. Also, you shouldn't try to cover up large gaps in your résumé by stating you were a consultant, unless you actually did consulting work. It's okay to have a gap in your résumé. Don't lie to cover it up."

Is there any value in an applicant including a letter of recommendation or reference?

"The ideal letter of recommendation is from your previous boss. If you're going from one sales job to another, for example, getting a letter or two from your customers might help, but you should bring those letters to the interview. Don't attach the letters of recommendation to your résumé."

How important is a cover letter to you?

"The cover letter should be short. It goes without saying that everything should be spelled correctly and the punctuation should be correct. Be sure to verify the spelling and exact title of the person whom you're sending the cover letter and résumé to. It's amazing how many cover letters and résumés I receive that contain typos, misspellings, and other obvious errors. Within the letter, clearly identify the job you're applying for, and provide one or two good reasons why you're suitable for that job. By the time you're ready to send a résumé and cover letter, you should know enough about the company and the job being offered to be able to clearly state the position you're applying for. The information you include within the cover letter should not repeat the résumé. I don't have time to read the same information twice. Like the résumé, the cover letter should never be more than one page."

Assuming you don't know anyone who can provide an introduction, what's the best way to get your foot in the door of a company?

"The best approach is to call or go in person to the human resources department and ask specifically what jobs are currently available, and what jobs they anticipate having to fill in the near future. If nothing is available at the moment, ask if you can come in for an informational interview, so that you can be considered for future job openings. When you're making contact with a company, you should be persistent, without becoming annoying. If you're applying for a clerical position, for example, but the human resources department is currently doing a massive search to fill a position within the accounting department, they might not have a lot of time to spend with you. Say something to the extent that you're very interested in working for their company, and you'd like to know what it would take to get a job there. Then, ask when the best time to make a follow-up call would be, if the person you contact says he or she is busy. Remember, how you act during the hiring process is seen by the employer as indicative of how you'll be as an employee if you get hired. You want to come off as being assertive, but not aggressive. If you act up or are obnoxious to someone in our Human Resources department, I would hate to see how you'd act with one of our guests."

How can someone make the best impression during an interview?

"Presentation is extremely important! I probably dismiss a significant number of people based on the first four minutes of the interview. As the interviewer, I pay careful attention to how applicants say hello, introduce themselves, how they're dressed, the way they sit down, and how they present themselves. Be prepared to answer questions that you're asked, but also ask intelligent questions that demonstrate that you've done your homework about the company you're applying to. One of the things that very few applicants ask during the interview, but I feel is very important, is about the culture within the organization. Every workplace has a unique culture, and understanding that culture will help you determine if you'll fit into the company."

What's the best way to determine if you're going to like a job, before you accept it?

"In the hotel business or in retail it's very easy. You can walk into the hotel or store and talk directly with the employees. Ask them how they like working for the company. Find out if the work experience is what you're looking for, and examine the culture. You can learn a lot simply by observing the people at a company. You also want to know exactly what you would be doing if you get the job you're applying for. Find out what your responsibilities will be, who you will be working with. You want to find out as much of this information as you can, so when you accept the job, there will be no surprises. Ask if you can spend some time meeting the people you'll be working with, before accepting a job. I am a firm believer in finding a job that you'll enjoy. Life is too

short for you to not enjoy what you spend many hours per day doing."

What has enabled you to be successful?

"I am a big-picture thinker. Not only do I think about the details and specifics of what I'm working on at any given moment, but I also pay attention to the big picture and to the future. Early on, I learned how important it is to have a general understanding of the jobs that other people are doing. Developing my listening skills and the ability to make quick decisions has also been beneficial. Once I make a decision, I have to be prepared to act on it. I also have a long-term goal to always keep learning, and that includes learning about other people's jobs."

Do women face different challenges in the workplace than men do?

"That's a very hard question for me to answer, because I have never been a man. As a woman, and because I was working for my family's business, I always felt that I personally had to strive to be better than other people. I feel that women face more of a need to prove themselves in the workplace, and sometimes have a tougher time building their credibility, especially among male peers. By the time I took on the position of President at Sonesta Hotels, I had proven myself by holding many other positions at all levels of the company, so I didn't really have anything more to prove."

LAST WORD

"Be sure to verify the spelling and exact title of the person whom you're sending a cover letter and résumé to. It's amazing how many cover letters and résumés I receive that contain typos, misspellings, and other obvious errors."

LOREN J. HULBER
PRESIDENT & CEO
Day-Timers, Inc.

COMPANY BACKGROUND

Since 1947, Day-Timers has helped people become more productive and organized by using one or more of the company's more than 100 different products including Pocket Day-Timers, Day-Timer Organizers, and the cutting edge Day-Timer Organizer software. For people who are still in school, Day-Timers also offers its extremely popular Student Planner, which is designed to help even the most unorganized person learn to become a better student. Day-Timers' products are designed to help people working in virtually any occupation manage their schedules, prioritize tasks, and develop long- and short-term goals.

Based in Lehigh Valley, Pennsylvania, Day-Timers, Inc. is a subsidiary of ACCO World Corporation, a core business group of American Brands, which is a multibillion-dollar global consumer products holding company. Day-Timers' products are available through the company's own direct mail catalog, or from many different office supply stores, such as Office Depot, Office Max, and Staples. The company's Day-Timer software product is available from Computer City, CompUSA, Egghead Software, and wherever computer software is sold.

Day-Timers' customers include people of all ages, working in all types of occupations, and from a wide range of large and small companies including American Express, Coca-Cola, Microsoft, and Nike.

⏱ DAY-TIMERS, Inc.

PERSONAL HISTORY

Loren J. Hulber has years of experience working as a top-level executive in various corporate environments. Looking back, Loren credits his parents for helping him grow into someone with the passion for being a high achiever. "My parents were both high achievers, and I went to schools that demanded a lot from their students. I've always been a competitive individual, and I've always tried to achieve excellence in whatever it is that I set out to accomplish."

Loren's father was an executive at a large commercial printing company in the Detroit area. "I used to work there during school vacations throughout my high school and college years. Early on, I considered becoming an attorney or a dentist, but it was business that I decided held the greatest opportunity for me. As I continued working for my father's printing company and was about to graduate from college, I started networking by getting involved with and meeting members of the Graphics Arts Association of Michigan. This was a trade association made up people working in all aspects of the graphic arts field. When I met the executive director of this association, he was impressed with my motivation, interest,

**TOPICS DISCUSSED
IN THIS INTERVIEW**

☞ **Learning and mastering time management techniques**

☞ **Setting job-related goals**

☞ **Networking to find job opportunities**

☞ **Overcoming fear and anxiety during the job interview process**

☞ **What information to include within your cover letters**

What is the key to your success?

"I strongly believe that the key to my success has been my passion for life. I look at my career as an opportunity to make a difference and to make a lasting impact on other people's lives. I approach everything I do with a strong passion. I've always studied other successful executives whom I believe possess these qualities, and I learn what I can from them. Having a dedication to achieving personal excellence and doing things that have never been done before are what has

"I approach everything I do with a strong passion."

and energy, which led to him writing a profile of me in the association's newsletter. The result was that I received numerous job offers and made many new contacts in the industry. A CEO from a large binding company contacted me after reading the article that appeared in the newsletter, and I wound up working for that firm. Five years later, I became the general manager."

allowed me to succeed. One quality that I feel makes me a good leader is that I have developed the ability to inspire the people around me to also believe in achieving personal excellence and to develop their own passion for life and their work.

"Don't define your job from the job description. Constantly think of ways to identify opportunities and add value. If I

> *"First, you must develop goals. Then, you have to develop plans for achieving those goals."*

look back over my career, in every case I achieved the top-level positions that I have held by thinking outside of my current area of responsibility, and I worked hard to make a greater impact."

According to Loren, there are two things that you must do if you want to accomplish something. "First, you must develop goals. Then, you have to develop plans for achieving those goals. These two steps apply to just about anything, whether it's finding a first job, obtaining a promotion, or completing a work-related project." One important objective when applying for a job is to differentiate yourself and establish a competitive advantage. "Set yourself apart from the rest of the pack and be creative. I got myself written about in a newsletter that was read by the executives from companies within the industry I was interested in working in. That article helped to set me apart from other young people who were looking for a job."

"We at Day-Timers make a real impact on people's lives because we help them with planning and time management, which allows them to stay on the fast track and achieve personal success. No matter how successful you are, you can't get more than 24 hours in a single day, so you have to make the best use of time as you can. At Day-Timers, we call this Four Dimensional Time Management—

Focus, Plan, Act, and Team Up. If you do these four things effectively, then you'll be successful in almost everything you undertake."

How important is networking?

Networking has proven to be a fundamental element of Hulber's success throughout his career. "Getting back to the fundamentals of defining goals and then developing strategies for achieving those goals, when I graduated from college, I had the goal of finding a job and launching my career. The plan I created to help me achieve that goal was to utilize the background I already had in the graphic arts field. I developed an 'action plan,' which included speaking with as many people within the industry as I possibly could. From a contact standpoint, I tapped the knowledge and resources of those people with whom I had come into contact during my summer jobs, and then I used networking to extend those contacts by getting involved with the Graphics Arts Association of Michigan. When you network, you're marketing yourself in much the same way a company markets a product. You need a strong brand in order to get people interested and curious enough to give it a try. When it comes to networking, you have to meet people, impress those people with your accomplish-

> *"No matter how successful you are, you can't get more than 24 hours in a single day, so you have to make the best use of time as you can...focus, plan, act, and team up."*

"When you network, you're marketing yourself in much the same way a company markets a product. You need a strong brand in order to get people interested and curious enough to give it a try."

ments, abilities, and positive attitude, and then sell those people on the idea of having you as an employee who will greatly benefit their company."

Networking refers to making and using contacts who can help you in your career. Since most young people don't have too many contacts with top-level people in the industry they're interested in working in, one excellent place to start is by contacting the people you already know. Talk to your parents, relatives, friends, and friends' parents to see who might know someone who works at the company or within the industry you're interested in entering. Contacting professional associations, or groups that are based within the industry you want to enter, can provide you with valuable contacts and job leads. If necessary, check the reference section of your local library for a directory of professional associations and organizations. "I think it's proper to use every opportunity that you have. I've seen statistics that show that up to 80 percent of all job openings are never advertised. You have to meet as many people as you can, and impress the people you meet with your skills, personality, and qualifications."

How can young people learn to master organizational skills and time management?
Many students learn basic organizational skills and time management in school, as they juggle the work and study requirements for multiple subjects, while at the same time attempting to have a fun and exciting social life. If you focused more on the social aspects of school and never actually developed time management skills or figured out how to keep yourself organized, it's not too late. "It's never too late to learn time management, personal organization, and goal-setting skills. One of the biggest problems with education today is that these skills are not taught as often or as well as they should be. Day-Timers is able to help thousands of students who use our Student Planner, which is specifically designed to help almost any student develop these three basic skills. Our research shows that when people enter into the workplace, nearly two-thirds of them feel rushed or under stress most or all of the time. It's a proven fact that the people who are the least rushed and the least stressed out are the ones who become the most successful, so by getting yourself organized, you too will be less stressed."

What does it take to be an organized and stress-free person?
"There is always more to do in a day than any of us can accomplish. One way someone can master time management, personal organiza-

"UP TO 80 PERCENT OF ALL JOB OPENINGS ARE NEVER ADVERTISED."

tion, and goal-setting skills is to use an organizational tool, such as a Day-Timer Planner. We have in place the system and the steps that people need to learn. Everyone has to develop a time management system that's custom tailored to their specific needs. However, if you're going to develop a successful system, you need the right building blocks and basic knowledge. Part of becoming organized is first defining what your needs and habits are."

appropriately for the interview and ultimately how you conduct yourself during the interview will also demonstrate to the potential employer whether or not you have your act together."

What's the difference between a job and a career?

"I would hope that everyone would approach finding their first job as starting their career. If the job is worth investing your time and

> "If the job is worth investing your time and energy in, then it should be a building block to something, or at least a learning opportunity."

How can you show a prospective employer that you've mastered time management, organizational, and goal-setting skills?

"Simply having these basic skills won't help you get a job unless you put them to use while you're searching for a job, and then demonstrate to potential employers that you have mastered these skills." Obviously, showing up to an interview early (or at the very least on time) is one way you can begin to demonstrate that you have the ability to manage your schedule. Simply showing up to a job interview on time isn't going to set you apart from the other applicants, however. "You want to demonstrate that you have a system of self-management. By taking notes in an organized fashion during your interview, you'll show that you are interested in what the other person is saying, and you know how to record and develop information for follow-up purposes. Dressing

energy in, then it should be a building block to something, or at least a learning opportunity. I would advise against taking a job unless you can see that it will enhance your personal development, or somehow help your career. If your goal is to have some type of career that will eventually lead to a top-level management or executive position, but the job you're about to take doesn't in any way help you to take a step closer toward achieving your goal, then you should carefully reevaluate that opportunity. When you go out and begin looking for a job, you should do so with some type of strategy in mind. Ask yourself, 'Where is this going to lead?' or 'Where am I going to go with this?'"

What qualities do you look for in a potential employee?

Successfully managing a group of employees is one of the most important tasks of a top-level executive. For a company to be successful, all of the employees, including the executives, must be able to work together to achieve the company's goals. Loren strongly believes that there are five qualities that most, if not all, employers look for in a job applicant.

1. **Qualifications of the individual—Can he or she do the job? Will the person be able to fulfill the responsibilities of the position?**

2. **Chemistry—Will the job applicant be able to work effectively in our company's environment?**

3. **Potential—Is the applicant a good investment? Should we spend the money or resources necessary to train that person? Will he or she be able to advance within the company?**

4. **Contribution—Will the applicant be able to make a contribution to the company quickly? "We're in a performance-driven work environment. People need to hit the ground running and be able to make contributions quickly."**

5. **Spirit and Enthusiasm—Will the applicant add to the enthusiasm and overall morale of the company? "There are lots and lots of good students, but far fewer people have the enthusiasm and the spirit to be successful in a performance-driven company. Having genuine spirit and enthusiasm can, and will, set an applicant apart from others."**

Never act phony! "Most companies don't hire someone based on a single interview. At Day-Timers, we'll see an applicant on at least three different occasions, and we'll have multiple people involved in the interview process. We ask a lot of leading and open-ended questions. We also ask a lot of questions that appear to be casual; however, we have a real purpose in mind, and we listen carefully to the applicant's responses. Through this interaction, we get a pretty good idea of what applicants are made of, and whether or not they're putting on an act. We can almost always determine someone's enthusiasm and what type of commitment they have. Sincerity is the most important thing. You have to want to do well, and you have to be committed. Distinguish yourself as someone who is honest and committed, and you'll be in a much better position when applying for a job."

How can someone demonstrate that they're going to be a good employee?

"You have to believe in yourself, have confidence, be sincere, be committed, and be trying to do good things for other people." Applicants who exhibit the five points Loren outlined are the ones who make the best impression during the interview process.

How important is a résumé and cover letter when applying for a job?

"A strong résumé and a strong cover letter are both important tools when applying for a job. Someone's résumé has to be organized and portray a positive profile of the individual. I think equally important is the cover letter. I would strongly encourage people to custom write each cover letter, and even edit

> "You have to believe in yourself, have confidence, be sincere, be committed, and be trying to do good things for other people."

their résumé so that it targets each specific company where the applicant is applying for a job. The résumé and cover letter should portray the applicant as the ideal person to fill the position they're applying for."

Loren stresses the importance of personalizing the cover letter to the individual you're attempting to gain an audience with. By personalizing the letter, he means use the recipient's full name and job title. "Applicants will have better results if they first use their networking skills to obtain some type of referral or introduction through a mutual acquaintance. Developing some type of connection or common interest with the recipient of your résumé and cover letter is also important.

"Use the cover letter to briefly highlight your specific skills and describe how those skills can benefit the company you're requesting an interview with. In describing those skills, focus on the related job experiences you have. If an internship or summer job has given you skills that will be required for the job you're applying for, use the cover letter to describe those experiences in more detail than what's listed in your résumé." Your cover letter should be concise, well written, and personalized to the person it's being sent to.

Will you enjoy the job you're applying for?

During the interview, ask probing questions. "Just as employers are trying to find the best possible person to fill their position, the applicants should be looking for the best possible position to help them meet or exceed their career-related goals. The questions an applicant asks during the interview provides the employer with a lot of insight into what that person is all about. Technical skills are one thing, but you have to be able to implement those skills, often by working with other people. Being able to work as part of a team is as important as being able to accomplish something on your own." By asking the employer questions, you'll be able to better determine if the job opportunity is really right for you, and whether or not you'll be happy in the job if it's offered to you and you accept it.

What do you ask the employer during the interview?

"Once you have begun selling yourself to the interviewer, and you can clearly sense a spark of interest on their part, then begin to ask specific questions about the work environment, future opportunities, and the types of training and development programs that are available. I'd also ask the employer for advice on what I could do as an applicant to get a better understanding of the company."

Do research about the company before you apply for a job. This research should be completed before you fill out an application and go in for an interview. "Applicants should have a general knowledge about the company they're applying for a job at. By having even a basic knowledge of the company's background, you'll be showing respect for the person who is interviewing you. The more you know about the company, the more interest you are showing in that

> *"Distinguish yourself as someone who is honest and committed, and you'll be in a much better position when applying for a job."*

company. This will result in the company having a greater interest in you."

Follow up every job interview by sending the interviewer a personalized thank you note. This note can be typed or hand written, and should contain specific references to something pertaining to your interview. You can also use this note to briefly remind the interviewer of your interest in their company and your qualifications for the job. Even if the interview experience was a negative one, your thank you note should be polite, sincere, and sent promptly after the interview.

How important are internships?

Any type of job-related experience that you can obtain before graduating from school will make you a better applicant. "Internships, summer jobs, extracurricular activities, and volunteer work are all extremely important for obtaining job-related experience. Try to get involved with activities that are of interest to you, and that have something to do with the career you hope to pursue." If you've always wanted to be a lawyer, do an internship at a law office. Just by being in that environment, you'll learn important job-related skills. Perhaps you'll discover that you don't really like law, and based on that summer job or internship experience, you'll decide to pursue other interests. Internships and summer jobs also allow you to meet people who already work

in your area of interest. Upon your graduation, when you begin your job search, use your networking skills to contact the people you met during your summer job or internship. These people can provide introductions or referrals which could easily lead to a job opportunity.

"Before applying for any type of internship, spend some time talking with people who work within the industry you're interested in. Examine different types of internship opportunities within that industry, and try to narrow down what area of that industry you're most interested in. If you're interested in a specific company, see if you can spend your time during the internship working in that company's various departments, so that you get an overall understanding of what that company is all about." Most companies have established internship programs, because interns provide inexpensive labor. As an intern, expect to work hard and to do many of the tasks that the paid employees don't enjoy. Internships aren't supposed to be glamorous; they're supposed to be educational and your first exposure to what the business world is really like.

"The more you know about the company, the more interest you are showing in that company. This will result in the company having a greater interest in you."

What if I earned poor grades in school? Can I still get a good job?

"Internships and other work-related experiences become even more important to a job applicant who doesn't have an A+ average in school. Are the grades you achieved in school a function of your ability or your commitment? Most employers look at more than just someone's grade-point average. Looking at someone's grades and SAT scores is just one way to measure someone's potential. There are a lot of highly successful people who were just average or even below-average students academically, but these students excelled in other areas. If you have poor grades but you have achieved success in other areas, those are the areas you want to bring to the attention of the person making the hiring decisions. If your poor grades are an indication of your commitment, that could be a drawback when you're applying for a job, so it is important that you demonstrate how committed you have been in internships, summer jobs, extracurricular activities, volunteer work, or other activities outside of the academic environment."

What topics should be avoided during the interview?

"Don't begin by asking questions about financial compensation and job benefits. These questions should be brought up in the later stages of the hiring process, once the company has established an interest in you, and you have established an interest in working for the company. At all times, I'd avoid topics of an extremely personal nature. I'd never ask the person conducting the interview anything they might consider to be inappropriate or offensive."

The most important thing to avoid is lying! "Never lie on a résumé or at any time during the interview process. The most important things any of us have are our personal integrity and identity. Never misrepresent yourself or your background. If you lie, more often than not it will be discovered, and then your integrity will be totally gone. Obviously, in the early stages of the process, you want to represent yourself in the best possible light, but lying in order to do this is not acceptable, and is probably the worst mistake you could make."

"Before applying for any type of internship, spend some time talking with people who work within the industry you're interested in."

"There are a lot of highly successful people who were just average or even below-average students academically, but these students excelled in other areas."

How can you overcome anxiety before and during a job interview?

A job interview can be an extremely stressful experience, especially if you're a recent graduate with little or no experience in the real world. Fear and anxiety can be detrimental to you unless you know how to deal with them, and maybe even use them to your advantage. "Nervousness about any situation is a function of confidence. Confidence is a function of expertise, and expertise is a function of training and preparation.

"I recommend that people set aside time, ideally first thing in the morning, for a daily planning, prioritizing, and goal-setting session. Spend about 15 or 20 minutes per day doing this, and you'll save at least one hour per day because you'll be more productive. I do this religiously, each and every day! By planning my day, I gain efficiency, but more importantly, it focuses me on the key things I must accomplish that day. If you approach your interview preparation efforts in this way, you'll focus on what your goals are for that interview, what you'll wear, how you're going to present yourself, and what kinds of things you want to say. You should also practice answering questions with a friend, or even in front of a mirror in order to gain confidence and practice. Preparation and practice will lead to improved confidence going into the interview, and having more confidence will eliminate anxiety."

"You want to represent yourself in the best possible light, but lying in order to do this is not acceptable, and is probably the worst mistake you could make."

How should I organize my job search?

Begin your job-search efforts not only by establishing goals, but by setting a start time and a deadline for yourself. "If you're going to be writing and sending cover letters and résumés, making phone calls to set up appointments, and sifting through 'Help Wanted' ads, set a start time and a deadline time for each of these activities. Be sure to prioritize your daily action or to-do list. By prioritizing your to-do list, you'll determine what tasks must be accomplished that day, and what tasks can be done after other

"**NERVOUSNESS** about any situation is a function of confidence. **Confidence** is a function of expertise, and expertise is a function of training and preparation."

important tasks have been completed. If the tasks that are placed at the top of your list are the ones that have the biggest impact toward you achieving your goals, then each time you complete one of those tasks, you'll be that much closer to your ultimate objective. I personally set multiple sets of goals. I have work-related goals, personal goals, family goals, and personal development goals.

"Organize yourself and you won't become overwhelmed. By understanding what your goals are, and exactly what it's going to take to achieve those goals, you will build up your confidence, which will greatly reduce anxiety and stress. People get overwhelmed when they have more choices about things to do than their time will allow them to complete. By prioritizing those choices,

you'll gain control over your life. By organizing yourself, setting goals, and doing the things I've discussed, you'll become a happier and more productive person, and that'll lead to your success."

What should you wear to an interview?

Making a good first impression is important. "You have to look at your job search just like a marketing campaign. You have to sell yourself, just like a company sells a product. The most successful products are the ones with attractive packaging. Looking your best and dressing in accordance with the company's dress code will make you more attractive to an employer." Do some research before your interview to find out what the dress code is for the company you're applying to.

"By prioritizing your to-do list, you'll determine what tasks must be accomplished that day, and what tasks can be done after other important tasks have been completed."

LAST WORD
"We need to recognize that every day of our lives should be leading somewhere. If we're just leading our lives, or marking time, then we have wasted time. We are all given just 24 hours per day, and you must choose how you are going to use those hours. You can use your time to better yourself or better the world, or you can just let the hours go by. When you allow time to slip by, then you've let something go that can never be replaced."

NICOLE MILLER

PRESIDENT, FOUNDER & DESIGNER

BUD KONHEIM  CEO

Nicole Miller, Inc.

COMPANY HISTORY

In 1982, Nicole and Bud bought P.J. Walsh from its parent company, and changed the name of the company to Nicole Miller, Inc. Four years later, the first Nicole Miller boutique opened on Madison Avenue in New York City.

In February 1990, Nicole Miller began branching out into the men's industry, offering silk boxers, robes, pajamas, bomber jackets, umbrellas, beach shirts, and, of course, ties--all featuring the colorful and lively imprints and patterns that have made Nicole a household name. Today, Nicole Miller has over 21 boutiques located across America, and her designs are sold at major department stores throughout North America.

52

PERSONAL HISTORY

Nicole Miller has been described as "the princess of prints," and as "an innovator in her field." *Crain's New York Business* recently ranked Nicole Miller as one of the 75 most influential women in business, and Robin Leach called her one of New York's most prominent society figures.

As a fashion designer, Nicole's career began in 1975, when she earned the position of head designer for P.J. Walsh, a contemporary dress and sportswear manufacturer. After she graduated from the Rhode Island School of Design, for seven years Nicole worked under the direction of her future business partner, Bud Konheim, during which time she established herself as a premier silhouette designer.

Bud Konheim has been involved in the fashion industry for over 40 years. "Most people think that successful people are motivated by money. In reality, most successful people set out to do something extremely well. Their motivation is to achieve perfection in whatever it is that they're doing, and as a result, people are willing to pay for that superior product or service, and that's when the money comes along. I believe success comes from knowing how and when to recognize opportunities when they present themselves, and then knowing how to maximize the benefits of those opportunities," explains Bud. "You also have to learn how to minimize the impact of mistakes that you make along the way."

"The biggest skill you're going to need is determination."

TOPICS COVERED
IN THIS INTERVIEW

☞ **Making career choices**

☞ **Making the best impression during an interview (what to wear and how to present yourself)**

☞ **The worst mistakes you can make during the interview process**

☞ **The importance of internship experience**

How should someone approach their career search and make career choices?

Nicole: "Many women are raised with the idea that they have to find a rich guy who will support them. I think that's been the biggest detriment to women in modern times. Women should be independent and establish their own careers, and they should stick with their goals and ambitions. The biggest skill you're going to need is determination. You'll need practical skills, of course, but I think the biggest thing you need in order to have a successful career is determination. Also, everyone likes a self-starter and a creative thinker, but nobody likes an overbearing person. When looking for new employees, I look for people who are capable in a lot of different areas. I like people who have diverse enough talent that you can throw a bunch of different types of projects at them."

Bud: "Work is where you spend most of your time. So you've got to figure that at the bare minimum, you're going to be spending from 9:00 A.M. to 5:00 P.M. on the job. The real fact of the matter is that as you get more involved in your career and take on positions that require brains, ambition, and dedication, then an 8-hour day becomes a 12-hour work day. Knowing this, you have to decide to pursue a career where you absolutely love the work you're doing. If you find this type of work situation, you have a far greater chance of being successful than if you accept a job doing something you're good at, but you don't love. First, decide what really feels good to you and have a good understanding of what type of job and work atmosphere you're looking for. Before you begin your job search, determine for yourself what types of things you like and don't like. The types of questions you should ask yourself are:

☞ **Do you like working with people?**

☞ **Do you like a busy and loud work environment, or a small and quiet environment?**

☞ **Do you like a corporate atmosphere or a more casual work atmosphere?**

☞ **Do you want to work for a large company, a medium-sized company, or a small company?**

"The day your job is labeled in your mind as 'work,' then you're not going to do well at it. People do not do well in work environments

that they don't like. Think about the types of things that you love to do, that you could enjoy doing all day long, then find jobs that involve those skills or activities. If you happen to be a computer genius, but you hate the status of being a 'computer nerd,' and you don't enjoy sitting for hours at a time in front of a computer screen, don't accept a computer-related job. No matter now good you are at using or programming computers, the guy who works next to you who absolutely loves what he's doing is going to beat you out every time, even if he's not as smart as you are, because he doesn't mind being on the job 18 hours per day. He'll love every minute he spends on the job."

What should someone do if they accept a job, but they absolutely hate it?
Nicole: "Very often jobs are misrepresented, but it's not a good idea to change jobs too often because that looks bad on your résumé. Large gaps on your résumé also look bad. If you wind up in a job that you really don't like, either leave immediately, or stick it out

"The day your job is labeled in your mind as 'work,' then you're not going to do well at it. People do not do well in work environments that they don't like."

> *"When you're taking an interview, you want to convey the idea that there is no place else that you'd rather be, because you love that company's product or service."*

for as long as you can. It will look a lot better if you're at a job for a year than if you were only there for three months. Also, it's a lot easier to apply for a new job while you still have a job, so don't quit until you've lined up another job."

What advice can you offer about the interview process?

Bud: "Let's say that you've found the thing that you love to do, and you found a company that has jobs where you'll be able to utilize your skills and do the things you really enjoy. For this example, let's say you love playing guitars, so you go to the Gibson Guitar Company, and you say, 'I love guitars. I'm not the greatest musician in the world, but I love everything about guitars. I love to listen to guitars, and guitars are my life.' When you say that to someone at Gibson Guitars during a job interview, chances are that you're talking to a person who has spent their entire professional life in the guitar business. What that person wants to do is find employees who love guitars as much as they do. When someone comes to Nicole Miller, Inc. and applies for a job, what I'm

looking for is someone who loves fashion and design, and particularly loves Nicole Miller's products and designs.

"When you're taking an interview, you want to convey the idea that there is no place else that you'd rather be, because you love that company's product or service. You want to convey that you're interested in almost any job within that company, as long as it gives you the chance to work there and offers opportunities to move upward. Once you're in the door, even if you're working in a position that you didn't originally want, you can work your way into whatever position you ultimately want, as long as you're patient and work hard. You have to demonstrate that you're willing to work hard and that you're totally excited about working for the company you're interviewing with.

"At Nicole Miller, Inc. we've never hired a genius from the outside to take a management or executive-level position. We build from within. As a result, we look for interns and entry-level people who can have a long-term future with our company."

How can someone make the best impression during an interview?

Nicole: "Before the interview, you have to figure out what the company is like, and determine what its image is. If you don't know what a company's image is, don't go for the interview. I have interviewed people over the years who came in to an interview with me and didn't know what I did or what my company was like. I certainly wasn't interested in hiring those people. Make sure that you dress appropriately for the company you're applying to. Dressing appropriately can mean a lot of different things. You have to feel confident about what you're wearing. If you're not sure about your outfit, change before the interview. To make a good impression, you don't have to wear designer clothes. I've seen plenty of people put themselves together well with clothing that they bought at a thrift shop, because they knew what they were doing and how to make it work. Whatever you do, you want to look your best for an interview.

"If you want a job at a company that's sort of funky, then you should appeal to them and dress a bit funky. You're not going to appeal to that company if you show up at the interview dressed in formal business attire. I expect people working at my company to look hip. You have to understand the personality of the company and learn about its products or services before the interview."

Bud: "Be yourself. There is no point trying to act out a part that you think you should be playing. You want to look alert, dress appropriately, and go into the interview with a good background knowledge of the company. During an interview, you want people to pay attention to what you have to say, not to how you look. You want to be seen as a person by the people interviewing you. You don't need four earrings in your ear to make a personal social statement. That's

distracting to an interviewer who might not wear an earring. If the interviewer spends the entire interview looking at your earrings, then he or she is not spending the time looking at you as a person. Don't call attention to anything other than your ability to perform well in a job. You should look clean and neat. An interview is not about making a statement with your clothing or accessories, unless you're applying for a job as a fashion model. If you're applying for a job at Giorgio Armani, then it might be a nice idea to wear one of his suits to the interview. If you're applying for a job at JC Penney, wear something from their store, to show you have a familiarity with the company's products and that you use them. If someone comes to Nicole Miller, Inc. for an interview, it's always nice if they're wearing a Nicole Miller dress or one of our ties, for example. This won't guarantee you a job, but it will be looked upon favorably."

During the job interview, what should the applicant ask the employer?

Nicole: "During the interview, you want to determine what the hours are and what your responsibilities will be. After someone gets a job, if I tell them that the hours are 9:00 A.M. to 6:00 P.M., and that person has their coat on at exactly 6:00 P.M. every night, that's not going to impress me. As an employer, I like people who are over-performers —people who do more than what they were told to do.

"You have to feel confident about what you're wearing. If you're not sure about your outfit, change before the interview. To make a good impression, you don't have to wear designer clothes."

"Don't ask too many questions about things like sick days, overtime, vacation days, and benefits. If an applicant seems too concerned about these things early in the interview, I don't consider them to be a good bet. Some questions like that are appropriate, away. Thus, I believe your education is the most valuable asset you can ever invest in. It's something you should always keep building on through work experience. While all work experiences are interesting, early in your life you should be looking for work experiences

> ## "You don't want to have a work experience that is so beneath your intellectual level that it's not stimulating and you're not learning anything."

but don't ask too many questions along those lines. Also, don't try to get a vacation too soon after you start a new job."

Bud: "You want to know what the future opportunities at the company are. Does the company have a policy to promote people from within? Will you be able to learn on the job or get extra training? As far as starting salary goes, that's pretty much already set in the employer's mind, so don't try to negotiate for a higher salary early in the interview process. Save the discussions about financial compensation and benefits for later. Right now, you're interested in learning more about the company, and letting the potential employer learn about you."

Once someone graduates from school, should they be looking to immediately start their career, or should they begin by just looking for a job?

Bud: "There's no such thing as bad work experience. Education and work experience are assets that you can't lose. Money, a house, a car, a boat, and even your clothes can all be lost. However, your education and work experience are something that can't be taken

that are also learning experiences. You don't want to have a work experience that is so beneath your intellectual level that it's not stimulating and you're not learning anything. You want to begin getting work experience that's related to whatever it is that you want to pursue for your career as quickly as possible, because after four or five years working in an industry, you're going to get labeled as working in that industry by future employers. What I mean by this is that if after college, you spend four or five years working at a steel factory, and then you apply for a job at a soap factory, the human resources people at the soap factory are going to look at your résumé and say, 'You work in the steel industry; why are you talking to me? What do you know about the soap industry? Now, if you tell the interviewer that you really love soap, his response is going to be, 'If you love

soap so much, why did you waste five years working in the steel industry? You're someone who likes to waste time.' While all experience is important, get experience in the field that you like or in a related field. At the very least, make sure your work experience doesn't get you labeled so that you won't be able to pursue something you know you'll want to pursue in the future. Also, when you're in an interview situation, be prepared to give good reasons for why you pursued your previous work experiences. What was it about those experiences that made you want to pursue them?"

How important is internship experience while you're still in school?

Nicole: "If you're willing to be an intern, you'll have a much better chance of getting your foot in the door at a company if you start off by supplying your services for free. If you're going to do an internship, it should be within a field that you're interested in pursuing, or at least in a related field or industry. I think internships are very important. If you get out of school and can't find yourself a job, one thing you might consider doing is accepting an unpaid, short-term internship position. This gives you the opportunity to prove yourself to a company, and you might be offered a job as a result."

Bud: "When you're working in an internship, bring to that experience enthusiasm, willing-

ness, aggressiveness, and creativity. If you can bring that to an internship, and you demonstrate that you're a hardworking person, you have a very good chance of getting hired by that company when you graduate. At Nicole Miller, Inc. we always look for people that excel during their internship period. We look at the internship experience as an extended interviewing process, where we really get to know about the applicants. Some interns become so indispensable at our company that we can't wait for them to graduate so they can work for us full-time. If you can make yourself indispensable as an intern, you have a 99 percent chance of being offered a job at that company when you graduate.

"During your internship, every time you're given a task to do, complete it with 100 percent accuracy, as quickly as possible. If you're not given an assignment, look for someone at the company who looks overworked, and offer to assist them."

What advice can you give someone about achieving long-term success?

Bud: "Once you have a job, periodically you should evaluate yourself and your accomplishments. Every day should be a productive day for you. At the end of a week, think about what you've accomplished. At the end of each month, again look back and see what you've accomplished. Then, at the end of the year, determine if you accomplished more and

"If you're willing to be an intern, you'll have a much better chance of getting your foot in the door at a company if you start off by supplying your services for free."

learned more during that year than you did in the previous year. Look at your accomplishments and compare them to other people's you work with. How does your career path compare to theirs? Everything you do in terms of learning new skills and moving forward in your career helps to build yourself. Having a successful career is all about continuously building and seizing opportunities. You have to be patient, dedicated, and continue increasing your skills."

LAST WORD

"One of the biggest mistakes I see young people make is that they look for high paying entry-level jobs. With big salaries come big responsibilities and big demands upon you to perform. That's not something you want to deal with very early in your career, while you're still learning. You're better off starting at a lower salary, proving yourself, and working your way toward a higher-paying job with more responsibilities. If you begin in a high-paying job, the employer isn't going to tolerate you spending the first week or two on the job getting acquainted with your new surroundings. They're going to expect results from you immediately, because that's what they're paying for. If you don't live up to an employer's expectations, you're going to get yourself fired."—Bud Konheim

BILL DeVRIES
PRESIDENT & CEO
Foot Locker

COMPANY BACKGROUND

Foot Locker was created in 1974 as a chain of athletic-shoe specialty stores. The company is a wholly owned subsidiary of Woolworth Corporation, which has its corporate headquarters in New York City. In 1982 the Lady Foot Locker chain was established, followed by Kids Foot Locker in 1987. All three chains, composed of over 1,830 stores, operate under the leadership of Bill DeVries.

Other retail store chains that are owned by Woolworth Corporation include: Woolworth's, AfterThoughts, Reflexions, Kinney (Shoes), Champs Sports, Northern Reflections, and The Bargain! Shop.

PERSONAL HISTORY

Bill began his career selling shoes at a Kinney shoe store while he was still attending college. "Early on, I knew I wanted to be a store manager. To do this, I had to work hard, size up the competition in terms of the people, and develop the skills needed to take the next step."

On graduation, Bill entered into management at Kinney, and began working his way up the corporate ladder to becoming a district manager. "As I was working my way up within the company, I kept reestablishing my goals, reanalyzing the competition, and renewing my commitment to continued learning."

After a stint as a buyer for the chain, he transferred to the importing division. His career at Kinney continued as he joined the marketing side of the manufacturing division, and then went into retail when Woolworth Corporation launched the Champs Sports chain. Bill was one of the

driving forces behind the launch of this Florida-based chain. Later, he returned to New York to help Kinney reorganize. Soon after that, he was promoted to President and CEO of the Kinney Shoe Corporation. When Woolworth Corporation divided Kinney Shoe Corporation into two separate companies, Bill became President and CEO of the athletic footwear and apparel division, which owns and operates the Foot Locker, Lady Foot Locker, Kids Foot Locker, and Champs Sports chains.

TOPICS COVERED IN THIS INTERVIEW

☞ **Launching your career in retail**

☞ **Choosing the type of company you should work for**

☞ **The importance of the résumé and interview when applying for a job in retail**

☞ **Dressing for an interview**

☞ **Questions you should ask during an interview**

What tips can you offer for choosing companies to apply to when looking for a job in retail?

"Analyze each company and the industry that the company is in. It's like picking a stock. You want to pick companies that you like and that are well positioned for growth in the future. When I graduated from college, I had worked for Kinney, and at the time, they were in the beginning of a growth spurt. I had an opportunity to join the company full-time and go into management. It is important to be selective, instead of finding any job to start off with and then hoping you'll move up from there. Next, you want to evaluate where you think you can go within that company. I think young people coming out of college today know more than they give themselves credit for. By doing a little investigation, you can easily pick out some companies that you can relate to and would like to work for.

"Once you accept a job, you have to be aggressive if you want to have a career track that moves upwards. Instead of sitting back and waiting to learn the skills you'll need to move up, get right into the water, and get yourself involved. Force yourself to learn everything that you possibly can."

If you want to work for a retail chain, but know that you eventually want a management or executive-level position, what's the best way to get started?

"You have to get a job working for a retail store or department store in an entry-level position. If you're going to make it in management, you have to have a good understanding of how a store operates. Once you reach management level, you can branch off and follow any one of many career paths within the company that interest you. If you're still in school and you're interested in a career in retail, take a part-time job or summer job at a store, and start gaining experience now.

"In retail, there are several interesting formats: department store and specialty store are two of the most prominent. Both deal with the same consumers but operate in very

"Choose a company that's well positioned in the marketplace, and that you think has a good future."

> *"In retail, there are two types of work experience—department store retail experience and specialty store retail experience. Both deal with the same consumers, but operate in very different ways, have totally different environments, and require you to master a different set of skills."*

different ways, have totally different environments, and require you to master a different set of skills. The people who have the highest level of success working in retail are the ones who really enjoy working with other people."

Did you learn everything you needed to know in school before you launched your career?

"I think I got good background knowledge of what business was about from my education, but nothing can take the place of on-the-job training. Actually working in a retail environment allows you to take what you learned from textbooks, about marketing, sales, advertising, accounting, and other aspects of running a business, and put that knowledge to good use. To succeed in a retail company, you have to have a strong willingness to learn and be dedicated. If you accept a job, but for whatever reasons you're not happy with that job, you always have three options:

1. You can quit.

2. You can say to yourself, "I can do this job, and change what I don't like about it," and then do whatever it takes to really change it so that you're happy.

3. You can try to change what you don't like, and allocate a specific time period to your efforts, such as three or six months. Then, if things don't work out, you can leave.

"Changing something about a job that you don't like is sometimes very easy, but it totally depends on what it is about the job that you're not happy with. The management of the company will have a lot to do with how flexible the work atmosphere is. That's why it's very important to learn as much about a company as you can, before accepting a position. You want the company's philosophies and practices to fit with your personality."

How important is networking when you're looking for a job?

"It can be very helpful. Any time you know someone who knows someone, it's worth checking out what assistance that person can provide in regard to making an introduction for you into a company. In today's employment marketplace there is a lot of competition, so it's the people with an extremely positive attitude and that show a willingness to try that get the best jobs. Don't think of a job in terms of dollars and cents. Sometimes you're better off accepting a lower-paying job that offers more opportunity for promotions in the future than you are to accept a higher-paying job where you will have to spend a lot of time before being considered for a promotion.

"Once you're actually working for a company, especially a large company, networking is critical. You want to meet as many people within the company as you can. It's important to be liked and respected by everyone."

For launching your career at a retail organization, how important is the résumé?

"I think the résumé is important, but a good personal interview is what gets you the job. How you interview is much more important than what your résumé says about you. If your job will involve working with customers and other people, the interviewer is going to be looking closely at your personality and your ability to communicate. If you're applying for a job in retail, make sure your résumé lists any retail experience you've had in the past. You want to demonstrate to the employer that you understand what working in retail is all about. Retail isn't for everybody. During the interview, be open, be pleasant, and answer the questions by putting your personality into what you're saying and how you say it.

"When creating your actual résumé, I think it's important to keep it simple and straightforward."

When applying for a job at a retail-oriented company, how should someone dress for the interview?

"Twenty years ago when I went on my first interview, it was important to wear new shoes, a suit, and a tie. Today, however, showing good taste in casual clothing is acceptable. It would depend on where the interview is taking place. If your interview will be taking place within a retail store at the mall, you should look nice, but casual. If you're applying for a job at a department store, for guys, a suit and tie is appropriate. If you're applying for a job at the corporate office of a retail chain, or you'll be meeting with a district manager at their office, then more formal business attire is appropriate."

What questions should the applicant ask the employer during an interview?

"In a nice way, you should put the interviewer on the defense and ask why they think you should come work for their company. Ask what the interviewer thinks the future of the company holds, and what type of work environment you can expect if you accept the job. Try to learn as much about the work environment as you can. You definitely want to avoid topics that are controversial, and never get into an argument with the person who is interviewing you."

What are the worst mistakes you've seen people make when applying for a job?

"People either come on too strong or are too intimidated. You have to show a certain

"Sometimes you're better off accepting a lower-paying job that offers more opportunity for promotions in the future than you are to accept a higher-paying job where you will have to spend a lot of time in that position before being considered for a promotion."

amount of confidence, without being arrogant. During the interview, if you have the interviewer speaking as much as you're speaking, then you're having a good conversation, and that's very good. If you're doing all of the talking, or if they are, then it's much harder to evaluate how you're doing."

What do you think are the biggest obstacles an applicant will have to overcome when trying to launch their career?

"Don't get discouraged. Don't just apply for one job at one company. Find several companies that you'd like to work for and apply for jobs at all of them. The worst thing that could happen by doing this is that you'll receive multiple job offers and have to make a choice about which one to take."

What are the qualities that you possess that have allowed you to achieve your success?

"I would say that I'm a self-starter. I'm aggressive, and I'm a good listener. I learn from my mistakes, and I have worked hard to become a good people person. I try to treat everyone in a way that I'd like to be treated. People are either self-starters or they're not. I think there are ways to improve the skill sets that you're lacking; you have to pinpoint your weaknesses and then find ways to overcome them. If you lack basic work-related skills, make sure you apply to companies that offer good training programs, and learn as much from this training as you can.

"Too many people go into an interview with the feeling that if they don't get the job, their life will come to an end. In the market today, you have to be open to different opportunities. If you really want to work for a specific company, but that company doesn't have any openings in the department or division you want to work in, then you should consider being flexible and accept a different job within that company. Who knows, you might enjoy that job. Later, you can always transfer within the company to the position that you originally wanted. Have the attitude that you're willing to give any opportunity a shot, and be willing to work hard."

LAST WORD

"When you reach the point in your career that you're satisfied, then it's over because you won't go any higher. Set your goals high and don't get discouraged if you don't land your dream job right away."

NATASHA ESCH  PRESIDENT
Wilhelmina Models

COMPANY HISTORY

Founded in 1967 by the Dutch supermodel Wilhelmina, Wilhelmina Models is based on Park Avenue in New York City and now represents over 900 models worldwide. Over the years, the agency has represented some of the world's most famous people, including Whitney Houston, Kevin Costner, Pamela Anderson Lee, Jessica Lange, Tom Berenger, Beverly Johnson, and Kim Alexis. Under the leadership of Natasha, the company has become an industry leader in the management of male models. Wilhelmina Models currently represents over 80 percent of all male models used today, including Calvin Klein's former print model, Michael Bergin, who also has a successful acting career.

Natasha's main responsibility is the promotion and development of all of her agency's clients in the highly competitive fashion and beauty industries. Her ultimate aspiration is to make Wilhelmina Models the top agency in the world, while playing an active role in assisting young adults in reaching their own personal and professional goals.

One of the new directions Natasha is currently steering her company in is working with well-known models and helping them to launch and manage their acting careers. "There are a lot of exciting things happening in our industry right now. I have tried to find new ways to do business. Wilhelmina Models was one of the first agencies to have a presence on the Internet's World Wide Web (http://www.wilhemina.com). I've tried to approach doing business within this industry a little bit differently from everyone else because I've had to. I'm a young person who had to establish myself in a different way than everyone else. I've tried to take a new and interesting approach to everything I do."

PERSONAL HISTORY

Imagine for high school attending a British boarding school in Switzerland, and then attending and later graduating early from a top undergraduate business school in New England. Then, at the age of 21, being made owner and President of one of the world's leading modeling agencies. Well, that's how Natasha Esch kicked off her career in early 1993, when her family purchased Wilhelmina Models and placed her in charge of the company.

"In 1989 my family acquired Wilhelmina Models, and during vacations from school I worked at the various divisions within the company, in both California and New York. One of the biggest obstacles I faced was that I was young, and the people who I was working with had been in the business for many years. It was very difficult to make decisions and implement new things with people who had a certain way of doing things. Of course, back then I had zero credibility. As a young person, I always had fears of working for a giant corporation with a lot of red tape. I knew that I wanted to be involved in the business world, but I also wanted to do something that had a lot of creativity involved with it. I wanted to work in an industry where young people could be successful. The modeling and entertainment industries offer a lot of opportunities for young people. These are industries that accept young leaders."

Coming out of school and stepping right into the management of a company, Natasha felt extremely lost and overwhelmed at first. "I continue to utilize the knowledge I acquired in business school. At the time I was learning it, I didn't think this knowledge was all that important. Only when I actually began running a business did I realize that what I was taught in school actually had some real-world relevance."

In addition to running Wilhelmina Models and representing many of the world's most recognizable faces, Natasha has written several books about how someone can break into the modeling business. Her latest book, *The Wilhelmina Guide to Modeling by Natasha Esch*, was published in June 1996 by Simon & Schuster.

TOPICS COVERED IN THIS INTERVIEW

☞ **The skills you'll need in business that you won't learn in school**

☞ **How to break into a highly competitive industry**

☞ **The biggest mistakes young people make when applying for a job**

☞ **Creating a résumé that works**

☞ **Making the best impression during an interview**

☞ **Dressing appropriately for the job you're applying for**

You went right from college to running a business. What skills did you find that college didn't teach you?

"Schools are really no good at relaying the real-life experience of working. When you enter a working environment, your entire lifestyle changes drastically. If I were running a college, one of the things I would force students to do is take internships and work during the summer, because that's the only way someone can obtain real-world experience and get a taste of what the work environment is all about. It's very hard for a school to prepare you for what the real world is all about. When you're working for any company, there are a lot of internal politics that you have to deal with in regards to how you interact with certain people, and that's something you can only learn by actually doing it. When you're in school, you don't get a true appreciation of just how competitive the business world can be. The modeling industry, like just about every other industry, is extremely competitive. I think a lot of people graduating from school don't have a realistic comprehension of what to expect when they begin working.

"Another thing I don't think they teach you in college is about all of the interesting job opportunities that are available when you graduate. I attended a well-respected undergraduate business school, and I don't ever recall hearing from a professor that the modeling industry might be an interesting industry. There are a lot of opportunities that aren't necessarily obvious. Many of these opportunities have tremendous growth potential, yet they go unnoticed. The truth is, if you look carefully, you can find job opportunities that don't take 10 or 15 years for you to work your way up to a high-level position."

What's the best way to break into a highly competitive industry, such as the modeling industry?

"If you want to be an agent at a modeling agency, for example, the very first thing you should do is get some experience. When you start at an agency, chances are your salary is

"If you have experience when you're applying for your first full-time job once you're out of school, that makes you much more valuable as an employee."

"Many recent graduates put absolutely everything they can think of on their résumé, and I think that's wrong."

going to be extremely low. One reason why the pay is so low for entry-level people in this business is because there's a lot of training involved. I recommend that while you're still in school, you use your summers and vacations to take internship positions that will allow you to get some of the learning out of the way. If you have experience when you're applying for your first full-time job once you're out of school, that makes you much more valuable as an employee. I think that a lot of people graduating these days from college waste a lot of time starting their 'career education' after college, when they can get a major head start while they're still in college. While you're in school, taking an internship position or summer job for little or no pay is usually a lot easier than taking this type of work once you graduate. While in school, chances are that you're still being supported by your parents, or you have fewer financial responsibilities so you can accept low-paying or no-paying work. Companies like to hire people recently out of college that have at least some experience in a related field. If someone spent a summer working as an intern for a fashion magazine and then applies for a position at my company, they have a much better shot at getting the job than someone with no experience.

"The other thing about highly competitive industries, like modeling, is that most people get their first jobs based on who they know within the industry. These days, who you know is everything. People always want their work to be easier, and one way they make it easier is by working with people that they like and know. In my business, when the qualifications of model A and model B are the same, ultimately it's going to be something else that determines who gets a specific job. In most cases, it will be the model (or the model's agency) that has some sort of relationship with the client. Networking, however, is something that's important in virtually every industry."

What are some of the biggest mistakes you see young people making when they begin applying for their first job?

"A lot of people coming out of school don't do the necessary research to learn about the industry they are interested in working in. When I interview people for entry-level spots, I find that many of them know very little about the modeling business. When you're applying for a job, you should have a basic understanding of what you're getting into. Find out who the industry leaders are, and what challenges the company you're applying to faces. There's also a big difference in what you can expect from a job based on the size of the company you're going to be working for. In the modeling industry, there are large agencies and very small agencies. There are pros and cons to working for large, medium, and small companies. At the larger agencies, as in most large companies, there is more structure and the benefits are usually better. Working for a smaller company will be more relaxed and you'll have more freedom to experiment and incorporate your own tastes into the job."

How important is the résumé as a tool for getting a job?

"For me, a good résumé lists a lot of quality work experience. Even if someone is fresh out of college, I want to see that the applicant has done something with his or her free time that was productive. I use experience as a measure of how much benefit an applicant can offer to my agency. When I look at a résumé, I'm much more impressed by someone who did an internship for a few weeks or months than I am with someone who spent years participating in school-related clubs or lots of nonwork-related extracurricular activities. Many recent graduates put absolutely everything they can think of on their résumé, and I think that's wrong. Before sending your résumé to a company, research what that company is looking for and then customize the information on your résumé to that company. Leave out all of the nonrelevant information. Listing basic skills, such as the ability to use a computer, is always valuable.

"If you don't have the ability to network your way into a company, the only thing you can do is send your résumé to the right person within a company, which means that your résumé is even more important, because it has to capture someone's attention."

What does it take to make a good impression during an interview?

"I always laugh when I see people just out of college on an interview, because they usually have an extremely corporate look. They're often wearing a nice suit and have their note pad and résumé in hand. For many jobs, dressing and acting to fit a corporate image is important, but in an industry like modeling or entertainment you should know that the dress code is more casual. If you come dressed in corporate attire, that shows me right away that you haven't done any research about my company or the industry, and that's a big mistake." Almost any type of job within the entertainment industry is probably an exception for not having to fit into a corporate or business-like image when applying for a job. "Don't come dressed sloppy, but don't look like you're applying for a job at IBM.

"If you want to make a good impression, you should come across as aggressive and forward. You should have a general idea about what you think you can add to the business. Within five minutes after an interview begins, I have a good idea of what that person is all about, and whether or not he or she will fit in well at Wilhelmina Models."

During the interview, what types of questions should the applicant ask the employer?

"You'll eventually want to discuss the job's benefits and how salary reviews work, but these topics should not be brought up early in the interview. More than asking about the specific job, I like to see people asking

"For many jobs, dressing and acting to fit a corporate image is important, but in an industry like modeling or entertainment you should know that things are a lot more casual."

"All the interviewer can judge you on is how you look and how you present yourself starting from the moment you walk in the door. Showing up late demonstrates you're not prepared or responsible."

intelligent questions about the industry as a whole. I think people are afraid to ask questions, because they're worried it will show their ignorance. If your questions show that you have at least some understanding of the industry, and demonstrate your strong interest in the industry and the company, then you won't be perceived as being ignorant.

"During an interview, I always ask the applicants why they want to enter into this business, and I always get very interesting responses. No matter what type of job you're applying for, be prepared to answer this question."

Other than dressing inappropriately, what other mistakes can someone make when applying for a job?

"Probably the biggest mistake is when people show up late for their interview. First impressions are the lasting ones. All the interviewer can judge you on is how you look and how you present yourself starting from the moment you walk in the door. Showing up late demonstrates you're not prepared or responsible. Even if it means arriving to the interview one hour early to ensure that you won't be one minute late, the extra effort is well worthwhile. During the interview, be open, alert, and enthusiastic. Don't slouch in your seat."

How important is having top grades in school when it comes to applying for a first job?

"In most industries grades aren't too important. It's much more important to demon-

strate that you're a well-rounded person. I personally had horrible grades during my first semester in college, and then I earned excellent grades in my later years. There are many reasons why some people don't do well in certain classes, and if you mess up during a semester that brings down your overall grade-point average. I would never base a hiring decision upon someone's grades. Obviously, I'd think twice about hiring a straight-D student, but if someone has a B average and also has some real-world job experience, he or she is a very attractive applicant."

Is it possible to determine if you're going to like a job before you accept it?

"Not really. When someone enters college, and at the age of 18 or 19 is forced to declare a major, chances are they don't have a clue about what it is they want to do with their life after graduation. Someone coming out of school has very little real-world experience. It is extremely difficult to predict what a job is going to be like. The only way you're going to learn if you like a job or not is by actually

doing it. If you don't enjoy a job, you can always switch jobs, but if you do enough research and know what types of things you enjoy doing, then you should be able to find a position that suits you. It's never a good idea to jump from job to job too often. One thing you can do to get a preview of what to expect from a job is spend some time with the people you'll be working with on a day-to-day basis. Are these people like you from a personality standpoint? The more you know about what you're getting into, the less shock you'll have when you start a new job."

Being a female executive, do you face more challenges then men in your position?

"No. The entertainment industry, specifically the modeling industry, is one where women traditionally earn a lot more money than men. Being a woman in this business is actually an advantage. I don't know if this applies to all industries, however."

LAST WORD

"I recommend that young people read a lot and learn about all of the different opportunities that are out there. No matter how good of an education you get, it's going to be limited, because no school can teach you about all of the career opportunities that are available in the business world."

SIDNEY SWARTZ

CHAIRMAN, CEO & PRESIDENT

The Timberland Company

COMPANY BACKGROUND

Timberland was founded in 1955 as Abington Shoe Company. The company name was changed to Timberland in 1978. The Timberland Company designs and manufactures premium-quality footwear, apparel, and accessories that are sold in over 50 countries worldwide through specialty stores, a growing chain of Timberland-owned concept shops, and better-grade department stores. Annual sales during 1995 for the company, which now employs over 6,000 people, were reported at $655.1 million.

In 1987, Sidney orchestrated the company's first public offering, and in 1991, he moved trading of Timberland stock to the New York Stock Exchange (NYSE: TBL). In 1994, Timberland was hailed as the "premier brand" in the outdoor market by the *Wall Street Journal*. It is recognized internationally, as it was in *Business Week*, as one of the "hottest" brands globally.

In partnership with City Year, the Boston-based youth "urban peace corps" and model for national youth service, Timberland has actively supported community service for the past six years. In 1992, Timberland made a $1 million investment in City Year. Later, in 1994, the company announced an unprecedented $5 million investment. Part of the company's involve-

Timberland®

ment includes employees spending their time doing community service work that's coordinated by the City Year program.

"As a company we have both a responsibility and an interest in engaging the world around us. By doing so, we deliver value to our four constituencies: consumers, shareholders, employees, and the community. Philanthropy is not enough. As a responsible corporate citizen, we must actively engage in the community."

PERSONAL HISTORY

While Timberland is a public company, it is a family business that was started by Nathan Swartz, Sidney Swartz's father. "My dad was an immigrant from Russia whose expertise was working with leather. He worked for many years in Boston, which, years ago, was the hub of the footwear industry in the United States. Eventually, my father opened his own shoe factory."

Sidney started working for his dad's company in 1955, as a trainee on the company's production line. In 1966 he assumed the position of treasurer, and began to oversee the company's marketing, advertising, distribution, finance, and manufacturing activities. "My father actually tried to talk me out of getting into the shoe business. He tried to encourage me to stay in school and get a technical background so that I could pursue a career in something like accounting or engineering."

When Nathan Swartz retired, Sidney and his brother took over the company. In 1986, Sidney's brother also retired, leaving the company to Sidney, who has been growing the company and expanding the popularity of the Timberland brand name ever since.

> ## TOPICS COVERED IN THIS INTERVIEW
>
> ☞ **Tips for entering into your family business**
>
> ☞ **Proving yourself after entering a family-owned business**
>
> ☞ **What makes a good employee/job applicant**
>
> ☞ **Making a good impression during an interview**
>
> ☞ **Getting a job at a specific company you want to work for**

If you know you're going to enter into a family business, what's the best way to prepare?

"I would encourage people entering into their family's business to stay in school and learn the skills you'll actually need to run that business, before you take it over. When I began running Timberland, I didn't have all of the knowledge and skills that I needed.

"Even if you know there's a job waiting for you in a family business, take some time and get yourself a job working for another company in an associated industry after you graduate."

Luckily, I was surrounded by many very talented people.

"Even if you know there's a job waiting for you in a family business, take some time and get yourself a job working for another company in an associated industry after you graduate. If you're interested in marketing, go work for a large marketing company and gain some experience. It's much easier to gain experience working for a company where you're not recognized as a member of the family that owns the business. Education and experience are vital before you take any position within a family business.

"I don't know if leaders are born, or if along the way you have to invent yourself, but if you know that eventually you're going to be running your family's business, be sure to perfect your listening skills. You have to learn to listen to people very carefully, and encourage people around you to do their best work. A large part of running a business is being able to build teams and be willing to delegate responsibilities. The Timberland Company is a public company, but it's family controlled. I would like to see my two sons, who now work in the business, eventually take it over. I did not pressure my sons to join the business, nor will I insist that they be the ones to keep it going if they choose to do something else. One of the things you have to do when working in a family business is find ways to ensure that family members don't wind up killing each other when they work together."

When someone actually enters into their family's business, are they going to have to prove themselves?

"Definitely. I believe that it's far harder to work in a family business than it is to work for another company. Relatives are always held to a much higher standard by both management and the other employees. Chances are, when you enter into a family business, you're being given a much higher-level position than someone with your same skills would get if they walked off the street and applied for a job. You're probably going to get some preferential treatment, and you should be prepared to deal with how other employees feel about that. I look at my two sons and expect more from them than I do from everyone else."

What types of employees do you hire?

"Since Timberland manufactures and sells a lot of products targeted to people who enjoy the outdoors, and a lot of our products are used by backpacking and hiking enthusiasts, many of our applicants have a strong interest in these types of activities. I like applicants who have chosen to pursue their interest by getting involved with the company that makes products they use. Some of our most successful employees are people who use our products as part of their leisure activities and hobbies. These people take great pride in our products, and as a result, we have become a much better company. For someone launching their career, the advice I'd like to share is that they should definitely find something that they enjoy doing. If you really enjoy backpacking or hiking, for example, apply for a job at a company like Timberland, L.L. Bean, or Eastern Mountain Sports. These companies offer jobs that involve things you have a strong interest in.

"Some people graduate from school and have absolutely no idea what type of career they're interested in. My advice to these

> "I personally believe that most of the time, sending your résumé blindly to companies isn't going to work."

people is to take some time and try different things." One way to get exposure to a variety of different jobs and career opportunities is to work for a temp agency and get yourself placed at a variety of different temporary work assignments.

"At Timberland, I definitely prefer to hire someone who is a user of our products because they become much more emotionally committed to the company and to the products. Of course, we also have many people working for us who aren't serious hikers or backpackers, but during the job interview process I know that someone who makes it clear that they are seriously interested in an activity, such as backpacking, will have an edge."

What's the best way to get yourself noticed at a company you'd like to work for?

"Personal contact is critical. I personally believe that most of the time, sending your résumé blindly to companies isn't going to work. Sure, you may get lucky and someone might read your résumé and invite you in for an interview, but I think if you're sending your résumé blindly to a company, you're counting on luck to get noticed. I think you have to pick yourself up, go to the company in person, and introduce yourself. Go directly to the human resources department and request an interview, or try to make contact with other people within the company.

"Obviously, if you know someone at a company you're interested in working for, that helps. I think everyone knows people out there who can provide introductions for them into companies. I personally receive

calls from people that I haven't seen in 25 years, asking me to interview their son or daughter who is interested in working for Timberland. If I receive this type of call, at the very least I'll go through the motions and invite that person's child in for an interview. If you network correctly, you should be able to at least get your foot in the door at a company and get yourself an interview.

"At Timberland, we basically get two types of applicants. The first type come into their interview and clearly demonstrate that they have done research about our company. The more knowledge you have about the company you're interviewing with, the more favorably you'll be looked upon by the employer. The second group are people who haven't done research. They come to an interview unprepared, and they seldom get whatever job they're applying for."

What tips can you offer for making a good impression during an interview?

"What really grabs me is when someone comes right out and says, 'I really want to work for your company because...' Those simple words are more important than most of the other things you can show on your résumé or talk about during the interview. If the person that I'm interviewing with looks me in the eye and says that they really want to work for my company and they show some passion in their statement, that has an enormous impact on me. There's something about actually asking out loud for the job. Obviously, sending a résumé and showing up for an interview implies that you want to work for a company, but very few applicants actually come right out and ask for the job that they want.

"During an interview, I look for emotion. I have spent most of my life living by my instinct and my gut. This may not sound too scientific, but that's how I am. I respond well to people who have some passion and emotion in what they're doing. When I ask an applicant why they want to work for my company, I want to hear more than, 'Because it's a really great company with a great financial history.' There's got to be more to their reason than that.

"Even if you're applying to a company with a casual dress code, you should certainly look professional when you come in for an interview. I'm personally delighted when someone comes into an interview wearing Timberland shoes, boots, or clothing. We recently had an advertising agency pitch us because they wanted to represent the company. When they came in to present their ideas and their firm, everyone was wearing a Timberland outfit. They were all dressed from head to toe in our products. This is taking it to the extreme, but it certainly caught our attention. We all started to laugh when the people from the advertising agency walked in, and that made them stand out in a positive way. If this is applicable to the company, during your interview, you want to demonstrate somehow that you are familiar with and use the company's products."

Research

What are some of the mistakes that you've seen applicants make when applying for a job?

"I receive up to a dozen letters per day that are addressed to me and marked 'Confidential' on the envelope. When I open the envelope, all that's enclosed is someone's résumé. When someone pulls a stunt like that, it's almost as bad as sending a résumé addressed to 'To whom this may concern.' Almost all of those résumés that are sent to me marked 'Confidential' are tossed in the wastebasket, because I don't have time to review them. When you send your résumé to a company, don't expect that piece of paper listing the education you have to generate a phone call from that company inviting you in for an interview. Most of the time you have to do more, such as show up at the human resources department and ask for an interview, to get a company's attention."

How can someone get the job they really want within a specific company?

"If working for one specific company is important to you, then the smartest thing you can do is to take any legitimate job you can within that company. I have this belief that if you really want to be successful at a company, getting in the front door is the most important thing you can do. Take any

"WHAT REALLY GRABS ME IS WHEN SOMEONE COMES RIGHT OUT AND SAYS, 'I REALLY WANT TO WORK FOR YOUR COMPANY BECAUSE...'"

"It's always easier to work your way up in a company that's growing quickly. Joining a company that's smaller and leaner almost always means faster promotions to qualified people."

entry-level job at that company, then work hard to capture the attention of your superiors. Plan on working your way up the ladder to the position you really want. This approach works for any company that offers employees the opportunity to move up through promotions.

"When you choose the company you want to work for, make sure that it's growing. Timberland, for example, is a fast-growing company, which means we have many new opportunities opening up within the company on a regular basis. It's always easier to work your way up in a company that's growing quickly. Joining a company that's smaller and leaner almost always means faster promotions to qualified people. At my company, we tell employees that there is no limit to what you can achieve. If you have an interest to do something that's beyond where you're currently at, we'll be happy to work with you."

During the interview process, what should the applicant ask the interviewer?
"Ask about the company's goals and objectives. Sure, you can read a company's financial statements, but that's not the same as getting someone's point of view about the company. If you learn that a company has no growth planned, or how things really are isn't like

what was described in the company's literature, then you want to know about this before you accept a job. Also, before accepting a job, always make the effort to speak with several people who already work for the company, other than the people who hired you. Ask these people what it's like working for the company and what you can expect. Ask the employer if you can spend some time at the company before accepting a job. Have lunch in the company cafeteria. Meet and talk with as many people as you can in order to get the best picture of what the company is all about."

Looking at your career, what are the qualities you possess that have allowed you to succeed?
"I think more than anything, I'm a very open person. I am willing to share the stage with other people. Companies, teams, and organizations that work well are the ones where groups of people work together. Within the company, I try to encourage people to voice their ideas and opinions. In meetings, employees are welcome to disagree and to state their objections. We don't always act on someone's disagreements, but we make the forum available for people within the company to make their thoughts known.

"To be successful at anything in life, you really have to be patient. Success comes to very few people quickly."

I think this management philosophy makes my company a better place to work."

What other advice can you offer to someone about to enter into the workplace?

"I would preach patience. Most people want instant gratification for everything they do. To be successful at anything in life, you really have to be patient. Success comes to very few people quickly. As you start a career, you have to understand that you're going to have to pay your dues, get your hands dirty, and work your way up the corporate ladder. You have to go out of your way to be special and outperform others, and believe that those qualities will be seen by the people around you. Patience is one of the great traits that separates the winners from the losers in the workplace. I think most people have talent, and most people work hard, but they don't stick it out. They get very frustrated and don't like being asked to do things that infringe on their time. You have to be willing to make sacrifices. You don't have to work 18 hours per day, 7 days per week, but you have to be prepared to dig in and prove to the company and to yourself that you're a valuable asset to the company. People who go that extra mile and put themselves out more than other people do are quickly recognized by management. That's the first step toward earning yourself a promotion."

LAST WORD
"For someone launching their career, the advice I'd like to share is that they should definitely find something that they enjoy doing."

JOHN J. McDONALD PRESIDENT

Casio, Inc.

COMPANY BACKGROUND

In **1947**, Tadao Kashio started a Tokyo-based machine shop called Kashio Manufacturing; he was later joined by his brother. In 1950, Toshio began developing an electric **calculator**, and the remaining Kashio brothers, Yukio and Kazuo, joined the company. The Kashio brothers incorporated in 1957 as Casio, and the company released its first **electric** calculator. By 1965, the company used transistor technology to create the first electric **desktop** calculator with **memory**; five years later Casio began exporting its products to America.

CASIO®

Today, Casio has 60 subsidiaries and affiliate companies located around the world, and is responsible for manufacturing and marketing electronic calculators, electronic musical instruments, pagers, portable phones, personal digital assistants, timepieces, multifunction watches, cash registers, liquid crystal displays, video printers, pocket TVs, word processors, label printers, blood pressure monitors, and hundreds of other products. Based in Dover, New Jersey, Casio, Inc. is the U.S.-based subsidiary of Tokyo-based Casio Computer Co., Ltd.

PERSONAL HISTORY

John J. McDonald began his career at Sperry Rand Corporation (now Unisys Corporation) as a salesman, was promoted to local product manager, then to branch sales

81

manager. Eventually, he moved to the company's home office after earning the position of product manager. He then worked overseas as a general manger for Europe, the Middle East, and Africa. When he returned to the U.S. office, he was promoted to vice president of product development.

About 22 years ago, Mr. Kashio, the founder of Casio, offered McDonald the position of President of Casio Europe. After about 17 years, he returned to America as the President of Casio, Inc. "I worked my way up to an executive-level position at Sperry Rand Corporation, then was recruited by Casio. Looking back, within the first year of being a salesman at Sperry Rand, I learned that there were two types of people—those who are active and that want control, and those who are passive and don't want control. Some of my colleagues were salesmen who wanted to spend their professional life staying salesmen. I, however, decided that I wanted a voice in running the show, so I decided that I wanted to move out of the job I was in and eventually earn a top-level position. I didn't make this decision based on the money. I was single at the time, and as a salesperson I was earning plenty of money. I simply wanted more responsibility and control."

TOPICS COVERED IN THIS INTERVIEW

☞ **What mistakes to avoid when applying for a job**

☞ **Finding jobs that will provide the best learning opportunities**

☞ **Developing a résumé that works**

☞ **Making a good impression during an interview**

☞ **The importance of being organized**

☞ **Working for a foreign-owned corporation**

What mistakes have you seen people make when launching their careers?

Very few people begin their career by making a career choice and sticking with it. Sure, there are some professions, like being a doctor, where someone makes a career decision early in life and then spends years training for that career. In business, however, most people decide that they want a job in some business-related profession, such as sales, accounting, marketing, or personnel, and then they accept whatever job they can get. Instead of falling into a job, approach your first job as a learning experience for whatever it is that you'd like to eventually pursue.

"When I started, people were encouraged to spend their life with one company, and companies made a big deal out of how many 25-, 30-, and 35-year employees they had, and awarded those employees plaques and gold watches. I don't know of a single company today that still has a 25-year club. Computers have changed how we do business. People say that because we're now in a global economy, companies have been forced to downsize. But I believe that computers have caused even more downsizing, because this technology has automated many types of jobs and has eliminated the need for many levels of people on both the manufacturing and administrative sides of business. Today, companies can't say with any degree of predictability what jobs will be available 10 or 20 years down the road. As a result, people coming out of school today aren't tied to the concept of choosing a company that they'll remain at for their lifetime.

"In today's business world, it's important to pick a first job in which you will have the opportunity to continue learning and have meaningful experiences. It doesn't matter if you enter into a small company and become a jack-of-all-trades or work for a large company and become a specialist; the important thing is to select a position that will continue teaching you."

How can someone find the best learning opportunities available when selecting a first job?

"I don't think the specific company you wind up at is anywhere near as important as the industry you select. Unless you have a bent toward a specific industry, I would highly recommend finding and working in a growing industry, because that's where you'll have the best long-term chance for growth and success. Select a company that offers training and upward mobility. Choosing a small company versus a large corporation is

entirely up to you, and should be based on your own personality. The culture and work environment are different at various size companies. In a small company, there isn't as much opportunity to move around, but you will have more responsibilities and a much broader job title. At large corporations, you have to be more of a politician to deal with the internal politics at that company. Your job will be far more structured and defined."

What's the best way to find job opportunities?

"I recommend working with your school's career placement office. Often, companies will come to your school to conduct interviews. As soon as you begin thinking about finding your first job, visit the job placement office at your school and obtain a schedule of the companies that will be visiting. Next, arrange to set up interviews with those companies that interest you. Once you have a few interviews arranged, go to the library and start doing research about those companies. You might also want to visit a local stock brokerage office and pick up the annual reports of the companies that are public. If the companies you're interested in aren't recruiting at your school, you can pick up the phone and call, fax, or e-mail the companies and find out about the jobs they have available.

"If you know alumni from your school who are now working at companies you're interested in applying to, you might want to contact them and ask them to put a word in for you at the company. Networking isn't as critical with entry-level jobs, but it will prove to be extremely important when you're ready to change from one job to another later in your career. Obviously, you should take full

advantage of any contacts you have within a company you want to work for.

"If you're approaching a company on your own, you'll probably discover that the human resources offices that you contact receive dozens, if not hundreds of résumés per day, especially during the spring season when college students from all over are also starting their job searches. In doing your research about companies where you want to work, try to find the name of someone you can contact directly at the company. If you're interested in accounting, for example, find out who the company's CFO is, and call them directly or send a personal letter. To find out who the best person to contact is, you can call a company's main switchboard, read their annual report, or check one of the business directories that are probably available in your school's library. If you can get an interview with someone at the executive level of the company you want to work for, then you have a much better chance than going through a company's human resources department. You'll probably find that most business leaders will take telephone calls and respond to letters from students and recent grads because they have kids of their own, and they themselves have been through the whole job search. If the person you contact forwards you to someone else within the company, ask him or her to make an introduction on your behalf."

Is it ever appropriate to do something outrageous to make yourself and your résumé stand out from the other applicants?

"I think that it could help, but only if you have an outrageous personality. If you can't follow through, then doing something outrageous to get attention will backfire. Doing something outrageous really requires the actor in someone to take over, and I think damn few people can pull it off effectively. If you want to make a good impression, be honest, sincere, and demonstrate that you're prepared to work hard and learn."

What should someone wear to an interview?

"The age-old phrase of wearing an 'interview suit' to an interview still applies. That's the best advice. Many companies have a more casual dress code either on Fridays or all the time, but unless the company that invites you in for an interview specifically states that you should be casual, then wear your nicest business attire. You want to promote a professional image at all times during the interview."

What are some questions that the applicant should ask the employer?

"Ask about the opportunities for advancement that exist within the company, and ask what a new employee can do to help the company to achieve its goals. Also ask about the company's long- and short-term goals. Don't bother to ask about salary, vacations, and other benefits, because when you're applying for an entry-level position, the company has predetermined what they are prepared to offer and they won't be willing to negotiate too much, if at all. If there is going to be a salary negotiation, you probably won't get the employer to change their offer by more than one or two thousand dollars for an entry-level job. That is, unless you're the 1 person in 100,000 that has exceptional skills. There will be a natural point in the discussion during your interview when the topic of financial compensation and benefits will come up."

What advice can you offer for creating a résumé that works?

"Whole books have been written outlining the pros and cons of various résumé formats. In my opinion, when you're applying for an entry-level position your résumé should be kept to one page. It should be clear, clean, and contain the minimum amount of verbosity. It should list what your accomplishments are, what work experience you have, and what your goals are. The things you want to highlight on your résumé are the achievements and experiences that you are most proud of and that you want to call attention to. The cover letter you submit should also be brief. It should stress that you're willing to learn new skills, and that you're a hard worker. The letter should be courteous. In my view, the worst thing is when people clutter their résumé and cover

letter with too much information that doesn't apply. Don't go overboard trying to magnify a minimum amount of work experience. The most important think you can do it make your résumé sound truthful and be true to yourself."

Is there any information you should leave out of your résumé?

"If there's anything negative in your history, you should probably leave it out of the résumé, but keep in mind that there is a very good chance that it will be discovered by the employer. I always operate on the theory that there are no secrets in life, and sooner or later everything comes to light. If there is something negative in your background or something that you're not too proud of, eventually you might want to bring it up during your interview, so that you have the opportunity to put a positive spin on whatever it is. The only time when your college transcript might be a factor is when you're applying for a first job, and even then, it will only carry a lot of weight if you're applying for a highly technical position. The people who do interviews understand how schools grade, so you don't have to explain that the B you earned at Harvard, for example, is equivalent to an A at just about any state college. The applicant's personality and perceived ability to fit in at a company will almost always carry more weight than your transcript."

During an interview, what's the one question that you ask that applicants should be prepared to answer?

"I always ask applicants what their major was in school, and why specifically they selected that major. I like to hear why people chose their major and discover what they got out of it. In my experience, I have found that an undergraduate with a liberal arts degree brings more to a company than a business graduate, because liberal arts are based on ideas and force students to be creative and to think. Business at an undergraduate level is more structured, and doesn't encourage students to use their mind to challenge management ideas, for example. An under-graduate business education deals more with learning procedures."

What skills do you possess that have led to your success?

"Consistency. Early on, I realized that I could not accomplish everything in a day that I was asked to do. As a result, the first thing I did every morning, starting when I began my career at Sperry, was to take a few minutes and think about everything that I had to do that day. I would then write down the 10 most important things that I absolutely had to accomplish. Once I wrote down the list, I would organize each item based on its priority, from most important to least important. I would always put the most unpleasant things at the top of my list, so once I got those things finished, it would feel like I was coasting through the remainder of the day. By doing this, I basically accom-plished a lot, because I was able to eliminate all of the unimportant tasks and focus on the important things that had to get done. Because I spent most of my time dealing with the important issues, it caught the eye of management and helped me to earn promo-tions. Many people work long hours every day, but they spend almost all of it doing

things that would be number 99 or later on their list of important things to do. By the end of the day, these people don't accomplish too much. My philosophy is that there is no point in showing up for work each day if I'm not going to accomplish anything. Every single day of my business life, I have started my day by sitting down and making a list of the most important tasks I have to accom-plish, and then prioritizing that list. I strongly believe that this organization has been a major contributor to my success.

"In a business, every single person in the company is a salesperson. Whether you're a janitor, you work on the assembly line, or you work in the marketing department, everyone has to sell the company's product or service. You won't actually be hawking the product to customers necessarily, but you are viewed as a representative of the company in much the same way the sales organization is viewed. Everyone you encounter while working for a company should be dealt with in a way that you would want to be treated, because how you act impacts how your company is perceived by the customer and the public."

In today's global economy, are there any pros or cons of working at a large, non-American-owned corporation?

"There are national cultures that are reflected in business, but most Americans working for a foreign company will wind up working for the company's American-based subsidiary. That's very different than working for the parent company. Casio, Inc. is owned by a Japanese company, but working here is very similar to working for any large American corporation. Any company doing business in the United States not only complies with all local laws, but most of them go out of their way to fit in and adapt their management philosophies. If you have a second language skill, and you really like to use that language, then there may be additional opportunities open to you in a company that's based overseas. It doesn't matter if you're applying to Casio, Panasonic, Sony, or General Motors; the basic hiring practices of every large corporation are going to be pretty similar. If you are applying to a Japanese company, for example, and the person conducting the interview is Japanese, he or she may stress loyalty, or want to hear you stress loyalty as one of your virtues. If you know you're going to be working with executives from a foreign country, anything you do to make yourself familiar with their language and customs won't go unnoticed."

LAST WORD

"I haven't found a college yet that teaches common sense. That's the one thing that many first-time job seekers lack. Also, many recent graduates are under the impression that they can change the world. I'm not saying that you can't change the world, but companies that are looking at you as an entry-level employee are more interested in someone who is level-headed and practical. Running a business isn't equivalent to rocket science. It's all about having common sense and being able to deal with situations without getting rattled."

JACK CHADSEY
PRESIDENT & CEO
Sunglass Hut International, Inc.

COMPANY BACKGROUND

Calvin Klein, Jean Paul Gaultier, Revo, Donna Karan, Fendi, Gianni Versace, Ray-Ban, Guess, Oakley, Giorgio Armani, and Diesel Shades are just some of the manufacturers of high-end, designer sunglasses. They're all available at Sunglass Hut International retail locations.

Sunglass Hut locations are in virtually every mall in America, as well as in airports and in the shopping districts of most major cities. Sunglasses sales are a $2.5 billion per year industry, and Sunglass Hut International continues to be the retail leader in this industry.

Founded in 1971 by an optometrist in Miami, Florida, Sunglass Hut International is a Coral Gables, Florida-based company that is now the leading retailer of sunglasses in America.

PERSONAL HISTORY

Jack started out his 25-year career in retailing at May Department Stores. From there, he moved to Dayton Hudson Corporation, a $15 billion company that owns (or has owned) several malls, large retail chains, and mass merchandising chains including: Target, Marshall Field's, and Marvyn's.

Working for a mass merchandiser, his job was to develop innovative ways to take

business away from traditional department stores. As a result of this experience, Jack became interested in specialty retailing, and in 1989 was offered his current position at Sunglass Hut International, Inc., a retail chain that specialized in selling middle- and high-priced sunglasses.

When Jack took over Sunglass Hut International, the chain had approximately 200 retail locations and a strong strategy. "What the company lacked was a strong infrastructure and the management talent to take the company to the next level," explains Jack. "The average male owns three pairs of sunglasses, and the average female owns five pairs of sunglasses. Over the course of their lifetime, the average person buys between 30 and 40 pairs of sunglasses. Our goal is to build relationships with the customer, so they keep returning to our stores to buy their sunglasses from us." No matter where you live, finding a Sunglass Hut International retail location shouldn't be too difficult, considering that since Jack took over the company he has expanded it to 1,800 retail locations. The company also has a fast-growing mail order catalog business, and allows you to buy products on the Internet. "The industry is broken up into three segments: sports, fashion, and the traditional segment. Our business is a leader in the sports and fashion segments of the retail sunglasses business," states Jack.

TOPICS COVERED
IN THIS INTERVIEW

☞ Launching your career in retail

☞ Is retail right for you?

☞ What type of person is best suited to work in retail?

What does it take to start your career at Sunglass Hut International?

"We're not looking for rocket scientists. Successful retailers are people who have good common sense. You don't have to be a straight-A student in school to launch a successful career at Sunglass Hut International and work your way up the corporate ranks. We're looking for people who are extremely energetic, flexible, and positive. The culture at Sunglass Hut is one that moves extremely fast. Specialty retailing is fast-moving, but our company is on a growth spurt, so everything moves at warp speed. We're a company that sees itself with over 5,000 retail locations worldwide. Recently, we launched a new line of stores that offer eye wear specifically to young people, and we've launched a chain of specialty watch stores. As a result, entry-level employees at Sunglass Hut have incredible growth potential within the company. Someone can start as a sales associate or store manager, work their way up to an area manager position, get promoted to a district manager, and continue to move their career forward with a promotion to become a regional director. From that point, the career path is at the corporate level."

"If you're the type of person who has to have a policy and procedure book in front of you to tell you how to do things, then you're probably not going to do well in the retail environment."

From the day someone starts as a sales associate in one of your stores, how quickly can they move up, assuming they work hard?

"It could be as little as six months to one year, if you're sharp and really do your job. In other retail environments, this fast-moving career path might not be possible, if the company you join isn't growing as quickly as we currently are."

What does it take for someone to be successful working in a retail environment?

"Good retail organizations move with the customer, which means the people who work for a retail chain must be flexible and able to adapt to a changing environment. If you're the type of person who has to have a policy and procedure book in front of you to tell you how to do things, then you're probably not going to do well in the retail environment. Working in retail is very different from working in a corporate environment. To be successful in retail, you have to be 100 percent dedicated to providing superior customer service. Almost everyone who applies for a job in retail is qualified to do the job itself, but what we look for is personality. We look at the applicant and ask ourselves if they will fit the culture of Sunglass Hut."

If someone wants to break into retail, what's the best way to find the opportunities available?

"Most of us who are in senior positions at a retail company got our start working for a traditional department store. Working at a

traditional department store will teach you the basics of retail. If you think retail is what you want to do with your career, starting off working for one of the major department stores is an excellent strategy. Make sure, however, you choose a quality company. Find a retail store that is well respected and in a growth phase. You don't want to begin your career at a company that a few months down the road will be laying off people. When evaluating job opportunities in retail, look for companies that offer the most extensive training programs. Nobody comes out of college knowing how to run a business, so the more training you can get for yourself, the better off you'll be. Also, look at career opportunities available at the retail chain you're applying to. How quickly will you get promoted? Also, look carefully at the benefit package that's being offered."

How should someone coming out of school go about setting job-related goals?

"First of all, you have to be realistic about what your goals are. Set goals for yourself that will keep you challenged, but that are not overwhelming. You don't want to hit a midlife crisis by the age of 30. As you develop long-term goals, think about what will happen if you don't achieve those goals for reasons that are beyond your control. If you get into retailing, during your career you will have many opportunities to move upward. The key is that you want to be exposed to as many different areas as you can within a company."

"Working at a traditional department store will teach you the basics of retail. If you think retail is what you want to do with your career, starting off working for one of the major department stores is an excellent strategy."

In the retail environment, how important is networking?

"If you want to reach the top at a company that's based in a retail environment, networking is important. Interact with people from other parts of the company. If you're in merchandising, for example, you'll be able to do a much better job if you interact and work with the people in the field organization, because they're the ones pushing your product. Likewise, if you work for the home office, you should have a good relationship with your managers. If you go into a store and you see the sales associate abusing the customer, you can be sure that the management of that company abuses that sales associate. That's a situation you want to avoid."

How important is the résumé for someone who wants to break into retail?

"There is no question that the résumé is important. The thing to remember, however, is to keep your résumé short and to the point. Provide the highlights of your experience and be very specific about the kind of job you're applying for. If you're at all general, your résumé will get tossed into a pile with hundreds of other résumés that don't get read. Also, don't just address your résumé to someone in the human resources department of a company. If you know that a company has a specific job opening, for example in the field organization, send your résumé and a cover letter to the vice president of store operations at the company. Likewise, if you want to work in merchandising, send a copy of your résumé and a cover letter to the general merchandise manager at the company. Everyone sends their résumé to the human resources department. Unless you know the president or CEO of a company, or have some sort of contact with that person, don't send your résumé to that person, because they're usually too busy to read résumés and will simply pass it along to human resources or the personnel department. Remember, the résumé should be customized specifically for the job you're applying for."

What are some of the mistakes people can make when preparing a résumé?

"In addition to keeping it short, never use wild-colored paper. When someone in the hiring position reviews résumés, they're looking for energy—someone who is reasonably aggressive without being too assertive. You want to sell yourself quickly, because when you're actually working in retail, you don't have a lot of time to interact with customers and win them over. If someone's résumé doesn't hit me between the eyes

"If someone's résumé doesn't hit me between the eyes quickly, and tell me what that person's skills are, then they're not going to get a job."

quickly, and tell me what that person's skills are, then they're not going to get a job. List the skills and experience you have that pertain to the job you're applying for."

In addition to having a concise résumé and a personalized cover letter, what else can someone do to get their foot in the door at a company?

"After you've sent in your résumé, follow it up with a telephone call. Calling the person you sent your résumé to shows that you have an interest and you are aggressive. After you've had your interview, immediately follow it up with a brief and personalized thank you note. This keeps your name on the mind of the person making the hiring decisions. If two people are equally qualified for a position, sending a thank you note could be the one small thing that gets you selected instead of the other person, because it shows you made the extra effort."

What does it take to make a perfect impression during an interview?

"Make sure that you act totally professional from the moment you walk in the door of the company you're applying to. You must have a neat, clean, and professional appearance. During the interview, make eye contact. Whatever you do, don't ramble. One of my best interviewing techniques is that I'll sit back and not say a word. I watch to see how long people will ramble on about nothing. Rambling could be deadly. By the same token, you want to supply more than 'yes' or 'no' answers. Answer questions in complete sentences, and stay to the point as you answer each question. Don't get intoxicated by your own verbosity.

"If you're applying for a job at a retail store, or for a job within a company that's retail-oriented, before the interview, make sure that you've spent some time visiting the actual store(s). During an interview, we'll always ask, 'Have you ever been in a Sunglass Hut store?' If the applicant says 'no,' that's a big turnoff. If you go through the trouble of coming in for an interview and taking up our time, the least you can do to prepare is to first visit one of our stores and become familiar with what we offer. If the applicant says they have visited one of our stores, then we'll ask follow-up questions, like, 'What did you think about the service? What would you have done differently? How did you feel about the design of the store? Did you feel that the store offered a positive environment for customers?' We listen carefully to the answers applicants provide to these follow-up questions, because this is when the applicant can demonstrate an understanding of the company and our products. If someone came into an interview wearing a pair of sunglasses that they clearly purchased from one of our stores, I'd say that would be a bit trite."

What types of questions should the applicant ask the employer during the interview?

"It's always good to ask about the vision of the company and what the company's long-term strategy is. Especially if you're being interviewed separately by multiple people, you can learn a lot from asking these questions to each person. If the answers are pretty similar, that's good news, because it shows that the company is doing a good job communicating with its employees and that people are working together toward a common goal. You want to work in a culture where people are communicating and working toward the same goals. In the early stages of the interview process, never ask questions about salary, vacations, and benefits. These are topics that should be discussed around the time the company is actually making a job offer to you. Right now, concentrate on selling yourself to the company and learning as much as you can about the company."

How can someone find a job they know they're going to be happy in?

"It's a rare occasion when people graduate from school and know exactly what they want to do. It's important to be flexible and keep yourself open. There are a lot of opportunities available in retail; however, after spending time in this environment, you might discover that it's not for you. You might decide that once you reach the level of district manager, the job requirements involve too much travel, for example. As you work your way up, you might become interested in the point-of-sale machines and find you'd be happier working for a retail organization's M.I.S. division. If you have an interest in retailing, the only way to find out what it's really like is to work for a retailer. While you're still in school, if you can participate in internship programs or work for a retail store during summer vacations, that experience will prove beneficial. When you're working in retail, the one thing you

want to determine as early as possible is how the management treats its people. Working for a traditional department store will provide a very different experience than working for a specialty retail chain, like Sunglass Hut International, so you have to decide for yourself what type of experience you're looking for."

What skills will someone need to be successful in retail that they might not have learned in school?

"Communication and marketing skills are important, and these aren't always formally taught in school. I don't care what your job is; you're always going to be marketing something to somebody. You have to learn how to communicate, listen, and sell. When you reach the management level, listening skills are critical. If you didn't obtain these skills in school, or by working at a summer job or internship, there are all sorts of books, videos, computer software packages, and seminars you can use to enhance these skills."

What are the biggest obstacles you've had to overcome in your own career?

"I've had to discover for myself how to learn from my mistakes. When I graduated from school, I wanted to get involved with a segment of retailing that was growing fast, and at the time, it was mass merchandising. The good news is that in this type of environment, you get promoted quickly. The drawback is that eventually, things slow

"When you're working in retail, the one thing you want to determine as early as possible is how the management treats its people."

down. Eventually, I was forced to sit in the same job for a few years. When this happened, I began to think something was wrong with me, when in fact my career track slowed down because of what was happening within the company and industry I was working in."

In today's business environment, is it possible to have an interest in retailing and achieve success owning and operating your own store that isn't part of a large chain or franchise?

"That's becoming more and more difficult. Unless you have a very unique concept that nobody else has tried, owning and operating your own independent retail location is becoming extremely difficult. A lot of our growth at Sunglass Hut has come at the expense of what we call 'mom and pop' stores. Because we have the financial strength, operating efficiency, and the buying power, we can use that leverage to compete at a level that 'mom and pop' stores simply can't. If you're an extremely creative person, you may be better off in the long run to find a company that will allow you to utilize that creativity as opposed to going out and trying a retail concept on your own."

What are the skills and qualities that you personally possess that have allowed you to achieve success?

"My vision. I have learned over time to build on my successes. I take one success at a time and build around it. One of my strengths is that I'm a strategist. I've developed the ability to attract and hire a quality team. Any good manager has people around him or her that complement them. You can't build a successful company by yourself. It requires expertise in a lot of different areas, and you have to know when to sit back and let other people do their jobs. When you run a company, you must be focused on the horizon, not just on the road. I'm involved in the day-to-day activities of my company, but I'm also responsible for developing the long-term strategies that will keep the company growing three to five years down the road."

LAST WORD

"You need to manage your expectations. Be realistic. Set realistic goals and measure yourself against them. Always be flexible, and don't get frustrated. If you're not taking risks, you're not moving forward. Even if you try something and you fail, it's still momentum. You want to create constant momentum and to continuously move yourself and your career forward."

RUSSELL A. BOSS
PRESIDENT & CEO
A.T. Cross Company

COMPANY BACKGROUND

Tracing its history back to **1846**, A.T. Cross Company is the nation's **oldest** manufacturer of fine writing instruments. The company was founded by Alonzo Townsend Cross, whose father, Richard Cross, uncle, Benjamin Cross, and step-grandfather-in-law, Edward W. Bradbury, made **writing instruments** and jewelry. The Cross family was originally from England, but moved to Providence, Rhode Island. In 1964, the company moved its headquarters to Lincoln, Rhode Island, where it has been headquartered ever since.

Sales for 1995 were $191.1 million. During the company's 150-year history, it has maintained its position as an industry leading manufacturer of premium ballpoint pens, soft-tip pens, rolling ball and fountain pens, pencils, desk sets, and accessories. The shell castings for these prestigious writing instruments are made from many different materials, including stainless steel, chrome, titanium, platinum, sterling silver, 10k-gold filled, 22k-gold electroplate, and solid 14k gold. The writing instruments manufactured by A.T. Cross Company are sold throughout the world.

CROSS® 1846 150 YEARS 1996

PERSONAL HISTORY

Russell A. Boss began his career at A.T. Cross Company in 1965 after graduating from Dartmouth College and spending three years with the U.S. Coast Guard as an officer. "When I was about to graduate from college, I had the option of either being drafted or participating in an officer's training program. After three years as an officer in the Coast Guard, I began working for my family's business, A.T. Cross Company, which was purchased in 1916 by my grandfather. My father offered my brother and myself a job in the production department of the company." He worked his way up within the company and in 1979 he was named President.

Outside of his professional interests, Russell is active in civic affairs and is a strong fund-raiser and contributor to his alma mater, Dartmouth College. He was recently chairman of the Alexis de Tocqueville Society of the United Way of Southeastern New England and is a director of the Narragansett Council, Boy Scouts of America. In addition to being involved with many professional organizations, Russell is an active golfer, tennis player, and sailor. Over the years, he has been the president of two yachting associations and a country club. Russell is married and has three daughters.

"I would highly recommend... some work experience outside of the family business before entering into it."

TOPICS COVERED IN THIS INTERVIEW

☞ **Preparing to join a family-owned business**

☞ **Setting career-related goals**

☞ **The importance of advanced degrees, such as an MBA**

☞ **The worst mistakes applicants make when applying for a job**

When you were growing up, did your father put a lot of pressure on you to join the family business?

"No. My father always made it clear that the company was there for us if we wanted it, but there was never any pressure to join the company. While I was in college, I spent several summers working at the company's manufacturing plant. During that time, I learned about the company from firsthand experience. My father always had an outstanding relationship with his employees, so when I joined the company and began working in the Production Planning division, I was accepted by the employees and received superior on-the-job training from them. In order to prepare for a career at A.T. Cross Company, I studied business in school. Dartmouth and Amos Tuck School of Business had a special MBA program at the time I attended, so I spent three years at Dartmouth and was supposed to spend two years at Tuck in order to graduate with an MBA. However, after one year at Tuck, I only had a C+ average, so the school suggested I

"Before you begin searching for a first job, you have to at least have a general idea about the type of job you're interested in pursuing."

take a year off and work. I went to Officer Candidate School, and I never returned to school. These days, most graduate schools won't admit people right out of college. They insist on people getting some work experience before entering grad school."

What's the best way to go for someone graduating from college or finishing graduate school who is planning to enter into a family-owned business?

"Both my brother and I went into the military and spent several years getting excellent training. From this experience, I learned how to manage people from all walks of life. The military was a wonderful training ground for me. If someone isn't planning on joining the military, I would highly recommend that they get some work experience outside of the family business before entering into it. My oldest daughter graduated from Harvard and went to work for a year on Wall Street before joining A.T. Cross as a supervisor in the production department. She is now a product manager."

What advice can you offer recent graduates who are trying to set career-related goals?

"Most people don't remain at the first company that they go to work for after they graduate. In fact, many people eventually move to other industries, after they have spent a year or two at a job that they haven't really enjoyed. My advice is that people coming out of school should accept the job they think looks the most promising. They

should stay at that job for two or three years, and then either move within the company to another position, or if they're not happy in the profession they chose, they should reevaluate their career path now that they have some experience under their belt.

"For someone who has absolutely no idea what type of career they want to pursue when they're getting ready to graduate, I'd suggest looking into those tests that they have to help people determine what types of careers they're most suited for based on their abilities and interests. Taking one of these tests might give you some direction. I would also recommend setting up appointments with the career counselor at your school. Before you begin searching for a first job, you have to at least have a general idea about the type of job you're interested in pursuing. Do you want to work behind a desk in an office? Do you want to be out on the road selling? Someone coming out of school and about to enter the workplace for the first time has a lot to think about before they actually begin their job search."

How important is having an advanced degree, such as an MBA, if you want to have a successful career?

"It all depends upon what type of industry you want to work in. In some occupations, an advanced degree is critical if you want to go beyond a certain level in your career. In other types of occupations, however, an advanced degree isn't important. In my opinion, going to business school at the

Responsibility

> *"By talking to people, you can learn a lot more about a company than what's published in its annual report."*

graduate level is an excellent way to perfect your skills, obtain additional maturity, and learn responsibility. Don't think, however, that just because you have an MBA when you begin applying for jobs you will automatically get many high-paying job offers. You'll still have to set yourself apart from the other applicants and demonstrate to the employer that you're the best person for the job."

What should applicants look for at the various companies they're looking at?

"Talk to people in the local community where the company is located and try to learn about the company's reputation. Also, talk to people who actually work for the company and find out if they like working there. Ideally, you'll want to meet the people you'll actually be working with, including those people who will be your supervisors or your immediate boss. By talking to people, you can learn a lot more about a company than what's published in its annual report. Of course, you'll also want to do research about the company and study whatever information you can find."

How can someone find the best job opportunities available?

"I would recommend taking full advantage of your school's on-campus recruiting program. When you meet with a company that sends someone to your school, don't ask them what job openings they have available. It's your job to find out what jobs the company has available before your interview. When you go into the interview, tell the interviewer exactly what job you're interested in. If the company you're interested in working for doesn't visit your school, then you'll have to do some additional work and start sending out your résumé in order to obtain an interview. This is a much more difficult path to follow."

Another way of generating job leads is to ask your school's career guidance office or alumni office for a list of companies that currently have alumni from that school working in high-level positions. Many alumni are willing to help recent graduates from their alma mater to find a job. Now, when you call up one of these alumni, even if you don't know them, you have something in common—the college or university you've graduated from. If you want an opportunity to meet top-level people, like Russell, who are still active in their alma mater's alumni council, find out when the alumni group is sponsoring a meeting or special event, and attend that event with the idea of using your networking skills to generate some job leads.

"WHEN YOU GO INTO THE INTERVIEW, TELL THE INTERVIEWER **EXACTLY** WHAT JOB YOU'RE INTERESTED IN."

How important is networking in the job-search process?

"Networking is very important when it's up to you to track down the companies you're interested in working for, and you have to find a way to get yourself invited in for an interview. Using any connection you have is the best way to get your foot in the door at a company in order to get an interview. If you know someone who can make an introduction for you into a company, at least you can be sure that someone there is going to read your résumé. Sending an unsolicited résumé to a company's human resources department is the least effective way of getting yourself an interview."

During the interview process, what's the best way to make the perfect impression?

"A job interview is a two-way street. You have to answer the questions that the interviewer asks, but you are also going to be evaluated based on the questions you ask the person doing the interview. The interviewer wants to use their time with you to learn about your personality, how mature you are, and how hard you want to work. Your communication skills are also going to be evaluated. As the employer, we want to know how you performed in past work experiences. There-fore, any reliable references you can provide from past employers from summer jobs or internships, for example, will be beneficial. How you performed in a previous job is a major indication to us about how you will perform in the job you are applying for. That's why a recommendation from a past employer is important.

"Good personal hygiene is important. You have to act interested in the job you're applying for, know about the company, and

show that you're motivated to work hard. During the interview, be sure to inquire about the career paths that are available. Some companies hire people for a specific job, but don't offer that employee the opportunity to move their career forward in the future after they've proven themselves. You don't want to accept a job that's a dead-end position."

When you go into an interview, bring with you at least one or two copies of your résumé, a list of potential questions you might want to ask the employer, your letters of recommendation, personalized business cards (if you have them), and a pad and pen. All of this information should be carried neatly (and in an organized manner) within some type of folder or portfolio. Having access to a pad and pen during the interview will help to demonstrate that you're an organized person and that you're interested in keeping track of important points that come up during the conversation. During the interview, be sure to jot down notes to yourself about follow-up questions you want

"During the interview, be sure to inquire about the career paths that are available."

to ask, or important job-related information you want to remember.

If you go into virtually any business environment, you'll often see that the middle- and upper-level people carry with them a good-quality writing instrument, manufactured by a company like A.T. Cross or Mont Blanc. For many people, the pen they carry is considered to be a corporate status symbol. Thus, if you've been given a nice pen set as a gift for graduation, bringing it along to the interview is yet another way to give a subtle boost to your overall professional image.

LAST WORD

"If you've recently graduated from school and you don't have a lot of work experience, be prepared to discuss whatever other types of accomplishments you've achieved. Stress the skills that you have, and talk about how those skills can be applied to whatever job you're applying for."

JIM McCANN

PRESIDENT & CEO

1-800-FLOWERS

COMPANY BACKGROUND

The concept is simple--give people the ability to order **flowers and gifts** and have them delivered to anyone, anywhere, quickly (often within **24 hours**). The typical customers of 1-800-FLOWERS are business people on the go. The company continues to be one of the fastest-growing companies in America, because it caters to its customers by offering many **convenient** ways to order its products, including:

☞ **An international 1-800 telephone number that allows people to use any telephone to have flowers or a gift sent to anyone, anywhere**

☞ **The Internet and America Online (Keyword: Flowers)—Customers can use their personal computer to view flower arrangements and gifts, then have their selections sent to loved ones with the tap of a few keys on the computer's keyboard**

☞ **A fast-growing chain of retail stores**

PERSONAL HISTORY

How do you go about launching a business that within 10 years generates over $250 million in revenue? As the President and CEO of 1-800-FLOWERS, Jim uses a unique management style, which he created based upon his life experiences. This management philosophy has allowed his company to become extremely

1-800-FLOWERS SM

103

successful and has earned him several prestigious honors, including the Entrepreneur of the Year award from *Inc.* magazine.

Jim began his career as a social worker and administrator at St. John's Home for Boys in Rockaway, New York. "Working with underprivileged children, I had to create hope when none seemed to exist. From this experience, I learned how important it is to make people feel loved. I also learned a lot about working with other people."

Unfortunately, the salary Jim was earning as a social worker wasn't really enough to support himself, his wife, and three children, so back in 1987, Jim opened his first flower shop in New York, but he kept his job as a social worker. The flower-shop business grew into what is now 1-800-FLOWERS.

"I opened my first flower shop by accident. I was looking around for a business that I could afford to buy on my own while I was working as a social worker. Someone told me about a flower shop that was for sale. I was able to borrow the money I needed to buy it, so I did. I didn't know anything about the flower business, but I was willing to learn. From that point, I found that I really liked the business, and I continued to grow it."

TOPICS COVERED IN THIS INTERVIEW

☞ **Developing a career track for yourself**

☞ **Arming yourself with the tools you'll need to get a job**

☞ **Making a good first impression during an interview**

☞ **How living below your means will help lead to long-term success**

☞ **How accepting temp work can lead to a full-time job**

When should someone start thinking about a career track?

"Based on my own life experience, all of our later-in-life professional interests start with our early exposures. As a result, those seemingly meaningless part-time and summer jobs that almost all of us have had when we were in high school and college aren't actually that meaningless after all. Those jobs gave us insight into different industries and careers. Working as a kid in retail, I learned a lot about many different types of businesses. Thus, the more work exposures you had as a teenager, the more insight you have now into the job market and the opportunities that are available to you now that you're ready to begin your career. Anyone who has the opportunity to graduate from college has an incredible advantage. People who are graduating these days with computer knowledge have an even greater advantage.

"The days of earning a gold watch for a lifetime's work at a company are gone. If you have the tools, the right skills, the right attitude, and the ability to spot opportunities, then you're probably going to have multiple jobs and careers in your lifetime, and you're going to be successful."

"The days of earning a gold watch for a lifetime's work at a company are gone. If you have the tools, the right skills, the right attitude, and the ability to spot opportunities, then you're probably going to have multiple jobs and careers in your lifetime, and you're going to be successful. There has never been a more exciting work environment than there is today."

Young people shouldn't get too hung up on picking a career, because the new verb of the late 1990s is to constantly be *résumé-ing*. People are constantly changing jobs and careers. Once you begin a career, every year or so, you should take a look back and a look forward. If you look back and say to yourself that you didn't really do anything new that year, and you didn't do anything that really challenged you, then as you look forward, you should consider making changes by finding work that will challenge you and look good on your résumé as you develop new skills and experiences. This might mean changing jobs within a company, or moving to another company.

"Since a huge part of my business involves working with AT&T, I can tell you that the people I work with from AT&T who have been with the company for 20 or more years have all held 10 to 15 different jobs within the company. More and more companies, including my own, have woken up to the fact that their organizations are only as good as their people. The best way to develop good people is to push them, challenge them, move them around, cross-train them, and continuously stimulate them. This is a practice that you should be prepared to face once you begin your own career."

You mentioned the importance of having the right skills. What are they?

"You have to be able to express yourself both orally and in writing. You have to have a familiarization with technology and should know how to use a PC. You have to be able to learn quickly and adapt. Things are changing extremely fast in the business world, and with every change comes a totally new set of opportunities. Learn to identify and take advantage of opportunities."

How important is the résumé when searching for a job?

"What the résumé says about a person's experience is tremendously important. If someone sends me a résumé and it doesn't have a cover letter attached, the résumé won't get looked at. If the cover letter isn't custom-tailored and personalized, then both the letter and the résumé will wind up in the trash. If someone is going to send me a form letter and place my name in a blank, they shouldn't bother. As a growing company,

Jim McCann **105** **1-800-FLOWERS**

1-800-FLOWERS receives so many unsolicited résumés each week that if someone doesn't take the time to write a personalized cover letter and then customize their résumé to the job they're applying for, then why should we take the time to read what they send? The very best way to get into a company is through a personal reference. It's just like marketing; you have to find a way to cut through the clutter. No matter what the person's résumé says about them, we hire people based on their personality. I would rather hire a guy who has a ponytail, a flamboyant way of dressing, and a wonderful and outgoing personality than someone who is dressed right, drives up for their interview in their parents' Volvo, but has the personality of a clam.

"On the résumé itself, highlight the companies that you've worked for that have the best reputation. If the companies you've worked for have a reputation for hiring sharp people, that are aggressive and have high ethics and morals, that says a lot about who you are as a person. We're all a product of the company we keep. Likewise, the reputation of the company you're applying to is something that you should seriously examine before accepting a position there."

You mentioned how critical a personalized cover letter is. What should someone's cover letter include?

"The cover letter should be short, but it should be clever and capture my attention

right away. Within the letter, show that you've done some research and you know what the company is all about. Never say, 'I don't know too much about your company, but someone I know recommended that I send you my résumé and apply for a job.' The person who reads the cover letter and résumé receives many of them. You only have a few seconds to capture their attention."

How can someone find a person who can make a personal introduction?

"Ask a lot of people. It's amazing how easy it is for anyone to network into a company just by talking with people. We recently hired someone in our computer department who was recommended by someone who works for us on a part-time basis. That part-time employee came to us and said that a friend of a friend of hers was looking for a job. She had met this person and thought the potential applicant was a go-getter and full of energy, so she asked if she could drop off a résumé on this friend of a friend's behalf. Because we respected the opinion of this part-time employee, we took her recommendation seriously. Having a recommendation will help to get your résumé and cover letter to the top of the pile."

How can someone make a good first impression during an interview?

"It all comes down to how you carry yourself in the first few minutes. If you appear to be comfortable and relaxed, have a sense of humor, and can answer the questions that are posed, then you'll be off to an excellent start. When I'm involved in interviewing a potential applicant, I look for personality and for the quality of the dialog between myself and the applicant. My goal in an interview is to learn what the applicant is all about as quickly as I can. Demonstrate energy and interest.

"Before the interview, create opportunities to talk with current employees from the company and learn as much about the company as you can. Ask these people what the best and worst things about working for the company are. The more you learn about the company before the interview, the better impression you'll make during the interview."

What should someone ask the employer during the interview process?

"Ask questions that are of interest to you. Don't try to fake an interest in the company or in the career opportunity that the company has to offer. If the first questions out of an applicant's mouth are about salary, vacations, or sick days, then I'm going to be turned off. I would recommend asking about the challenges, opportunities, and educational resources that are available at the company."

What's the best way to overcome being nervous before and during an interview?

"Practice. Go on as many job interviews as you can. The first thing I would do is visualize what will happen within the interview and think about the answers to questions you think you'll be asked. Have your friends interview you as practice. The more practice you have, the more comfortable you'll be during the interviews for jobs that you're really interested in."

Do you think a head-hunting firm or an employment agency can help someone just out of school to find a job?

"Headhunters normally work only with people who have experience. Employment agencies, however, can be a useful tool to help someone find job opportunities. I am a strong believer in temping. By taking temp jobs, you might not work at the level you want, but accepting a temp job gets you into a company and gives you the opportunity to sell yourself and work for people who can offer you a full-time position. Doing temp work offers wonderful networking opportunities, and you get paid for the experience. Working in a temp position is one way you can get your foot in the door at a company."

What qualities do you possess that have allowed you to become a business leader?

"I have learned to recover quickly from mistakes. Everyone makes mistakes. The trick is to recover quickly and keep moving forward. Don't get hung up on past mistakes. I always learn from my mistakes and from other people's mistakes. Look, learn, listen, and steal good ideas. The definition of creativity or innovation is the adaptation of a good idea from another field into your field. That's creative. There aren't any new answers. There are only old answers that are repackaged. One of the best learning experiences I had was when I worked at a home for underprivileged teenage boys. I learned quickly that if I wasn't a leader, I was going to

"The trick is to recover quickly and keep moving forward. Don't get hung up on past mistakes. I always learn from my mistakes and from other people's mistakes."

"Waiting until you're older before starting a family allows people to take some chances and make mistakes without severe consequences when starting their career."

get run over. Part of being a leader is being proactive, showing care and concern for those you work with, and having an agenda. If people think you have a good plan and they trust you, they'll follow. I also read voraciously. I consume periodicals. I listen to books on tape, and I read a lot of books."

How can someone achieve their goals?

"I was taught as a child that it isn't good to fantasize or daydream. As I got older, I discovered that daydreaming about success is good. If you constantly continue to work, even at a turtlelike pace, to achieve your dreams, then what you dream about can eventually come true. It's amazing what fantasizing and imaging can do in terms of conditioning your mind as to what your lot in life is to be, assuming you're willing to work for what you want. Once you create goals, think hard about what it will take to achieve those goals, and then work toward achieving them. Early on, what I discovered about myself was that I liked to work in an organization with a lot of people around, in a casual, but hardworking environment. I like a lot of social interaction. Once I identified the atmosphere in which I work best, I worked hard to craft an environment that was in line with what I wanted. Since I was running the show, I had to find ways that would allow me to have a lot of people working at my company, so I could have the socialization that I wanted."

What other advice can you offer to someone launching their career?

"Young people today are getting married later and starting their families later. I am a strong believer in this because it allows those young people to be more responsible and to become better mates and parents, plus it gives them an edge up. Waiting until you're older before starting a family allows people to take some chances and make mistakes without severe consequences when starting their career. Having the extra responsibility of a spouse and children, you have to be much more careful when making career decisions, and you always have to make choices that will be safe to ensure a paycheck. If you don't have a family to support, the chances you can take are much greater, and you will have more opportunities to accept jobs which could lead to greater long-term rewards. With a family, you will have to think long and hard before accepting a promotion in the early stages of your career that will require relocation to another city or state, for example. From a career point of view, you'll have a major leg up if you wait until you have an established career before you take on the huge personal responsibilities of a family.

"Another piece of advice I can offer that's based on my own experience is that people should always live below their means. There is nothing sadder than seeing someone who has a good job and is living high on the hog, but loses their job and has no money put aside for emergencies. If you can afford to do it, live below your means so you can develop a nest egg and create an insurance policy for yourself. Ideally, you want to have enough money in savings so if you lose your job, you can live without changing your lifestyle for six months to a year. Having a nest egg in place will give you a different attitude and will give you more confidence when it comes time to taking chances. You'll sleep better at night and be prepared for whatever happens.

"When you graduate from school and begin your first job, consider moving back in with your parents to save money, or get an apartment with one or two roommates. Take the money you save and put it away. Over a few years, you'll create a good-sized nest egg for yourself. Do this even if you're making enough money in your new job to rent your own apartment. When I decided to buy my own business, I still kept my current job for 10 years. That allowed me to put food on the table and live a comfortable lifestyle, and at

"If you can afford to do it, live below your means so you can develop a nest egg and create an insurance policy for yourself."

the same time take risks so that I could grow my company into what it has become today. I wanted to run my own business, but I wasn't going to run the risk of not being able to support my family if the business ran into hard times. I wanted better for my family and I was ready to work my ass off to get it. It didn't matter to me that I worked seven days a week and worked nights, because I was doing things that I really wanted to do, and I was able to take some chances, because I still had my day job that would support my family. When I was maintaining two jobs, my family lived below our means, but we were comfortable. In the long term this strategy really paid off."

LAST WORD

"I have learned that the difference between people who do and the people who don't are the people who actually did. When my own kids are ready to enter the workplace, I will recommend to them that they spend a few years and take several different types of jobs at different-size companies. Working for a large company is like finishing school after you graduate from college or grad school, only you get paid for it. After holding a few different jobs, maybe they'll want to attend grad school and study what really interests them. After grad school, I'd suggest that they become consultants for a while, then go to work for a company that they really like, or take the entrepreneurial route and start a business using the knowledge and work experience they have acquired."

DR. AMAR BOSE

FOUNDER, CHAIRMAN & TECHNICAL DIRECTOR

Bose Corporation

COMPANY BACKGROUND

If you've ever been in the market for a home stereo system, a home theater system, speakers for your multimedia computer, or a car stereo system, chances are you came across speakers from Bose. In fact, even if you don't have a fancy home theater system with surround sound, but you happen to drive a car manufactured by General Motors, Audi, Honda, or another leading manufacturer, more than likely the stereo system built into your car includes Bose speakers.

Based in Framingham, Massachusetts, the company is the world's largest manufacturer of component-quality loudspeakers. Dr. Bose's goal was to set his company's speakers apart by offering technologically advanced products that are easy to use and compact in size. Bose has achieved this goal, and the company currently manufactures dozens of different products, ranging from the popular Wave Radio® and Acoustic Wave® music system to car speakers and high-powered audio systems that are used by major stadiums and arenas, such as Madison Square Garden, and hundreds of theaters and venues worldwide.

BOSE®

Better sound through research.

PERSONAL HISTORY

Research has always been Dr. Bose's passion; however, holding the title of Chairman, CEO, and Technical Director of Bose Corporation takes up the majority of his time, which is divided between running his company and working as a professor of electrical engineering and computer science at the Massachusetts Institute of Technology (MIT). As a professor, Dr. Bose continues to help instruct tomorrow's electrical engineers.

Back in 1956, Dr. Bose began a research program in physical acoustics and psychoacoustics at MIT. He now holds numerous patents in the fields of acoustics, electronics, nonlinear systems, and communication theory. In addition, Dr. Bose holds S.B., S.M., and Sc.D. degrees in electrical engineering, which he obtained at MIT, and he has earned honorary degrees from Berkeley College of Music (Doctor of Music) and Framingham State College (Doctor of Science).

Why did Dr. Bose start the Bose Corporation in 1964? He went shopping for a pair of speakers for his personal use but was disappointed in all of the loudspeakers he tested. Having spent seven years studying the violin, and years studying physics and electronics, he was acutely aware of the limitations of the speakers he tested when they were required to reproduce the sound of string instruments.

His disappointment in the products available at the time led Dr. Bose to investigate the relationship between reproduced sound as perceived by people and sound as measured by electronic equipment. Dr. Bose and his students performed many psychoacoustic studies and later determined that existing measurements for loudspeakers did not correlate with human perception. New measurement techniques had to be developed. Like most successful entrepreneurs, Dr. Bose pinpointed a need and worked to fill that need with an innovative new product.

Having discovered the problem of imperfect loudspeakers, Dr. Bose spent many years of research with his colleagues. More than a decade after Bose first shopped for the speakers, Bose Corporation released its first product—stereo speakers—which dramatically changed the way speakers are designed and manufactured. Today, Bose Corporation continues to set new standards in audio equipment.

As a professor, Dr. Bose deals with some of the smartest young people in the world—they attend his classes and lectures at MIT. Over the years, Dr. Bose has hired many of his students as employees at Bose Corporation, including Sherwin Greenblatt, who studied under Dr. Bose at MIT in the early 1960's and is now the company's president.

TOPICS DISCUSSED IN THIS INTERVIEW

☞ **Learning how to think and solve problems**

☞ **Choosing a career**

☞ **Finding a job you'll be happy in**

☞ **Surviving the job interview process**

☞ **Finding a job opening**

☞ **The importance of internships**

"Facts are important, but what people need is the ability to think, and there aren't too many universities that really teach people how to think and solve problems."

How do young people learn to think?

"At the end of every semester, I bring all of my students to Bose Corporation to spend a day here. This visit allows my students to discover firsthand what industry is like, from research to production. During their visit, we discuss what students will face once they graduate. Just about all educational organizations fill their students' heads with facts. It isn't the facts that will make the leaders. Facts are important, but what people need is the ability to think, and there aren't too many universities that really teach people how to think and solve problems."

Learning large numbers of facts and forcing students to regurgitate the information they read about in the textbook or heard during lectures might earn students a high grade in school and help to improve their memory skills, but it doesn't teach them how to examine a problem and be able to solve it on their own. "The thought process needs to be emphasized, because when you get out of school and you're in the real world, you won't be facing the types of problems you faced on exams in school. Problems in the real world have many more dimensions to them, and they have the human element as well, which is very complex. The most important skill someone should master is the ability to be a clear thinker. Knowing how to face a problem and knowing where or how to find the answer, are two things that I believe set successful people apart from the crowd."

How does someone learn how to think? According to Dr. Bose, one way to perfect your thinking ability is to study a subject that is quantitative. This can be done by taking courses in school that deal with mathematics and science. "Quantitative problems are not necessarily the type of problems you're going to be facing in life, but the beauty of these problems is that there's a known answer. If you don't get the correct answer, then you know that your thought process is wrong, and you have to go back, change your thinking, and try another approach for obtaining the correct answer. This sharpens your thinking. So, no matter what type of job or career you are planning to pursue, you should definitely have a good grounding in science, mathematics, engineering, or in a discipline that will teach you how to think clearly." Most colleges and universities require students to experience at least introductory courses in math and science. Even if these areas of study have nothing whatsoever to do with your own areas of interest, these courses can help improve your thinking and problem solving skills, which will ultimately prove to be vital.

How does someone choose a career?

"The most fortunate job candidates are those who have chosen a field of study that is close to their hobbies or interests and are able to select a career along the same lines. However, for many reasons, this does not always happen. In this event, it is up to the person to develop a strong interest in whatever career he or she has chosen. This can be done and it

THINK &
SOLVE PROBLEMS

"When you visit the company for an interview, go out of your way to meet people working at the company who you're not scheduled to meet."

will make an enormous difference in the happiness, creativity, and success of the person in that career."

How can you find a job you'll be happy in?

"The whole job-search process is very strange. Most people just out of school know nothing about industry; yet they are forced to go on job interviews and make decisions that will impact the rest of their lives. Going on a job interview is like going on a first date, and after that date you must decide if you're going to marry the person you've just met. At a job interview, everyone is on their best behavior, just as they would be on a first date. The job candidate is on his or her best behavior, and the potential employer is also on their best behavior as they discuss only the best aspects about working at their company. In reality, there's always another side to both the individual and the company."

How can someone determine if the company they're applying for a job at is one that they'll be happy with?

"Always ask the people interviewing you, 'What are the three things that you most like about working for your company?' After the potential employer or the person interviewing you answers this question, follow up by

asking, 'What are the three things that you like least about the company?' As the person answers this question, pay careful attention to the first part of the answer. You'll gain a lot of insight about the company by learning how the current employees feel about working there."

How else can you learn about the company during an interview?

"When you visit the company for an interview, go out of your way to meet people working at the company who you're not scheduled to meet. The people whom you are supposed to meet are programmed to create a certain appearance for that company. If you're able to speak with someone not involved in the hiring process, you'll probably get a more accurate picture of what the company is really like."

If you manage to meet one or more of the company's employees outside of an interview situation, what types of questions should you ask?

"One thing to ask is what that person's experience was like when they first started working for the company. Try to get the most information you can about the organization, and how it treats its employees. I'd also look closely at the quality of the people working for your potential employer. If the quality of the people is high, then you'll be forced to live up to those qualities and ultimately improve your standards. If the quality of the employees is very low, chances are you won't rise or develop further as a person. Study the character and the abilities of the people you could be working with. If you're lucky enough to already know some of the people you might be working with you'll have an advantage, because you can learn about what you should expect from the job and get some insight into the internal politics at the company.

"In my career, I am constantly facing obstacles and challenges. Originally, I never wanted to have anything to do with business, I just wanted to do research, but when you form a company you quickly find out that you have to learn the necessary disciplines. I have learned that the business disciplines I've had to master require just as much creative work and effort as the technical research I enjoy. One constant challenge in business is being able to overcome problems and to outperform the competition while maintaining a high ethical standard. I always learn from my mistakes. I personally pay a lot of attention to the human aspect of the business. Running a business is like running a sports team. You can have the best employees in the world, but if the morale and the interaction among the people aren't right, you'll be lucky to win a game. If the spirit and cooperation among everyone is right, then a company will most likely be successful. As you examine job opportunities, make sure you'll fit in and will be able to be a valuable team player before accepting a job."

How can someone survive the job interview?

"The biggest mistake you can make during a job interview is working too hard to impress the person who is interviewing you. If someone tries too hard, it becomes extremely transparent to the interviewer, and that doesn't help. If you go into the interview with a sincere interest in learning about the company, and you answer the interviewer's questions as truthfully as you can, without bragging, good companies will quickly recognize that characteristic and they'll want it."

When you're searching for a first job, Dr. Bose says you should try to find a job in a field that you're extremely interested in. "Unfortunately, jobs directly relating to someone's interests aren't always available. Often, recent graduates have an idea about what type of job or career they want to pursue, but what they wind up doing may be very different. If this happens, it doesn't mean you can't excel and enjoy what you're doing. If you generate an interest in what you're doing and work hard, then you'll be successful at it. If you think that there is only one type of job you'll be happy with, and you hold out for that job, you might find yourself very old before that perfect job comes along." Be open-minded when evaluating job opportunities, and be ready to accept different types of challenges than you originally set out looking for.

"During the interview, try to discover exactly what the employer expects from you, and at the same time try to give the potential employer an honest look at what you think you have to offer."

"Those who have internship experience have a much higher probability of getting a job that they want."

Based on your experience, how can someone make a good first impression during a job interview?

"That's easy. Don't try! Trying is transparent. Be yourself. During the interview try instead to discover exactly what the employer expects from you, and at the same time try to give the potential employer an honest look at what you think you have to offer. If, during the interview, you act like someone you're not, it will be obvious."

Dr. Bose goes on to say that it's virtually impossible to get a complete picture about a company from a job interview. "During the interview, do your best to discover everything you can about the company, and then if you accept the job, it's up to you to do the best that you can do with the hand that you are dealt."

How can you find out about job openings?

"Take full advantage of the recruitment office at your school. Most schools also have companies come to their campus in order to make presentations about the jobs they offer. If company representatives visit your school, I suggest you arrange to attend their presentation or set up a preliminary meeting with them. Personally, I am against someone getting a job based on who they know instead of what they know. Networking is an excellent way to obtain information about job opportunities and maybe get your foot in the door so that you can submit a résumé or obtain an interview, but to use a relative or someone you know to get you a job is a mistake. In the long run it'll hurt you, and you'll most likely be resented by others in the company once you join."

How important are internships?

"Taking part in internship programs while you're in school is a fantastic opportunity. Internships provide practical experience and will give you knowledge of the real world that you could not obtain simply by going to school and attending classes or reading. Participating in an internship program allows you to work with and learn from people who are already working in the field you're interested in. Those who have internship experience have a much higher probability of getting a job that they want, and they'll be able to adjust to their new job faster and easier. Internships also provide you with skills and knowledge that will make you more valuable to a potential employer. Based on my experience, nobody can preach to you about what it's really like in the real world. It's something you have to experience firsthand. I know of no better way to get experience than to get an internship in the field that you think you want to pursue as your career when you graduate."

LAST WORD

"Knowing how to face a problem and knowing where or how to find the answer are two things that I believe set successful people apart from the crowd."

JERRY YANG

Yahoo! Inc.

CO-FOUNDER & CHIEF YAHOO

COMPANY BACKGROUND

There are many ways that people communicate. Mail, telephone, fax, and the Internet are all substitutes for in-person meetings that are used daily in the business environment. In fact, if you're not totally familiar with every one of these communication methods by the time you begin your first job, then in today's corporate environment you'll be at a major disadvantage. Businesses of all sizes are turning to electronic mail (e-mail) as a preferred method of communication, and what ties computers throughout the world together is the Internet--the Information Superhighway.

Yahoo! is a sophisticated but easy-to-use search engine that helps people navigate their way around the Internet. Each day, over 800,000 people use Yahoo! as their home base for their adventure into cyberspace. While Yahoo! is a World Wide Web site unto itself, its main objective is to be the world's most intuitive, up-to-date, and efficient guide for information and on-line discovery.

Think of Yahoo! as an electronic Yellow Pages of Internet sites that you can visit using your computer. In addition to providing listings and direct links to over 160,000 World Wide Web sites and databases, this free service offers a powerful search engine, allowing you to type in key words or search phrases and instantly locate information on just about any topic.

The creators of this service have also helped to start an entirely new industry—

YAHOO!

WWW

Internet advertising. Just like commercial television, Yahoo! is sponsored by companies that place ads on-line. For a computer user, Yahoo! is a free service. All you need is a computer, modem, communication software, and access to the Internet.

Since it was created in 1994, Yahoo! Inc. has grown into a multimillion-dollar business. Now that major corporations have discovered the benefits of reaching the millions of people who are on-line, they've begun using on-line advertising that's designed to appear in this constantly evolving electronic medium.

In August 1995, David and Jerry needed venture capital to expand Yahoo! They either had to begin charging computer users to access the service or they had to find a way to get companies or organizations to pick up the tab. "There was a huge appeal for Yahoo! to be a free service, so we decided that offering advertising on-line was the best way to keep Yahoo! a free service but at the same time allow us to earn money. One of our main goals has been to ensure that the advertising we allow on-line isn't intrusive to the users. Originally, we didn't solicit advertising as a way to get rich. It was simply a matter of finding a way to earn enough money to keep Yahoo! going."

The company's Internet address is **http://www.yahoo.com**.

PERSONAL HISTORY

Jerry Yang is a Taiwanese native who was raised in San Jose, California. While still in graduate school at Stanford University, he and his pal David Filo co-founded Yahoo!.

Jerry was first exposed to computers in high school, but it wasn't until his college years that he developed a real interest in computers. This interest eventually led him to launch his career in the fast-growing on-line services industry. Yahoo! is Jerry's first job since leaving grad school, but while still in school he had a variety of different jobs, including mowing lawns and a job at NASA, which he held for three summers.

Before Jerry cofounded Yahoo!, he knew that he wanted to pursue a high-tech career at a start-up company; however, he had no idea that it would be his own company that would be his first job-related experience once he left school.

TOPICS DISCUSSED IN THIS INTERVIEW

☞ **Using the Internet to find a job**

☞ **Advice for would-be entrepreneurs**

What's this Yahoo! thing all about? How did you transform your ideas into a company?

"David Filo and myself are the two creators of Yahoo! We created this service while we were in graduate school doing our Ph.D.'s in electrical engineering. We were close to graduation when we became totally intrigued by the growing popularity of the Internet. This was in late 1993. As sort of a hobby, we started to collect Internet addresses that we thought were cool, and that's what led to the initial creation of Yahoo! At the time, the problem with the Internet was that once you found an interesting site, if you didn't remember the exact address for that site it was very difficult to locate it again. Likewise, there was no way to easily search the Internet for information based on a key word or phrase. That's why David started developing a database of the Web sites that we discovered."

Before Yahoo! was given its name, the database of Internet sites that David and Jerry created was known as "Dave and Jerry's Guide to the World Wide Web." "We decided we needed a better name. We wanted a name that started with the letters Y and A, which stood for 'Yet Another.' We opened the dictionary and looked at all of the words that started with 'YA', and *Yahoo* really stood out. We liked the word's connotation. At the time, we had no clue this was going to evolve into a business.

"One thing we learned is that you really can't plan on something like this becoming popular and evolving into a moneymaking business. What we offered was a core fundamental value for people, because we allowed them to easily navigate the Internet. Our goal was to make using the Internet easy, and at the same time keep up with the demand of the users by offering the information they wanted." One thing that sets the Yahoo! service apart from others is that all of the information and Web site links that are offered through Yahoo! are checked out before they are made available through the service. As a result, if you do a search using a key word, like *résumé*, you can be sure that all of the Internet sites

"Ya-hoo —
1: a member of a race of brutes in Swift's *Gulliver's Travels* who have the form and all the vices of humans. 2: a boorish, crass, or stupid person."
—*Merriam Webster's Collegiate Dictionary*, 10th Edition.

and database references that Yahoo! provides are somehow related to *résumé*.

In fall 1994, David and Jerry realized that they were onto an exciting business opportunity. It also become apparent that they could no longer use Stanford University's computer equipment to operate the service. "We were using up too much of Stanford University's computer system's resources. It became obvious that if Yahoo! was going to continue, we'd have to operate it without Stanford University's equipment and funding. It had to become a separate entity. This was at a time when nobody had yet discovered a way to make money using the Internet. The entire Yahoo! phenomenon happened through word of mouth. We never did any marketing or advertising for the service. People found it on their own and spread the word about it."

"The entire Yahoo! phenomenon happened through word of mouth. We never did any marketing or advertising for the service."

How has your interest in computers and your passion for your work led to your success?

"This experience has been very rewarding. I am the most happy when I'm growing or producing something that's affecting people in a positive way. Whatever I do next, after Yahoo!, will have to be something that also has a positive impact on people. I want to keep growing intellectually, and keep creating. At this point, I can't think of what my life would be like without Yahoo! The biggest challenge for me has been constantly facing the unknown and charting new territory in cyberspace."

How can someone use Yahoo! and the Internet to help them find a job?

"There are hundreds, if not thousands, of resources on the Net that pertain to jobs and careers. From Yahoo!, someone can access the employment section, which provides all sorts of career development advice, information about career and résumé services, and even job listings from companies located throughout the world. These listings can be sorted in a number of ways, such as by industry, job type, or geographical area. Using the Internet to help someone obtain a job has always been a popular use for this service, because it makes doing research extremely simple. Information about just about every public company, thousands of private companies, and virtually every industry can be obtained within seconds using the Internet. Thus, if you're applying for a job at a specific company, you can use your computer to quickly and easily learn about that company from a variety of sources. One way to use the Internet to learn about a company is to visit

that company's Web site. A growing number of companies are establishing a presence on the Web, and some are using their site for recruitment. If a company is actively using the Web for recruitment, you can often send e-mail directly to the human resources department at the company, and even submit your résumé via e-mail." Many résumé databases also exist on the Internet, where you can post your own electronic résumé on-line, where it can be read by employers.

Just about every college and university in America offers its students access to the Internet. This is a powerful resource that you shouldn't overlook when beginning your job-search process. "One way to look at the Internet is as a massive library. If you think of it as a library and use it as one, then it can be very helpful. Most people who are into computers can't imagine what life would be like today without the use of e-mail or the Web. Once people get their first exposure to what the Internet offers, they realize that it contains information that isn't available anywhere else. Over the next few years, the Internet will become a major part of corporate life, and it is critical that people who are entering into the workplace stay up-to-date with the latest trends."

What advice can you offer to other would-be entrepreneurs?

What does it take to create a company based on an original idea? "I think that a lot of it has to do with timing and looking for the right opportunities. Once you've decided what it is you want to do, don't give up too quickly if you're not instantly successful. You must be totally dedicated to whatever it is that you do, and be willing to stick with it.

Don't give up.

Before starting your own company, be sure to evaluate the risks. Make sure you understand how you'll manage the risks so that you don't burn yourself out too early. We were very lucky when we started Yahoo!, because initially we had the support of Stanford University, so we had the opportunity to thoroughly test our idea. I would say that it is very important for anyone interested in starting a business to first test out their ideas. There are any number of ways to do this. If you're going to make mistakes, you want to make them while someone else is protecting you, while you learn as much as you possibly can.

"Business, like everything else, relies a lot upon common sense. You have to be able to look at opportunities in a logical way. It's easy to look back and ask yourself 'What if I did that differently?' or to constantly try to second-guess yourself. The best thing you can do is to make a decision and then to rally around that decision and move forward. I know that in the past we made a few bad decisions, but what we did was to quickly put those mistakes behind us and move forward. Making mistakes is part of the process of starting a business. What you want to do is understand that you're going to make mistakes, but set yourself up so that the mistakes you make won't hurt you. Being able to perform good damage recovery quickly after making a mistake is important. This sounds like common sense, but when you actually try to put this advice

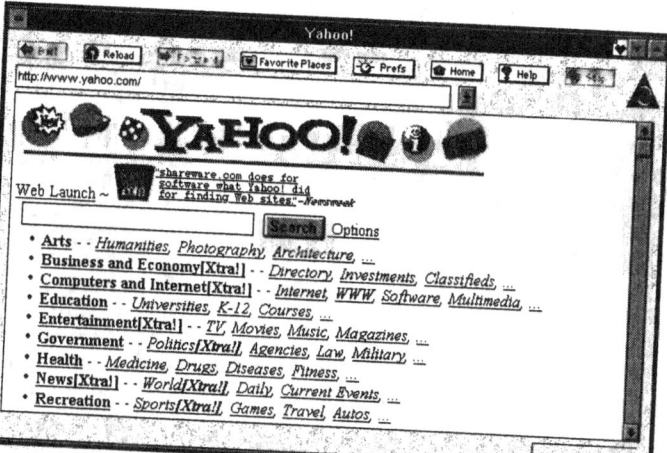

Once you have access to the World Wide Web on the Internet, the address for Yahoo! is: http://www.yahoo.com. In these examples, Yahoo! was accessed via the Internet gateway of America Online. At the opening menu for Yahoo!, you can search for a topic based on any key word or phrase, or you can click your computer's mouse on one of the highlighted menu topics, such as "Business and Economy."

into practice, you'll see that it's a lot harder than it sounds."

HOW CAN SOMEONE USE YAHOO! TO HELP LAUNCH A CAREER?

Simply by spending a few minutes exploring the various menu options that Yahoo! displays after performing searches based on job- and career-related key words, you'll find dozens of useful Web sites, such as JobTrak (http://www.jobtrak.com), which offers a selection of on-line resources targeted specifically to college students and alumni searching for jobs. In addition to offering job listings from over 150,000 employers, JobTrak offers company profiles, a guide to graduate schools, and tips for how to best locate a job opening on the Internet.

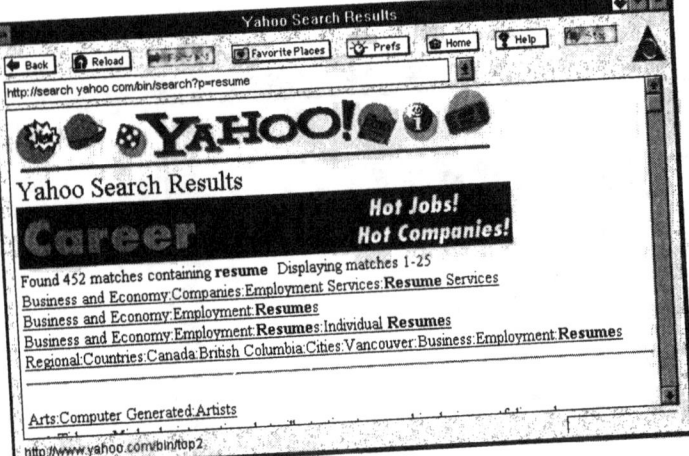

Since you're about to begin your job search, there are several key words that can be used to kick off your exploration on the Internet--Try using words like "Résumé," "Job," "Job Fair," "Job Listings," and "Career" to begin. On the day Yahoo! performed this search, using the phrase "Résumé," 509 Web sites relating to résumés were discovered. Simply by clicking the mouse on the first menu option, "Business and Economy: Companies: Employment Services: Résumé Services," another menu displaying a wide range of résumé preparation services and electronic résumé distribution services was displayed. If you're in the process of writing your résumé, or if you're looking to distribute your résumé electronically to as many companies as possible, this is an excellent place for you to begin your on-line exploration.

JobTrak lists over 600 new full- and part-time job listings per day. This is a free service to college and grad school students, because it's the companies that pay to post their job listings.

If you're looking to perform research on a specific company, you can enter that company's name at the Yahoo! search prompt to determine if that company has a site on the Web. If you'd like a directory of businesses that have Web sites, click the mouse on Yahoo's "Business and Economy" option. Even if a company you're interested in doesn't yet have an on-line presence, there are many independent databases that contain information about public and private companies. Another way to learn about a company is to use Yahoo! or another on-line service to access a database of newspapers and magazines. By searching these databases, you can read articles that have appeared about the company or industry that you're interested in.

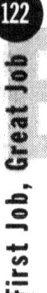

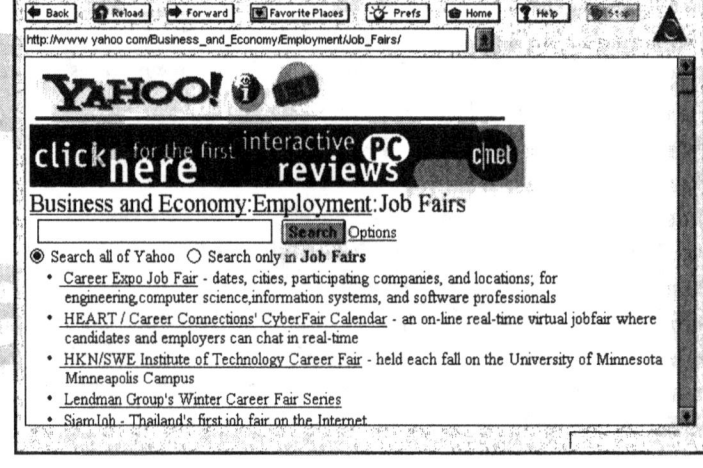

After using Yahoo! as your starting point,
several other job/career-related World Wide Web sites
that you might want to visit include:

First Job, Great Job	http://www.firstjob.com
The Monster Board	http://www.monster.com
Career Mosaic	http://www.careermosaic.com
CareerNET	http://www.careers.org
Career Magazine	http://www.careermag.com/careermag/
JobWeb	http://www.jobweb.org
College Grad Job Hunter	http://www.execpc.com/~insider/
CareerWEB	http://www.cweb.com/homepage.html
The Definitive Internet Career Guide (Oakland University)	http://phoenix.placement.oakland.edu/career/internet.html
Margaret Riley's Job Guide	http://www.jobtrak.com/jobguide
JobSource	http://www.jobsource.com
Career Center	http://www.netline.com
Kaplan On-Line Career Center	http://www.Kaplan.com

TIM KOOGLE

PRESIDENT & CEO

Yahoo! Inc.

Once Yahoo! began to take off as a business, Tim Koogle was hired as President and CEO of Yahoo! Inc., in part because of his experience in the high-tech business world.

PERSONAL HISTORY

Even as a child, Tim was an entrepreneur. At the age of 9, he was a newspaper boy. He later started a landscaping business at the age of 14. As a teenager, he held many jobs, including one at McDonald's. After college, his first job was with a large farm equipment manufacturing company. While in grad school, Tim launched an engineering design business and a race car engine rebuilding company. Upon graduating, he started and later sold several other companies, which ultimately led to his working for Motorola.

Tim now has over 15 years of experience working in executive management positions within the high-tech industry. Prior to joining Yahoo! Inc., he was President of

Intermec Corporation, a Seattle-based manufacturer of automated data collection and data communication products. Under Tim's leadership over a three-year period, Intermec's annual sales rose 50 percent, to over $300 million. Tim also served as corporate vice president of Intermec's parent company, Western Atlas, Inc., which has annual revenues exceeding $2.4 billion. Prior to Intermec, Tim spent almost nine years working for Motorola, Inc., where he held a number of executive management positions in both operations and the corporate venture capital group. Tim holds an M.S. and engineering degree from Stanford University.

TOPICS DISCUSSED IN THIS INTERVIEW

☞ **Preparing for a job interview**

☞ **How to make a good first impression**

☞ **What to ask an employer during an interview**

☞ **Mistakes people make when applying for a job**

When did you decide you wanted to be a top-level executive?

"I never planned to be the President of a company. I just did what I really enjoyed doing, which was engineering and design, but at the same time I kept taking on more and more business-related responsibilities. Coordinating the efforts of groups of people came naturally to me, and I was successful at it. This led to me taking on management-level responsibilities. All of my degrees in school were for engineering, not business. As I started my own small businesses, I was forced to wear many hats, which led to my learning about all aspects of business."

Many people attend high school, college, and even grad school before they're able to determine what type of career they're interested in pursuing. Tim, however, knew early on what he enjoyed doing. "It was in high school that I began forming an interest in engineering and design. I always did really well in math and science. In addition, my father had attended engineering school and he was sort of a mentor for me. Once I

actually entered into engineering school, most of my professors were practicing engineers. In my freshman year of college, I was very inspired by those professors who related real-world aspects of engineering to our education. It was in graduate school that I started learning about how products are designed and brought to market."

A major part of Tim's success has been a result of his setting job-related goals. "My father once told me to find something that I really like, and then to pursue that as a career. If you do something you like, you'll be good at it. That, of course, is easier said than done, but it's excellent advice. Based on my own experience, I found that having a variety of different types of after-school jobs, summer jobs, and internships gave me the experiences I needed to make smart career-related decisions as I got older. Through these jobs, I had the opportunity to speak with a lot of people who offered me guidance along the way. Of course, potluck also plays a part in finding a career you'll be happy and successful in."

How should you prepare for a job interview and make a good impression?

"When I hire someone, I always look for candor, openness, and honesty, along with a little bit of modesty and confidence in the applicant. People develop confidence over time. It is not something that someone fresh

out of school will necessarily have, in which case I try to discover if that applicant is comfortable with themselves. During an interview, I find out about the applicant's job-related experiences. One quality I look for is someone who is proactive about pursuing things. I look for this quality by speaking with the applicant, but also by studying their résumé. If someone coming out of school has a respectable list of summer jobs, internships, or after-school jobs, that means they took an interest early on in developing themselves. I see that he or she has taken a proactive role in launching their career, and I respect that."

What should a job applicant ask the employer during an interview?

"Ask the employer to describe exactly what you'll be doing if you're accepted for a specific job opening. Also ask who you'll be working with, and try to determine if you're likely to learn a lot by working with those people. I think that it's very important to have a good chemistry with the people you're working with, especially if it's your first real work experience. I would also ask the employer how well the business is doing. If a business isn't doing well, the working atmosphere might not be a good one. When you're applying for a first job it's important to ask questions and gather information about what you'll be expected to do. Also, it doesn't hurt to ask about the overall direction and vision for the business. The more you're able to learn about the business, the better opportunity you'll have to evaluate the job opportunity if a position is offered to you."

What are some of the mistakes you've seen applicants make when applying for a job?

"I've seen people be overly anxious to take a job and not spend adequate time evaluating a number of opportunities. If you have the luxury, I would not jump at the first opportunity that comes along, because once you start a first job, it isn't always easy to make a change. Obviously, if you accept a job and you're not happy there, you can quit and go someplace else, but you want to avoid this by evaluating the job opportunity before you accept a position. I've seen too many people ignore their intuition and accept jobs doing things they don't enjoy doing, and that is one of the major mistakes that sets you up for failure. Many people simply follow a career path that someone told them to follow, or they follow the money trail instead of following a career path that leads to jobs that they'll enjoy. If you enjoy your work and you're good at it, the money and success will eventually follow. Once I have all of the facts, I always rely on my intuition when making career- and business-related decisions."

Are there any skills that someone should have that they might not have learned in school?

"Definitely! I think the most important skill someone can bring to a job is interpersonal skills, and they're not often taught in school. The only way you can learn interpersonal skills is by working closely with other people on various types of projects. Many young people learn these skills by working on school projects in groups, participating in sports teams, or doing volunteer work in the community. Interpersonal skills have to be developed. They can't really be taught. Communication skills and computer skills are also critical in just about every job. By the time you graduate from school, if you don't feel you have acquired proper communication and computer skills, there are many types of classes and seminars you can take. Practicing these skills will lead to perfecting them." By communication skills, Tim refers to the ability to write well, hold intelligent conversations, and convey ideas to groups of people.

> **LAST WORD**
> "The more passion you have for something, the more successful it's going to be, because you'll be more critical of your work, and you'll enjoy it."—Jerry Yang

JEFF TAYLOR
FOUNDER, CEO INTERACTIVE DIVISION
The Monster Board (TMP Worldwide)

COMPANY BACKGROUND

The Monster Board is a career hub on the Internet's World Wide Web. It's a site that provides job seekers with a place to look for employers and career information, and a place where employers can represent themselves to candidates with a high degree of sophistication. The Monster Board offers an overview of employers, a section devoted to college students and entry-level candidates, and an easy "browse and select" interface that supports job searching by company name, location, discipline, industry, and specific job title. By using a forms application, the job seeker (that's you) can apply on-line for a targeted position, and e-mail a résumé directly to a company.

Other services offered by The Monster Board include: Résumé City, a national database of résumés that employers can search for potential candidates; a forum for human resources professionals to exchange advice, read current articles pertaining to HR issues, find updates on career events, trade shows, and editorial specials for targeted advertising; ROAR, an on-line forum for

129

college students; and The CEO Exchange, a forum for top-level executives.

To access The Monster Board, all you need is access to the Internet. If you own a personal computer, you can use an Internet service provider in your city to access the World Wide Web, or you can connect to the Web via one of the major on-line services (such as America Online, Compuserve, or Prodigy). If there's no computer in your life, visit the computer lab at your school or local library. You can also ask a friend to let you use their computer.

The Monster Board is available to everyone, 24 hours per day, 7 days per week, and it's totally free to use. Employers pay to promote their job listings on the service, so it's free to you, the applicant. Instead of spending countless hours in the library doing research about industries and companies, then going home to write dozens of résumés and cover letters, you might want to try taking a high-tech approach to your job search, using the many tools and services available to you on the Internet.

The Monster Board's Internet address is **http://www.monsterboard.com**.

PERSONAL HISTORY

After graduating from the University of Massachusetts, Jeff Taylor began working as a disc jockey, then later launched his career as a headhunter at Search, Inc., a Boston-based technical recruiting company. In 1989, Jeff opened a specialized recruitment advertising agency—one that was infused with leading-edge technology as a point of differentiation from the larger agencies. Adion Human Resource Communications grew to be one of New England's leading recruitment agencies

by 1993. While in school, Jeff studied advertising. Combining his talents and experience as a job recruiter with what he learned about advertising in school helped his company prosper.

It was in late 1993 that Jeff began to build an Internet presence as a means of offering a more sophisticated recruiting tool for his clients. This was the first incarnation of what would become The Monster Board, one of the most exciting and pace-setting "career sites" along the Information Superhighway. With his vision and aggressive use of interactive communication between candidates and potential employers, Jeff has pioneered a new wave of career tools that makes finding career opportunities easier than ever.

Jeff eventually sold his business and The Monster Board to TMP Worldwide, headquartered in New York City. Now, as the CEO of TMP Worldwide's Interactive Division, Jeff is working with the nation's largest companies to create new strategies as they strive to hire the best and brightest.

TOPICS COVERED IN THIS INTERVIEW

☞ **Using your computer and the Internet to get yourself a job**

☞ **Electronic résumé preparation and distribution**

☞ **Performing research on-line**

☞ **Using The Monster Board**

☞ **Traps to avoid when selecting a career**

"Life experiences come in all shapes and sizes. You can have an excellent experience doing something that you never plan to do again when you take a summer job."

In the past, you have worked for recruiting firms. Do you recommend that people graduating from college or grad school take advantage of the services offered by headhunters, employment agencies, and job-search firms?

"I think one of the challenges entry-level workers face is that most job-search firms, employment agencies, and headhunters won't talk to you, because you don't yet have real-world work experience. As a result, using one of these firms probably isn't going to be the best use of your time when looking for an entry-level job. Once you have established a career and want to change jobs, that's when a headhunter, employment agency, or job-search firm will be the most useful to you."

Is there a difference between getting your first job and launching your career?

"I think so. A lot of people decide to take the summer off after they graduate. During that summer, they get a 'job' that they think will be fun, before they actually pursue what they want to do for their career. Life experiences come in all shapes and sizes. You can have an excellent experience doing something that you never plan to do again when you take a summer job, such as working as a truck driver, waiter/waitress, or lifeguard at a resort. The more well-rounded you are when you begin your career, the better off you'll be. For example, being a waiter/waitress for a summer won't help you be a better accountant or

analyst, but it will teach you how to work with people, which is an extremely valuable skill."

When can you lie or stretch the truth on a résumé or during an interview?

"Never. If you held a job with a title that was unique to the company you worked for, then you have to repackage that experience so that your skills and experience better match up with what employers are looking for. Repackaging your skills isn't lying. It's repositioning for success. Being misleading, however, will put you in a defensive position during the interview process, and that could be deadly. When I'm interviewing applicants, I ask questions that test for consistency. If you lied on your résumé or during the interview, it could easily come back to haunt you, because the interviewers know how to ask questions that will eventually uncover the truth."

What's wrong with traditional paper-based résumés?

"Many large companies, and a growing number of midsized companies, now have computerized résumé management systems in place. When you send in your résumé, it immediately gets scanned into a computer. All of the key words are broken apart and analyzed to get right to the meat of your résumé. As a result, no human actually reads your résumé in its original form. In the past, a well-orchestrated résumé had a lot of flowery phrases and descriptive words to describe experiences and accomplishments.

Now, you might want to use key words and phrases like 'managed' or 'responsible for.'

"When describing your interpersonal skills and qualities within a résumé you know will be scanned into a computer, use key words like:

- ☞ **Accurate**
- ☞ **Assertive**
- ☞ **Competitive**
- ☞ **Creative**
- ☞ **Detail-minded**
- ☞ **Flexible**
- ☞ **High-energy**
- ☞ **Innovative**
- ☞ **Leadership abilities**
- ☞ **Organized**
- ☞ **Problem solving**
- ☞ **Self-managing**
- ☞ **Team player**

"The idea is that a computer picks out all of the key words in your résumé and summarizes you based on the number of key words that it finds. The computer will match up the key words in your résumé with the list of words that the employer put together to describe the job opening available. A condensed list of qualified applicants is then provided to the person doing the hiring. Now, instead of having to read dozens of full-length résumés from people who may not be qualified to fill the job opening, the computer scans the applicants and chooses only the best candidates for the human resources person to review. If you're going to be applying for jobs where computers are used to scan your résumé, you should become familiar with the 'key word process,' and adapt your résumé accordingly. Your descriptions should be quantifiable. Think about the skills you have that are marketable and package them in the résumé in ways that they apply directly to the jobs you're applying for."

How can e-mail be used to help someone get a job?

"Most midsize and large companies have e-mail capabilities, which means that you can often submit your résumé electronically. This can be a very efficient way to get your résumé out to a lot of companies quickly and cheaply. When using the Information Superhighway to distribute your résumé, the cover letter becomes antiquated. Using cool paper to print your résumé on is also something that no longer applies if you're distributing your résumé electronically. As a result, what your résumé actually says is more important then ever."

What are the dangers of sending a traditional paper-based résumé to a company that scans them electronically into a database?

"Many people print their résumé on fancy paper that's heavier than regular 20-pound paper. Sometimes they use colored paper, or paper that contains a watermark. If you're submitting a résumé to a company that will be scanning it into a computer system, then you have to be very careful because the computer scanners that are used don't react well to heavy paper stocks, fancy fonts and typestyles, or colored paper. In fact, if you

132

First Job, Great Job

use the wrong type of paper, or a nonstandard font, the scanner will create typos in your résumé which will be held against you. My advice is that when printing copies of your résumé, use good-quality white paper and a traditional typestyle."

Is there a difference in format if you're creating a résumé that will be submitted electronically, via e-mail?

"You still have to include your name, address, phone number, along with the usual information that would be included on any résumé. I recommend you also include an e-mail address, if you have one. In terms of the information you include in an electronic résumé, be concise and try to include buzzwords that apply. If you're using a specialized service that will distribute your résumé electronically, pay careful attention to the résumé format that's outlined for you by the service. When you submit a résumé electronically, it demonstrates to the employer that you know how to use a computer, which is a skill that many employers like to see.

"Having a concise résumé that lists whatever summer job or internship experience you have, along with your skills and goals, is probably better than a long printed résumé that has fancy fonts and graphics but lists no real experiences or skills. Having a flashy résumé isn't going to get the attention

of the employer. A résumé is a very personal thing. You have to have the horsepower to follow through and live up to what that résumé says about you."

If you submit a résumé via e-mail, what's the best way to follow up with the company you send the résumé to?

"I would suggest that you pick up the phone and give the company you e-mailed your résumé to a call. For any job, there are usually about 100 people that think about applying for that job, and 25 of those people are actually qualified. Out of that 25, at least half of those people won't follow up by contacting the company after they have sent their résumé. So, if you follow up, now there are only 12 people competing for that job. By making direct contact with the company, you're doing something to set yourself apart from the other applicants. I recommend that people use all of their resources to obtain an introduction to a company. You want to be professional, but you want to do anything and everything that's within your power to get that company's attention if you really want to work for that company."

In addition to listing job openings, what else does The Monster Board offer to job seekers?

"The Monster Board currently has more than 100,000 job listings in our database, most of which are exclusive. In addition, our service offers the ability to easily perform research on a company when you use the 'Employer Profile' section of the service. What's nice about our service is that you can locate and then apply to multiple jobs that interest you. Most people don't just apply to one college

"If you have a tongue post or belly-button ring, that's cool, but you'll want to remove it when you go for a job interview."

and then sit back and hope they get accepted. You should have multiple irons in the fire and apply for several jobs at once. As a career hub, The Monster Board is designed to be a fun place to come to, to find jobs, learn about companies, and post your résumé. If you have a computer, the Internet should be your first stop when your job-search process begins. In addition to visiting Web sites like The Monster Board, make a point to see if the company you're applying to has its own Web site. If it does, spend some time visiting that site to learn more about the company."

What are the biggest mistakes you've seen people make when applying for a job?

"We are in a dress-down culture at the moment. With things like body piercing, for example, those are forms of self-expression. There are times to increase your self-expression and times to be a bit more subdued in what you're doing. If you have a tongue post or belly-button ring, that's cool, but you'll want to remove it when you go for a job interview. Once you have the job, then it's up to you and the dress code at the company whether or not various forms of self-expression are appropriate. However, when you're applying for a job, in almost every situation you should dress professionally. To be successful in our society, you have to be like a chameleon and learn that there is a time and a place for everything. The interview process is the time you have to define who you are going to be on the job. You don't want to act too far off from how

you are in reality and fake your way through the interview process or you'll be miserable with the job you wind up with, but you might have to conform a bit to the atmosphere you'll be working in.

"If you're applying for a job where the office attire for men is to wear a suit and tie, then when you go for an interview you'll want to be wearing your best suit and tie. If, however, the job allows employees to wear street clothes, then when you go for an interview, you might want to wear a more casual sport jacket and a nice pair of pants. Don't wear your favorite torn jeans and a T-shirt.

"If you're not sure how people dress at the company you're applying to, visit that company the day before the interview and look at what the employees are wearing when they go in and out of the building. Then dress accordingly."

How is the job market changing as we approach the year 2000?

"I think the reactionary hiring process, where an employee leaves a company and then that company launches a search to replace him or her, is something that is changing. A lot more companies are laying off long-term employees and using temporary workers, consultants, freelancers, or an interim work force. The companies are doing this because they need to maintain profitability. As a result, employees will no longer be able to nestle in with a company and expect that the company will take care of them for their entire career. More and

"Organized"

First Job, Great Job

more people will have multiple careers during their professional life.

"You should think of yourself as a set of skills or a tool set that you are continuously developing. You should not stop learning when you get out of college. If possible, continue to take classes, take advantage of training programs at your company, and always try to be learning new skills that are marketable from the job you're in. So each time you change jobs, you become more marketable, because you have acquired new skills and experiences. Computers and technology are opening up the world, so it's vital that you keep up with the technology. Many people recognize that technology changes, but they don't really pay attention to it.

"Companies are also starting to keep databases of talent that they can turn to when jobs open up. Companies are taking a proactive approach to hiring, and using electronic résumé databases to find qualified applicants. Thus, a company may never actually post a 'Help Wanted' ad. Instead, they may sift through the résumés that are in a database maintained by a service, like The Monster Board, in order to select qualified applicants they want to invite in for an interview. Since posting your résumé in these databases is almost always free of charge, as an applicant you have nothing to lose and a lot to gain by uploading your résumé to these services."

How can someone go about setting job-related goals?

"One of the problems with college is that about 80 percent of the classes don't have a job title associated with them. As a result,

you're supposed to be analytical about your approach to classwork, but be able to apply what you learn to the real world. In an idealistic world, that's great. In the real world, however, if you were a sociology major in college, then you're going to be stuck when you get out of college because there are really no jobs with sociology in the job title. When you're doing your early career planning and setting your goals, think about the type of industry you want to work in. A lot of people don't realize that they have a choice of direction, because they just don't know how to channel their interests and talents into a job or career that they'll be happy in.

"Make a list of your talents and interests, then look at industries that hire people with those talents and interests. You should be able to narrow down your search to several different industries, and then do research to find specific companies that you want to work for within those industries. Don't narrow yourself to one company or a single industry. You have to go with what you love. I am a firm believer in having passion and direction. To be successful, you have to have both. If you're doing something that you love, as opposed to something you have to labor through, you'll excel.

"If you have an interest in fossils, you might not want to become an archaeologist but maybe you can get a job at a university or museum that has a good archaeology department. This may be painfully obvious, but when most people come out of school they stand there like a deer frozen in place by an oncoming car's headlights. They have no idea what to do because they haven't stopped to really think about and examine their own skills and interests."

What traps do people fall into when selecting their first job?

"There are a lot of jobs that allow you to make a lot of money, but it's short-term payoff with no future. Taking a job as a disc jockey or bartender, for example, allows you to work nights and make more money than you would in a typical entry-level position. The drawback is that there is no forward-moving career track as a bartender. Some people choose to follow the sun, going from ski-slope jobs to beach jobs on Cape Cod, then on to Florida, based on the season. It's an addicting lifestyle, but you'll wind up at the age of 35 making $20,000 a year with no future and no real skills. Pursue your dream, but have a long-term plan for yourself that will provide for future personal and professional growth.

"I had a friend who got a job in financial services and after a while she was making extremely good money. Within a few years, she decided she didn't like working in financial services and wanted a job in advertising. The problem was, the only advertising job she could get paid half of what she was currently making. The only way she could continue making the salary she was accustomed to was to stay in the industry she was already in. To do something that she enjoyed and would eventually have a long-term future in, she was forced to take a few steps backwards and accept a lower-paying job in advertising. The benefit was that she would be doing something she really liked in an industry she had an interest in. Eventually, she would be making a good salary once again, and she would be able to move forward in her career. This is a common situation, but it can be avoided with careful career planning and goal setting, after you have done some serious soul searching to determine your interests, strengths, and weaknesses."

USING THE MONSTER BOARD TO FIND JOB OPENINGS

One of the services of The Monster Board (http://www.monsterboard.com) is that it offers an ever growing and changing database of over 100,000 jobs that you can scan in a matter of minutes using your computer.

Once you're connected to the Internet and to The Monster Board World Wide Web site, choose the "Career Search" option to search the electronic "Help Wanted" database. Instead of reading newspapers, visiting your college's career placement office, and manually sorting through hundreds or thousands of job opportunities, you can save countless hours by letting your computer do the work for you. The result will be a list of job opportunities that meet the criteria, which you predetermine. Now, all you have to do is make contact with those employers and get yourself an interview.

LAST WORD

"I have seen many people be not at all realistic about the jobs they apply for based on their qualifications and experience. Someone who barely made it through school should not enter the job market thinking they are going to start in a management position with a $50,000-plus salary. The highest starting salaries go to the people who have the best qualifications and experience. If you're launching your first career, apply for entry-level positions, not management positions that require three to five years of experience that you don't yet have."

MICHAEL DAVIS — PRESIDENT & CEO

Motown Animation

COMPANY BACKGROUND

Motown Animation is a division of Motown Records. The company's first projects include publishing two lines of comic books--"Motown Comix" and "Motown Machineworks," which are distributed by Image Comics, one of the largest independent publishers in the comic book industry. Part of Motown Animation's objective is to develop and discover new intellectual properties that can be used in comic books, animated television, movies, and other media. Michael Davis uses the comic books published by his company to help promote literacy and get young people excited about reading.

PERSONAL HISTORY

Michael Davis is an artist, an entrepreneur, and a teacher. He's also the head of Motown's new animation unit, a company with the goal of producing entertainment and educational properties. Michael began his career as a commercial illustrator, designing advertising and promotional materials for CBS, NBC, Ford Motor Company, and many other companies.

Michael was born in Jamaica, Queens, New York, and grew up in a housing project. He graduated from the High School of Art and Design, and then from the Pratt Institute. In 1987, Michael entered the world of comic books by working on a project for DC Comics. At the time, Michael was a partner of a company that he founded, called Milestone Media (America's first black-owned comic book publisher to be distributed by a multinational entertainment giant).

Outside of his work, Michael has founded a unique educational program and often lectures around the country offering young people advice on how to be successful. "Many of the people I grew up with are either dead or are still there. It would have been very easy for me to become a thug.

"When most people have violence in their life, what usually happens is they themselves turn to violence. I, however, have a cousin, William T. Williams, who is a very successful artist. Throughout my life, my cousin has been my role model and a mentor. He has the motto of 'each one, teach one,' so when I was a child, he had me come to his studio on Saturdays to learn about art and being an artist. That kept me away from the wrong elements in the 'hood. My mother also took a mentoring approach toward educating me. As a result, when I got older I started talking to people about my experiences growing up. During my high school years, I got a summer job working for the Children's Art Carnival, which is an art school in Harlem that was started by the Museum of Modern Art. At one point, I substituted for one of the teachers, and that got me very interested in teaching young people. By the time I graduated from college I was being invited by many different organizations to be a guest speaker or lecturer. My goal is to get kids of color to stay in school and realize the importance of

education and literacy. I take a very different approach than other people to accomplish this objective."

TOPICS COVERED IN THIS INTERVIEW

☞ **Making a good impression during an interview**

☞ **Setting and achieving your goals**

☞ **Creating your résumé**

☞ **Avoiding mistakes applicants make during the job- search process**

How can someone make the best impression during a job interview?

"You've got to do your homework about the company. If you're applying for a job at IBM, you don't go into the interview talking about how much you love using an Apple Macintosh computer. Instead, you talk about where the company you're applying to is now, and how you can fit in. Most interviewers don't want to interview people; they want to hire people. They want to be impressed and excited about filling positions their company has available.

"When I applied for work as an illustrator, I made sure that my portfolio was impressive and that it demonstrated my capabilities. In the art world, your portfolio is your résumé. It is common when applying for a job as an illustrator to drop off your portfolio a few days before your interview, so that people have time to review it. I always put

> *"One trick I advise people to use before they start interviewing is to have personal business cards made for yourself, with your home address and phone number printed on them. Then, when you go in for an interview, give the interviewer both a copy of your résumé and your card."*

a special seal on my portfolio, so I could tell if it was actually looked at. When someone opened my portfolio, they heard music, because I inserted a special computer chip that played music. I also had a mini light box and magnifying glass built into my portfolio, so people could easily look at my slides. This set my portfolio apart from others.

"During the interview, ask the interviewer some questions about their company. When I was applying for jobs, after my interviews I immediately sent personalized thank you notes to the people I interviewed with. In about a week, if I didn't hear from the company, I would give them a call and thank them for giving me the opportunity to interview with them. I wouldn't ask if they had made a decision about hiring me. Never be cocky, but be confident.

"I think the biggest trick to doing well in an interview is knowing how to deal with people. During an interview, you have to be very excited about the job you're applying for, but not talk too much. You want to leave a positive impression. You also have to be well informed. I tell young people that no matter what type of business they want to get into, they should subscribe to and read at least two of the following publications: *Business Week*, *Forbes*, the *Wall Street Journal*, *Inc.*, or *Success*.

"One trick I advise people to use before they start interviewing is to have personal business cards made for yourself, with your home address and phone number printed on them. Then, when you go in for an interview, give the interviewer both a copy of your résumé and your card. This is something very few people do, but it goes a long way to make yourself stand out from other people. Applying for a job is like a game, but it's a game you can win!"

How do you set goals and then go about achieving those goals?

"I aim to be like the people that I'm most influenced by. I want to follow in their footsteps. Right now, I want to be like Michael Eisner, the CEO of the Walt Disney Company. When I choose a role model for myself, I try to learn as much as I can about them, and if possible, I try to meet with my role models and talk to them as often as I can. When someone gets a call from Mr. Eisner, no matter what they're doing, they take that call. I want to have that kind of access to people. The way you gain that sort of access is by building relationships, being good at what you do, and being true to yourself and to what you do."

"If you're interested in pursuing a certain occupation, such as being a lawyer, go out and find yourself a few lawyers to talk with."

What advice can you give to people about networking?

"Talk to everyone you know. If you know people in business, have them introduce you to other people. Just by talking to people, you can learn a lot about many different things. The people you meet and the knowledge you learn can lead to bigger and better things. If you're interested in pursuing a certain occupation, such as being a lawyer, go out and find yourself a few lawyers to talk with. Ask the lawyers you meet if you can spend a day with them to see what their jobs are like."

What makes a good résumé?

"Your résumé should be one page and printed in a relatively large and easy-to-read typestyle. Make sure you list your goals and aspirations along with your work experience. When I look at someone's résumé, I look for three things: a goal, something about the applicant's education, and short bullet points about previous jobs. I think that anyone who lists on their résumé why they left their previous job is an absolute idiot. That's just asking for trouble. If someone asks you why you left your previous job—which is a common question—have your answer prepared in advance."

How important are appearance and demeanor during an interview?

"Wear an outfit that you're comfortable with. Look neat, presentable, and clean. You want to dress for success, so dress according to the dress code of the company you're applying to. You want to show respect for the company. Your shoes and clothing have to be clean. Make sure your hands are clean and that you've brushed your teeth, especially if you've recently eaten." Since Michael looks young, he often makes it a point to choose clothing and accessories that make him look older. For example, he sometimes wears eyeglasses to subtly change his appearance, even though he has perfect vision.

Another mistake Michael believes applicants often make is to give the interviewer a subtle physiological advantage during the interview process. "Never ever sit down at the start of an interview before you are specifically asked to sit down. If you do, the interviewer has now assumed a sense of power that you don't want him or her to have. If you're sitting down and the interviewer is still standing, that means the interviewer is looking down at you, and that gives the interviewer a physiological advantage. You want to sit down at the same time as the interviewer, or after them."

> "I THINK THAT ANYONE WHO LISTS ON THEIR RESUME WHY THEY LEFT THEIR PREVIOUS JOB IS AN ABSOLUTE IDIOT."

"As you go through the whole job-search process, maintain your sense of humor."

Part of making a good overall impression during the interview process is watching the language and vocabulary you use. "If your vocabulary has a lot of slang words in it, don't use those words until after the interviewer uses them, and even then, use them extremely sparingly. If you're starting to feel too com-fortable in an interview, be careful. You don't want to feel too comfortable, because then you won't be at your best. Don't be afraid to talk about your failures. One of the worst mistakes you can make is trying to show to the inter-viewer that you're absolutely perfect."

LAST WORD

"Have a long-term goal for yourself. Make sure that it's a goal that's so big that even if you don't achieve it, you'll still be extremely successful. Along the way toward achieving that goal, you'll also want to set many smaller, shorter-term goals for yourself. Never lose sight of your goals. As you move around in your career, make sure that each step takes you closer to achieving your ultimate goals. Always maintain a positive attitude, and be excited about whatever it is you're doing. As you go through the whole job-search process, maintain your sense of humor. If you don't get a job, so what? It's a job you didn't have the day before."

JERI TAYLOR

CREATOR/EXECUTIVE PRODUCER

Star Trek: Voyager

COMPANY BACKGROUND

"Space...the final frontier..." For over 30 years, *Star Trek* has entertained millions of television viewers. The original groundbreaking *Star Trek* series has since been spun off into three additional and highly successful television series--*Star Trek, Star Trek: The Next Generation, Star Trek: Deep Space Nine,* and *Star Trek: Voyager,* plus a series of hit motion

pictures. Since the death of *Star Trek*'s creator, Gene Roddenberry, the entire *Star Trek* universe has been kept alive under the leadership of several talented individuals, including Rick Berman, Michael Pillar, and Jeri Taylor. These three people manage the cast and crews of the *Star Trek* series and movies that are currently in production and ensure that the series continues to satisfy its many fans around the world.

PERSONAL HISTORY

Jeri Taylor's story begins with a sense of desperation, but has a happy ending. During her career, Jeri has written, directed, and/or

produced some of the most popular shows on television including: *Quincy, M.D., Blue Thunder, Magnum P.I., In the Heat of the Night, Jake and the Fatman, Little House on the Prairie,* and *The Incredible Hulk.* She spent several years as a writer, supervising producer, and then co-executive producer for the award-winning syndicated television series *Star Trek: The Next Generation,* and

the fear of ending up behind the counter at a fast-food restaurant to support myself for the rest of my life. Before this major change in my life, I had spent some time working with a small theater company, doing some acting, directing, and teaching of acting. I didn't think I could make a living working for a small theater. I did, however, feel that I could somehow combine the education I had as an English major with my theater experience. After much thought, I decided to try writing for film and television."

Jeri had no previous professional writing experience, nor did she have any knowledge about how difficult it is to break into the Hollywood community as a screenwriter. "I had ignorance, fear, and some luck on my side. At the time, if I had had a clue about how difficult it would be to break into this business, I probably never would have tried. I sat myself down and started writing screenplays. After a while, I began the most difficult part of launching my career, which was hustling around trying to make contact with anyone and everyone I know, hoping to find someone who had something to do with the television or film industry. I asked everyone if they knew of an agent, or knew anyone who knew an agent who could assist me in selling my first screenplay. I eventually found an agent, and later found a first writing job. I spent

currently holds the title of Executive Producer for the top-rated television series *Star Trek: Voyager* (which she also helped to create). Jeri received her bachelor of arts degree in English from Indiana University, and her master's degree in English from California State University at Northridge.

"I am of a generation in which women never considered having a career. I was married and expected to spend my life as a homemaker and mother and never really trained for any type of career. For many years I was a homemaker and mother, until the mid-1970s, when I got divorced and was forced to find a way to support myself. At the time, I was totally unprepared for life as a career woman, and I was motivated mainly by several years writing television scripts on a freelance basis, and was able to make a living. Gradually, I worked my way into staff positions at shows like *Quincy, M.D.* In 1990, however, I found myself unemployed once again."

Jeri was forced to again use her networking skills to find another job that would allow her to support herself. "I made contact with a friend at Paramount Television, who was working on *Star Trek: The Next Generation.* She asked me to assist in doing a rewrite of a script. I had never seen an episode of *Star Trek,* or *Star Trek: TNG,* nor had I seen any of the movies. What I did have was a reputation in Hollywood as a screenwriter with strong character development skills, and that's what this episode required. I did a good job on that script, and was later asked to join the staff of *Star Trek: TNG.* I gradually worked my way up the ranks, and went from being a supervising producer to co-executive producer of *Star Trek: TNG.* When we were asked to develop a new *Star Trek* television series, which would become the United Paramount Network (UPN)'s *Star Trek: Voyager* series, I began working with Rick Berman and Michael Pillar as a creator and executive producer."

As the executive producer of *Star Trek: Voyager,* Jeri is totally responsible for all aspects of producing the weekly television series, which has a multimillion-dollar-per-episode budget. This responsibility includes managing a staff made up of literally hundreds of different people, each with different skills and backgrounds, who must work together as a team to produce each one-hour episode without going over budget or falling behind schedule. "This is a very labor-intensive, demanding and time-consuming job. I come to work about 7:00 A.M. and go home about 7:00 P.M. I always take work home with me, and I almost always work on weekends."

TOPICS DISCUSSED IN THIS INTERVIEW

☞ **Setting career-related goals**

☞ **Mastering your networking skills**

☞ **Qualities that employers look for in an applicant**

☞ **Getting the attention of an employer**

☞ **The worst mistakes you can make when applying for a job**

☞ **Advice for women entering a male-dominated workplace**

How do you set and achieve your career-related goals?

"I have always had a very detailed plan for achieving my goals. When I worked as an acting teacher, I developed a specific strategy and taught it to my students. One of the most discouraging things for most actors is the lack of structure in their lives. I devised this goal-setting system to help people in this situation, but the system works for people breaking into almost any career."

What is your goal-setting strategy?

1. **Take a piece of paper, and write down where you envision your career to be, and what you want your life to be like, five years from now.**

2. **Think about where you'd like your life to be at the end of one year, and write down these goals.**

3. **Now, consider where you need to be at the end of one month, in order to work your way toward achieving your one-year and five-year objectives.**

4. **Finally, list the specific things you need to accomplish in the next week, and then the next three weeks after that, in order to achieve your one-month objectives and goals.**

When you continue Jeri's process, and devise a list of many smaller, easily attainable, short-term goals that are designed to move you a step closer to your ultimate objective each time you accomplish one, just about any long-term goal or objective becomes possible to achieve, if you're willing to plan ahead and work hard at it. "All of this should be written down, so that you can constantly refer to your plans and review your goals. As you begin working toward your first goals, at the end of each day write down exactly what you did and analyze what needs to be done on the following day."

When Jeri was forced to launch her career, she followed this goal-setting strategy and still has the original papers in which she kept her journal. "I occasionally look back and see how lost, frightened, and alone I seemed to be in the beginning. I can now read my own notes and see how I eventually worked my way toward getting that first job, by setting and achieving many smaller goals that led up to my ultimate goal of writing for a television series."

What does it takes to master networking skills?

"When I began looking for work, I spoke with everyone I knew, because I needed an introduction to someone who worked in the business. Back then, I didn't realize that what I was doing was in fact networking. What I have done, in all aspects of my life, is always try to meet people and present myself as honestly as I can. I always treat other people in the way I'd like to be treated. I know this sounds like a cliché, but it's how I live my life.

"Often, when I meet an applicant, I base my hiring decision on my gut feelings about that person. If I feel someone has the qualities that will make him or her a good team player, then I will often hire that person."

"There are as many ways of breaking into an industry as there are people in it. I am a great believer in hard work. I think that the people who work hard, who are tenacious, and who don't quit are the ones who are going to succeed."

Good manners, common courtesy, compassion, and thoughtfulness are the qualities that I have practiced throughout my life. These are qualities that allow people to see me in a positive light. There is a delicate balance between selling yourself and representing yourself in a positive manner. You don't want to come off as arrogant or self-serving. I don't know how someone learns how to walk that tightrope, other than by trying it for themselves and learning from their mistakes. Overcoming obstacles is what makes us strong. One of the things that I always taught my own kids is that success doesn't lie in never falling down. It lies in getting up each and every time you fall."

What do you look for when you are hiring someone?
"I look for enthusiasm, a sense of responsibility, and someone who is centered and focused. When I am hiring someone who needs experience in a certain area, I look at their previous work experience, but I also hire people in entry-level positions. Often, when I meet an applicant, I base my hiring decision on my gut feelings about that person. If I feel someone has the qualities that will make him or her a good team player, then I will often hire that person. Working in episodic television is a very tough world, and

it is a collaborative effort. Everyone working in this field has to be a strong team player and be able to pull together with others without getting caught up in their own ego. Basically, when I interview an applicant, I am looking for an emotional connection with that person."

How can someone get the attention of the person responsible for hiring at a company?
"That's where the hustling comes in. You can always begin by writing a letter. In my current position as executive producer of *Star Trek: Voyager*, I receive many letters from people requesting jobs. I keep a file of résumés, so if a job opening comes along, I have someplace to begin my search for someone to fill that job. As a result, the way someone presents themselves in a résumé often proves to be important. If you are trying to enter into a highly competitive industry, which is for the most part closed to outsiders, talk with literally everyone you know and try to find someone with a connection to that industry, so they can make an introduction for you. When I was trying to break into the television industry as a writer, it was my neighbors who knew an agent, and they made the initial introduction for me. You have to begin by taking the first

enthusiasm

step, which might be writing a letter or it might be having someone you know make an introduction for you. With any luck, that first step will lead to a telephone conversation or a job interview. Unfortunately, I don't think there are any magic formulas you can follow. There are as many ways of breaking into an industry as there are people in it. I am a great believer in hard work. I think that the people who work hard, who are tenacious, and who don't quit are the ones who are going to succeed."

the point where they have actually made their point. I think that you should never go to an interview looking sloppy, and you should always be prompt. The first impression that the employer gets of you is going to be a lasting one. The first impression you make tells the employer a lot about who you are. If you arrive five or ten minutes late, that gives the employer a bad feeling right away. I know sometimes delays are unavoidable, but as the applicant you have to make sure you're

"The worst mistake you can make is to try too hard to sell yourself."

What types of questions should the applicant ask the employer?

"It is vital that the applicant develop a strong understanding of what their responsibilities are to be, how they will fit into the hierarchy of the whole organization, and what qualities and skills the employer expects them to have." To discover these answers, the applicant must ask the right questions during the interview process and do research about the company. "I don't think that the applicant should ask the person interviewing them a lot of personal questions. It all comes down to courtesy and good manners."

What's the worst mistake someone can make when applying for a job?

"Based on my own experiences, the worst mistake you can make is to try too hard to sell yourself. I frequently speak with people who are nervous, and while they are trying to make a good impression they go on and on about how terrific they are and what good workers they are. They soon go way beyond

going to arrive at an interview on time, no matter what, even if it means leaving for that interview extra early and arriving thirty minutes before the interview, as opposed to being just two minutes late.""

Talking too little during an interview can also be a negative. "If I ask an applicant questions, and all I get back are one- or two-word answers, that doesn't give me a window into that person's personality. It all comes down to honestly representing yourself and letting someone know who you are and what you're about without going overboard."

How can someone distinguish themselves from the competition?

"I have actually seen a lot people not get a job because they tried too hard. One young man comes to mind. He was applying for a production assistant position. I think he must have just completed a job interview course or something, because he was trying much too hard to let people know how much he would love the job. He actually talked himself out of getting the job. He should have tried to relax and let us see more of the nice young man that he actually was. Instead, he kept trying to impress people, and that wasn't at all impressive. You don't always have to be the most charismatic person in the world to get a job. You should never adopt a personality that you think someone wants you to have. Be yourself and be honest. Don't try to be something you're not, because that dishonesty will always show through."

If you feel that you have the drive and desire to succeed in the job that you're applying for, then you have to make that clear to the employer. "During your conversations, mention things like, 'I know what it's like to work hard,' 'I'm willing to work hard,' 'I respond well to a heavy work load,' or 'Work doesn't scare me.' If you say this type of thing simply and honestly, the employer will respect it and believe it."

Is there any way to determine if you're going to like the job before you actually get it?

"Whether or not an applicant will enjoy a job is not something that the employer can really predict. Applicants have to take the information that they learn, based on their research and the interview, and determine for themselves if that work environment is the best place for them."

What keeps you motivated on a daily basis?

"I have a huge sense of responsibility. I am not the type of person who allows things to slide or to slack off. I am very mindful that *Star Trek* has a very enlightened and intelligent audience, and an audience that we cannot and will not take for granted. People

always say to me that *Star Trek* has been around for over 30 years, and it will be around forever. My response is that it won't if we become complacent and we start turning out work that is less than our best. There is no reason in the world to think that the audience will stick with us just because we're there. I think that a sense of uncertainty is a good thing. It keeps the juices flowing and keeps the creative edge a little sharper. I don't ever want to be guilty of doing anything less than my very best work."

Do you have advice specifically for women trying to get a job in a male-dominated world?

"I absolutely feel that we're still living in a male-dominated world. I think it is very difficult for women to be treated equitably in the workplace. When I first started as a freelance writer, I would have said that there was no gender discrimination in Hollywood. I didn't realize at the time that women working in low-level positions aren't considered too much of a threat. It was when I began ascending the ladder of success, and earning higher and higher titles, that I began to perceive a sense of threat from some men. Achieving success as a female is a road that each woman must follow for herself, because I don't think there is a formula or an easy solution for being accepted as a female leader in the workplace. I have gradually learned to assert myself without being threatening. I am willing to yield and compromise when necessary, and I try not to use my position now in a way that would make any man that is subordinate to me feel like less than a human being. As I have already said, I treat all people how I would like to be treated, and I expect that back in return."

LAST WORD

"When I began trying to launch my career, at first I wasn't successful. Someone once said to me, 'Just don't quit. If you don't quit, you're going to make it, but if you quit, you know you'll never succeed.' Somehow, this advice rang true with me, and I was never willing to give up. If you want something badly enough, and you don't quit, then chances are you're going to get it."

SARINA SIMON | PRESIDENT

Philips Media Home and Family Entertainment

COMPANY BACKGROUND

Philips Electronics is the world's **third largest** electronics company; it was originally founded in 1891 by Gerard Philips in Eindhoven, Holland.

Computer games and family entertainment applications for **multimedia-based** computers have become a huge business, and Sarina Simon oversees Philips Media Home and Family Entertainment's **worldwide** development and production of all family and children's software for CD-ROM and Compact Disc-interactive (CD-i) platforms. To **discover** new and exciting content for these multimedia software applications, Sarina works with sister companies that are owned or partially owned by Philips Electronics, including PolyGram, A&M **Philips Media** Records, PolyGram Home Video, Philips Media Studios, SideWalk Studio, Insight, Kaleidoscope, Magnavox, Marantz, and Motown.

Philips has organizations in 60 countries around the world. The North American headquarters of the company, Philips Corporation, is based in New York City. Philips Media Home and Family Entertainment is based in Los Angeles.

PERSONAL HISTORY

Prior to becoming President of Philips Media Home and Family Entertainment, Sarina held the position of senior vice president of product development and planning for the company. Before that, she held a number of different positions and occupations.

Sarina holds a master's degree from Columbia University and a bachelor's degree from Sarah Lawrence College. She is currently one of the few female presidents of a high-tech company and is an accomplished writer, author, and mother of two daughters.

TOPICS COVERED IN THIS INTERVIEW

☞ **Setting career-related goals**

☞ **Being successful working for a large company**

☞ **The importance of networking**

☞ **Creating a good résumé**

How did you set your own career-related goals?

"I'd like to say that I've always had a very focused career plan, but that's not the case. In college, I very much envied people who had a clear idea of what they wanted to become. Some of the most blessed people on Earth are those who grow up with a passion. I had a liberal arts education and an interest in many things, but I had no clear direction about which way to go with my career. I knew that I wanted to do something creative. That was a very broad objective and could have led me to being an innovator in virtually any industry. I went from college to graduate school and originally studied medieval Italian literature. That lasted for a brief period of time, until I changed my focus to education. When I graduated from Columbia University, I was offered a teaching position there, so I didn't face too much of a job search. That led to my teaching in a public school system in Yonkers, New York, until the city ran into financial problems and I found myself in an out-of-work situation. Rather than seek another teaching position, I pursued a career in publishing. I had always had an interest in writing."

As Sarina struggled to find a career in which she could experience long-term enjoyment and success, she managed to support herself through the jobs she pursued. "While I was trying to find myself, I was not being supported by my parents. During this time in my life I spent a great deal of effort networking, and I eventually worked my way into the publishing business, first as a freelance writer and later as a full-time editor for several different major New York publishers. After several years, I went to work for the Walt Disney Company and moved from New York to Los Angeles. I found this job at Disney by responding to a blind ad. I read the ad and it sounded like a job that was created just for me, so I applied for it, not having any idea what company actually was offering the position. Disney was working on several educational projects, and they were looking for people with a teaching, writing, and publishing background. I learned a great deal working for Disney, and eventually moved on once again."

From Disney, Sarina went back into book publishing. During a lunch with a friend, she was discussing her work and her personal situation as a single mother. Her friend worked for a major children's video company, but she was being recruited by Philips to create interactive software for children. "My friend wasn't interested in changing careers, but I saw the opportunity to make more money by changing careers and applying for a job at Philips Media. This was when the whole multimedia industry was first forming, so entering into this type of business was very risky. After meeting with the company, I realized there could be a future for me there. From a career perspective, I had to choose either to remain in a publishing job that I was doing well in or change careers once again and trying something new."

Sarina saw the opportunities that Philips Media was offering and chose to accept a position as a senior vice president of product development in the children's area. From this point, she worked her way up within the company until she was offered the position

of President of Philips Media Home and Family Entertainment. "Thus far in my career, I had experience working as a writer, editor, teacher, publisher, and as a film maker. I had a broad palate of experience, and this job was perfect for me."

In recent years, Sarina says that she has found more direction in her life by analyzing what her strengths are. "I really enjoy giving birth to a product. I like to be involved in the conceptualization and then following it along as it's brought to market and finds an audience. I feel very focused in my life right now, and think that I will remain in the multimedia industry for many years to come."

Once you accepted a job at Philips Media, how did you work your way up within the company?

"It was through a tremendous amount of hard work and genuine dedication. My goal was to put together top-quality products, and that's what I did. Every time I accomplished something within the company, I was rewarded and moved up within the organization. If you look at any other media-related industry that targets children, whether it's publishing or television production, you will find that in these areas females have experienced a lot of success. In the multimedia industry, most companies grew out of companies that were already established with male leaders. At Philips, however, we were in a situation where we were starting this multimedia division from scratch. The company wanted to hire the most qualified people, whether they were men or women, and for the children's software division, many of the most qualified people were females. Right now, I think there are a lot of many different kinds of

> "The first thing someone has to do before they start looking for any type of job is to determine their true interests and skills. If your interests are all over the map, try to see if there is something that those interests have in common."

opportunities available within the multimedia industry for people of both sexes."

What does it take to be successful working at a large company?

"I think the trick is being able to work with many different kinds of people in a way that makes everyone feel comfortable with each other. You have to be willing to work as a team, no matter what your position is within the company.

"The first thing someone has to do before they start looking for any type of job is to determine their true interests and skills. If your interests are all over the map, try to see if there is something that those interests have in common. This will help you to narrow down your search. When I was younger I didn't really understand all of the different job opportunities that were available in the world. Once I got past the basic occupations of doctor, lawyer, and business person, I wasn't really that informed. I think young people today have to go out of their way to make sure they are informed about the opportunities that are available to them before they make any career decisions. In my day, if you didn't know what you wanted to do with your life

when you got out of college, you went to law school, because that allowed you to go to school and come out with a career. I applied and got accepted to law school twice, but I knew that I really wasn't interested in law. If you have a lack of focus, learn as much as you can about the many different ways people are making a living. Meet people and talk to them. Go around asking all types of people what it is they like about their jobs."

Once someone knows what type of career they want to pursue, how should they get started?

"First, do your research. Learn as much about the industry as you can, and then focus your research on the individual companies within that industry. Speaking now as someone who hires a lot of people at my company, it really astonishes me how many bright people apply for a job at my company, but they come into a job interview having done no research about what my company does, how their skills can benefit my company, or even how my company fits within the industry. If someone does their research and has a good understanding of the company they're applying to, then they will know exactly how their skills

and experience can benefit the company they want to work for.

"A while back, I had a young man apply for a job at Philips Media who had no previous experience in the job he was applying for. I didn't give him the job because I didn't see what he could offer to the company. After the interview, he went out and did some research. He went to his local computer store and actually tested all of my company's software products. He then wrote me a four-page letter showing me that despite his lack of experience, he had real insight into the kind of work that we do. The result was that I wound up hiring him. This is a situation where doing research about a company, although it was late, actually got someone a job.

"I have a friend from Baltimore who had a dream of moving to California and working for Disney. She was working for an advertising agency, but she spent time researching the hell out of the Walt Disney Company and analyzed each division within the company looking for places she would fit in. Based on her research and persistence, she wound up getting an interview and landing her dream job at Disney. The people that I have met who have accomplished a lot in their lives are the people who went that extra mile and took some risks along the way. I hate to sound like my grandmother, but hard work and perseverance are what it takes to succeed."

How important is networking for getting yourself a job?

"I think it's tremendously important. I got my first job in the publishing industry through a friend of mine who had a sister who worked for a publishing company. If you don't have a contact within a company, sometimes just getting yourself an interview at that company is the hardest part about landing a job. I think that young adults have more opportunities to network than they realize. When you're looking for a job, you have to put those feelers out and let everyone know that you're looking for a job. The number of people who get a job based on a personal introduction from someone is tremendous.

"In my own career, I have a huge network of colleagues in many industries. I constantly use my network of contacts to help people I like and respect to find work.

"The advice I can offer about networking is that it can be extremely beneficial, but don't become so aggressive that you become obnoxious and make people feel like you're taking advantage of them in order to get yourself ahead. You have to be careful. Don't become someone's best friend overnight just because they have a connection that you want to exploit in order to get yourself an introduction into a company."

What skills should someone master in order to get themselves a job?

"I am a firm believer in the importance of good writing skills. If there is one skill that is hardest to find in recent college graduates, it is the ability to write well. As a result, a well-written résumé and cover letter really stand out and get my attention."

Networking

"If there is one skill that is hardest to find in recent college graduates, it is the ability to write well."

What advice can you offer about creating a good résumé?

"Most people who are first starting out don't have a lot of experience, so they tend to use too many adjectives and hype when listing their skills and interests on their résumé. I think that a well-described objective at the beginning of a résumé is an important element. This objective should be changed and customized to match every specific job you're applying for. If you're not a good writer, get someone to help you create your résumé, and whatever you do, make sure that your final résumé contains no typos. If you are lucky enough to get your résumé into the hands of a busy person, that person could easily discard your résumé just because it contains a misspelled word or typo, especially if you have no real work experience.

"I personally believe that applicants should avoid including personal information in their résumé, such as their marital status or the number of children they have. Applicants need to ask themselves the questions, 'What are the needs of the employer?' and 'How can I meet those needs?' Based on the answers you have to these questions, your résumé should be written accordingly. Everything on your résumé should contribute to answering those two questions. Leave extra or unrelated information out of your résumé. If you're going to be creative, the place to be creative is in your cover letter."

Once you've created a résumé that you're proud of and you're ready to submit it to a company that you want to work for, to whom should you send the résumé?

"You can send your résumé and cover letter to a company's human resources department, but I don't believe that's the best approach you can take. I would recommend pinpointing an executive within the company who is in charge of the division you want to work for, and sending your résumé to that person. The problem, however, with sending your résumé directly to an executive within a company is that they could very well be too busy to read it. I think that it's perfectly acceptable to send your résumé to multiple people or to multiple departments within a company."

What are the biggest mistakes you've seen applicants make when applying for a job?

"There is a difference between convincing people that you can contribute to a company and telling them how to run their business. The younger you are, the more careful you have to be about that. You have to strike a balance between being confident and arrogant. Don't go into an interview with senior people and try to pretend that you're on the same level as them. Also, never be late for an interview. If you get invited in for an interview at a company, consider yourself lucky, because chances are there were many applicants who didn't get an interview. Don't blow your opportunity by being late. If two equally qualified applicants apply for one job, the person who was on time for the interview will almost always get that job. Don't let your being late become the deciding factor for the interviewer to give someone else the job.

Finally, if you don't know the answer to a question that's posed to you during an interview, don't make up an answer. Be honest and say you don't know the answer. You'll earn a lot more respect that way."

LAST WORD

"The people that I have met who have accomplished a lot in their lives are the people who went that extra mile and took some risks along the way."

MICHAEL D. ZISMAN
EXECUTIVE VICE PRESIDENT & CEO
Lotus Development Corp.

COMPANY BACKGROUND

Lotus Development Corp. was founded in 1982. By the mid-1990s, the company was offering a wide range of business and personal productivity software products. Today, Lotus computer software products include Lotus 1-2-3®, Lotus Notes®, SmartSuite®, Freelance Graphics®, Lotus Word Pro®, Lotus Organizer®, and Lotus Approach®. The company's Lotus 1-2-3 product is the world's most popular spreadsheet application with more than 20 million users worldwide.

Lotus's software products are available in more than 80 countries. In fact, over 44 percent of the company's revenue is generated from sales outside the United States. The company currently has more than 5,600 employees worldwide, and annual revenues of more than $1 billion.

In 1995, Cambridge, Massachusetts-based Lotus Development Corp. became a wholly owned subsidiary of IBM Corp. IBM paid $3.52 billion for this acquisition.

PERSONAL HISTORY

In October 1995, Michael D. Zisman became CEO of Lotus Development Corporation, a subsidiary of IBM. Prior to taking this position, Michael was the founder, President, and CEO of Soft-Switch, Inc., a company that

he started in 1979 and later sold to Lotus Development in 1994. "When Soft-Switch was sold, I accepted an executive position at Lotus. Ten months later, Lotus was then sold. Two months after that, the CEO of Lotus decided to leave, and I was offered the position."

Michael has also taught at the Sloan School of Business at the Massachusetts Institute of Technology (MIT) and at the Wharton School of Business at the University of Pennsylvania. "I always joke around that the question 'What do you want to be when you grow up?' is something you should be asking yourself until the day they bury you. I think people are always looking to the next thing. The very first day I was exposed to computers, it was in 1967, I was a chemical engineering student. I knew right away that my career was going to involve computers. Looking back, I never really had a goal to be an executive. I did, however, have a goal to be an entrepreneur. If you're an entrepreneur and your company grows, you evolve into an executive."

TOPICS COVERED
IN THIS INTERVIEW

☞ **How grad school may fit into your overall career picture**

☞ **How to find the best job opportunities available**

☞ **Creating a powerful résumé that will get attention**

☞ **Making the best impression during an interview**

☞ **Preparing for trick questions during the interview**

What do you think are the reasons for your success?

"I think more than anything, success comes from tenacity. The only thing that separated me from other people was that I refused to give up. I can honestly say that starting my company, Soft-Switch, was not an easy thing. It was something that I built up over a period of 15 years. It was not an instant success by any stretch of the imagination. Most people would not have had the tenacity to stick with it and keep going until a formula for success was eventually found."

What's the difference between getting a first job and actually launching a career?

"When I was graduating from college, I remember very clearly some advice that a professor gave me. What he said was that 'most people don't remain at their first job for too long, so I wouldn't worry a whole lot about it. You'll probably decide to go off to graduate school or move to something else.' In other words, when you accept a first job, don't think of it as the place you're going to stay forever. I don't think that someone's first job necessarily marks the start of their career. People need to be incredibly flexible and recognize that their interests may change. I often say that there is a God out there, and life is fair. The reality is that there are hundreds of opportunities available to every one of us every day, yet we fail to recognize them as opportunities. You've got to be willing to stay flexible and explore the opportunities that you discover."

In today's competitive business climate, how important is a graduate degree?

"It really depends on what you want to pursue. If you look at a company like Lotus,

"The reality is that there are hundreds of opportunities available to every one of us every day, yet we fail to recognize them as opportunities."

we hire many software people from both undergraduate and graduate levels. If you want to work for a top consulting firm, you'll need an MBA. I encourage people to get work-related experience before thinking about going to graduate business school. I have taught at two of the top graduate business schools in the world, and worked on the admissions committee at MIT. The average age of someone starting grad school at Wharton and MIT today is somewhere between 27 and 29 years old. A lot of grad schools have a policy not to accept students right out of college. They encourage people to get work experience first.

"One piece of advice I have given to my daughter, who is in junior high school, is that she shouldn't do things simply because they will look good on her record. What I tell her is to pursue things because she wants to do them and because she'll become a more well-rounded person. A lot of people today fall into the trap of fitting themselves into a mold that they think schools and companies are looking for. What both grad schools and employers are really looking for are smart and well-rounded people who have a sense of

direction and confidence about themselves. When I hear someone say that they joined the drama club in school because they needed to list extracurricular activities on the college application or résumé, I see that as a negative. It shows that person has a lack of confidence about themselves. They should have joined the drama club because it was of interest to them and was something they really wanted to do."

How should someone go about setting career goals?

"Young people need to think about the first three to five years of their professional life. If you're just graduating from college, you have to ask yourself if you're on a career path that will allow you to work for a little while and then go off to graduate school, or are you on a path where you probably won't attend graduate school?

"If you decide that you want to work for a few years and then possibly attend grad school, where you initially work will be irrelevant. What you should be thinking about is what you can do to maximize the likelihood of getting into a good grad school. Look for a job that will be a learning opportunity. Once you finish grad school and have a degree, then you've probably narrowed down the field of your interest and will probably pursue a career along the lines of what you studied. Now, you have to decide if you want to work for a large company or a small company.

explore

> *"The best references to use when applying for a job are from people you know within the company you're applying to."*

"If you're not planning on continuing your education after college you should look at the on-the-job training that the company you'll be working for offers. You might want to work for a while at a large company that offers better training and management programs."

Once you decide what you want to do, how can you find the best opportunities available?

"I think you have to pursue every avenue you can find. The most obvious avenue is on-campus recruiting. I receive tons of letters and résumés. Résumés coming across my desk don't get a lot of personal attention. They almost always get forwarded to Lotus's Human Resources department. As an undergraduate, you should pursue whatever personal contacts you have at various companies. If someone I know or work with calls me and makes an introduction for an applicant, then that applicant will often get personal attention from me. People looking for employment opportunities should not overlook the 'Help Wanted' ads and should attend job fairs. Lotus does a lot of on-campus interviewing and recruiting at job fairs. You have to make yourself available and visible."

If you're going to send your résumé to a company, but you don't have any personal connection with someone at the company, what's the best approach to take?

"If it's a large company, you're probably better off sending your résumé to the human resources department, unless you know an executive at the company or have an unbelievable statement that will get an executive's attention if you contact them directly.

"The best references to use when applying for a job are from people you know within the company you're applying to. If your cover letter says, 'You'll see that (insert name) from your company is on my list of personal references. I hope you'll take a few minutes to call (insert name),' that will get my attention, because I can call someone who I know and respect to find out more about you. Other good references are well-respected people within your community and past bosses from summer jobs or internships."

What makes a powerful résumé that works?

"For me, cuteness is a turnoff. I like to see résumés in a fairly standard format, and no longer than one page, particularly if the applicant doesn't have a lot of work experience. The résumé should be well written and printed on quality paper. Your résumé doesn't need to be printed on colorful paper using multiple fonts. What it does have to be is professional looking, crisp, and concise. A

> *"Your résumé must convey a sense of professionalism. There should be absolutely no typos in any way, shape, or form."*

résumé should allow me to quickly learn about someone's education experience, what school he or she went to, and what summer work experience he or she had. I also want to get an indication that the applicant is aggressive. I look for applicants that are well rounded, so be sure to include some of your personal interests. If your college or university has a predefined format for creating a résumé in order to participate in an on-campus recruiting program, I would recommend that you follow that résumé format.

"Some larger companies use computerized résumé scanning programs, so there is a good chance that your résumé will be scanned into a database and then picked apart by a computer based on key words. It is important to include the important key words in your résumé. If you were applying for a job in my industry, your résumé should include a line that says 'proficient in the following programming languages,' and then include a list of programming languages.

"I have looked at résumés that when I read the first few words, I thought to myself that this first series of words leading up to the first period is not a sentence in the English language. At that point, everything is downhill. On one résumé that I looked at recently, there was a word missing in the first sentence. Your résumé must convey a sense of professionalism. There should be absolutely no typos in any way, shape, or form. Focus on making a clear statement regarding what it is you want. What kind of job are you looking for? What are your goals? Ideally, between your junior and senior years at college you had a summer job or internship. Write about the experiences you had in that job. You want to demonstrate increasing responsibility and an increasing focus on your career goals."

What's the best way to make a good impression in a job interview?

"You want to present yourself well. Be professional and research the company before the interview. Read the company's annual report and any recent articles written about it in the media. One of the first things I would do if I were applying for a job and preparing for an interview is visit the company's Web site on the Internet."

Many companies, including Lotus Development Corp., now have a presence on the information superhighway. A growing number of companies even use their Web sites to post career opportunities and job openings that are available. The Lotus Web site (http://www.lotus.com), for example, lists information about the company and all of its products and features a database of press releases that the company has issued in the last few years. There's also a "Jobs" area that lists current openings within the company. Within minutes, anyone visiting this Web site can obtain just about everything they ever wanted to know about Lotus Development, day or night.

"ONE OF THE FIRST THINGS I WOULD DO IF I WERE APPLYING FOR A JOB AND PREPARING FOR AN INTERVIEW IS VISIT THE COMPANY'S WEB SITE ON THE INTERNET."

"The most important thing during an interview is to demonstrate that you've taken an interest in the company and have done some research to learn about it. You want to engage the interviewer in a conversation and be as natural as you can be. Don't ask silly questions.

"Even if the dress code at the company you're applying to is casual, you should probably come to an interview wearing business attire. That's a safer thing to do, unless you're specifically told by the company that the dress is 'business casual.' Business casual does not mean jeans and a T-shirt.

"Another tip I can offer is to respect people's time. If you have separate interviews scheduled with multiple people at a company throughout the day, assume that it's your responsibility to stay on schedule. If you're supposed to meet with someone from 10:00 A.M. until 10:30 A.M., and then with someone else from 10:30 A.M. to 11:00 A.M., but the first person is going on and on, take it upon yourself to say, 'It's 10:30 A.M., and I know I'm supposed to see so-and-so...' and then pause. Let the interviewer say that it's okay if you're a few minutes late, or offer to walk you to the next interview. You want to respect the time of everyone on your

schedule. Don't keep your 10:30 A.M. appointment waiting."

What types of trick questions are generally asked during an interview?

"I personally don't ask trick questions. I do ask questions, however, that will test to see if the applicant feels comfortable saying they don't know an answer. It's perfectly acceptable to be honest and say you don't know the answer to a question. One response you might use is, 'Gee, I should know the answer to that question, but I'm embarrassed that I don't.' Be prepared, because many interviewers will ask questions to see how well applicants can think on their feet. You have to be able to go with the flow."

If the interviewer asks a question that's totally off-the-wall or unrelated to anything, Michael suggests that you don't make the interviewer feel stupid for asking a question that you think is stupid. "Don't challenge the interviewer. Don't reject any question that seems unusual, because the interviewer probably doesn't care about your answer. They're probably testing to see how you respond to the question, not what you respond.

"When I was an applicant, I remember the interviewer saying, 'Michael, you're a

very smart guy who's probably going to get a lot of job offers. How are you going to decide which one to take?' This was a very good question, and he was able to learn a lot about my values based on my answer. A good response to this question is, 'I'm planning to do some more research about each company.'"

How can people figure out if they're going to enjoy the job they're being offered?

"I am delighted when we offer an applicant a position and before accepting it the person asks to spend a few hours, or an entire day, tagging along with someone in the department he or she may be working in to meet the people and get a taste of the atmosphere. This is something you can do, but be positive about it. Say that you're thrilled with the offer and you'd be excited to meet the people you may be working with. If you've been offered a job, hopefully you've done your research. You've already been through the interview process, so you should have a general idea of what the company is all about."

LAST WORD

"I think more than anything, success comes from tenacity. The only thing that separated me from other people was that I refused to give up."

JANE COOPER PRESIDENT
Paramount Parks

COMPANY BACKGROUND

Paramount Parks owns and operates the following amusement parks: Paramount's Great America (Santa Clara, California), Paramount's Canada's Wonderland (Ontario, Canada), Paramount's Carowinds (Charlotte, North Carolina), Paramount's Kings Dominion (Richmond, Virginia), and Paramount's Kings Island (Cincinnati, Ohio). Paramount Parks is the amusement park division of New York City-based Viacom, Inc., one of the largest entertainment and publishing companies in the world.

PERSONAL HISTORY

Jane began her career while still in high school, working summers at Paramount's Kings Island in Cincinnati, Ohio. At the time, she had no idea that, some 20 years later, she'd be in charge of running all five of Paramount's theme parks. After several summers, she was promoted from an entry-level employee to a supervisor. She continued working at Paramount's Kings Island through her college years, and was offered a full-time job there when she graduated.

"I would encourage everyone to get as much exposure to the real world as they can. Taking summer jobs that interest you is an excellent way to do this. Many high-school and college educators try to tell students that by the age of 18 they're supposed to know what they want to do with their life. In reality, most 18-year-olds have no idea what's out there, nor do they have the ability to make decisions that could impact the rest of their lives. If you go out and try a bunch of different things, it will become apparent to you what you really like and what you're good at. This will help you make a much better decision when the time comes to get your first real job and launch your career."

Jane is an example of someone who started in an entry-level position at a company and worked her way to the top. She says that there are several personal qualities that have allowed her to succeed. "I am very decisive, flexible, and aggressive. I believe that it's always better to make a decision, be wrong, and have to fix it afterward than it is to never decide anything at all. I also think I have good people skills." Jane believes that she wasn't necessarily born with all of these qualities. "I think it's half-and-half. Everyone is born with some qualities and then they develop others over a lifetime. I have been managing people since I was 18 years old, so I have developed good interpersonal skills. Management skills are an art form which can't totally be learned, but they can certainly be perfected and improved upon."

> ## TOPICS DISCUSSED IN THIS INTERVIEW
>
> ☞ **Setting career-related goals**
>
> ☞ **Networking to find the best job opportunities**
>
> ☞ **Mastering skills you'll need that weren't taught in school**
>
> ☞ **Choosing to work in a large corporate environment versus a small or midsized business**
>
> ☞ **Balancing your career and personal life**

How and when should someone begin setting career-related goals?

"It's never too early to begin setting goals for yourself. I think it's important for everyone to have a five year plan once they begin their career. When you're about to start a new job, ask yourself where you see yourself going, and where you see the job leading several years down the road. You need to be your own career manager as opposed to just accepting a job and waiting to see where it takes you. After you've been at most jobs for about 18 months, you probably have gotten everything you're going to get out of them.

At that point, it's your responsibility to decide if you want to keep doing what you're doing or if you want to learn something else. If you want to learn something else and move your career forward, then it's time to transfer within your company to a job that will require you to learn a new set of skills. You might have to consider finding another job altogether, if opportunities to grow within the company you're working for don't exist. Early on, even though I have been with the same company for over 20 years, I

all of the resources available to you, whether it's a contact you made several years ago as a summer employee, a neighbor, a friend of your parents, or even one of your friends' parents. There are a lot of people competing for jobs, but the fact is there aren't a lot of really good people out there. So when somebody comes highly recommended to me, I take that recommendation seriously. The marketplace is very competitive, so as an employer I want people who are enthusiastic, aggressive, and want to work hard. If

"In a corporate environment, you will never get a job that you don't ask for."

changed jobs every couple of years. I kept learning and obtaining experience in different jobs."

Jane admits that she always had an urge to move up the corporate ladder, but early on she had no plans to become a top-level executive. "Being President of Paramount Parks wasn't my initial goal. My goal was to work my way up three levels in the corporate infrastructure. After several years, I achieved this goal and spent about four years in that position. After that, I was ready to move forward once again and seek out new challenges. If the opportunity for me to continue to move upward in my career wasn't going to be available at Paramount Parks, I was prepared to go elsewhere."

How can someone find the best job opportunities available?

"The very best way to do this is by networking. Pick up the phone and call people. Use

someone comes to me and says that they know someone who they believe has these qualities and can fill a job opening, then I want to meet that applicant. I don't care what job title the person recommending the applicant has. Even if you don't know someone who is a top-level executive, chances are you know people who can help you by making introductions into companies on your behalf."

Jane says that the majority of applicants she agrees to see for job interviews come to her though some type of referral. "I get at least 25 résumés per week that are sent to me without a referral, and I don't usually have time to sort through them."

In her own career, Jane always used her networking skills to meet and spend time with people within her company. "I would create opportunities to spend time with senior-level people within the company. I made myself available to participate in

"If you're new to the work force and you really want to learn about a lot of different things, I'd recommend working for a small or midsized company, because you'll be exposed to a lot more in a short time."

special projects so I could work with those senior people, even if working on a project cut into my personal time. In a corporate environment, you will never get a job that you don't ask for. By spending time with people in higher positions than you within a company, you can sell yourself and your abilities, so when a job opening becomes available you know who to talk to about getting that job. This is how I have used networking to help me succeed."

What tips can you offer to help someone get the job that they're applying for?

"The best advice I can offer is to go into a job interview with a good understanding of the industry in which you want to work. Know who the key players are, and make sure that the industry you pick is a growing industry. Don't choose an industry that's on a downward spiral, or that could be where your career winds up."

Jane also notes that there's a major difference between the work environments of a major corporation and a small or midsized company. "The larger companies often offer better benefits, and there may be more opportunities to move up the corporate ladder. But things tend to happen much more slowly. A smaller company will be more entrepreneurial. In a small company, you'll have to wear multiple hats and do many types of jobs. At a large company, you will be hired to perform a single, well-defined job. If you're new to the work force and you really

want to learn about a lot of different things, I'd recommend working for a small or midsized company, because you'll be exposed to a lot more in a short time. If you want to be a specialist, such as a specific kind of accountant or analyst, then a larger company will probably be more suitable for you."

Are there skills that someone must have that weren't necessarily taught in school?

"Definitely! I think that schools don't focus enough on teaching communication skills. No matter what type of career you want to pursue, you will be more successful if you have good communication skills. There are many people out there who are very intelligent, but they can't communicate with other people, either on a one-to-one level or in groups. Any type of management job requires that you be able to deal effectively with people. If you want to be in business, you'd better learn how to speak in front of people. Also, being able to write a decent letter is critical to being successful in virtually every type of occupation. A growing number of college graduates can't even write a complete sentence, much less a business letter or some type of report." It is never too late to improve your communication skills; however, you must first evaluate your own weaknesses and then develop a plan to improve upon them. Obviously, this isn't something you can do overnight, but if you hope to move out of an entry-level position, you'll want to develop writing and public speaking skills.

In the old days, if you got a job working for a large company, such as IBM, you'd be able to plan on working your entire professional life for that company. With so much corporate downsizing going on, is this still possible?

"I've worked my entire professional life for Paramount Parks, but these days I think I'm the exception. I started at the bottom and worked my way to the top. There are still some industries, however, where this is likely to happen. Any kind of industry, like retail, that hires a lot of entry-level people like cashiers often provides opportunities

your résumé that says, 'I want to work with people' isn't going to get you hired. Working with people isn't a goal."

What qualities do you look for in an applicant that comes in for a job interview?

"I look for people who make a good general presentation. Applicants need to be articulate, demonstrate that they can be aggressive, and be flexible. Young people entering the job market have to be flexible and be willing to work hard. If you want to be successful, the days of working 9:00 A.M. to 5:00 P.M., Monday through Friday, no longer

"Applicants need to be articulate, demonstrate that they can be **aggressive**, and be *flexible*."

for people to work their way upward though promotions. If you're not working in an industry where this happens, you should not expect it to. It all comes back to managing your own career. If, after you've held a job for a while, you're ready to move on and there are new opportunities available to you within that company, then you should certainly take advantage of those opportunities. If not, you should consider moving on." During the job interview process, and when you're doing research about the company you're applying to, learn about the growth potential you'll have within the company and within the industry.

What tips can you offer to someone who is preparing their résumé?

"I believe your résumé should be fairly specific in terms of listing your goals and accomplishments. A general statement in

exist. I personally spend about 80 percent of my time traveling. If necessary, I work on weekends or at night. You have to determine for yourself what you're willing to invest in your career. If you're only willing to work 9:00 A.M. to 5:00 P.M., then that's the type of job you're going to get and you will eventually reach a limit to your career potential."

Jane stresses the importance of communication between employees and employers. "If you're not getting what you want out of a job, then go to your boss and explain that you're interested in doing other types of things. People have to pay their dues and spend time learning, which often means spending time doing things you don't enjoy or don't feel challenge you. However, you must not be willing to spend too much time in these situations. The best employees become successful people because they're willing to work and speak up for themselves. Don't be intimidated by the position someone holds. We're all people."

What types of questions should an applicant ask the potential employer during a job interview?

"Ask questions about what expectations the employer has for its employees. Ask what you'll be expected to do in the job you're applying for, and try to find out what that job can lead to in the future. During the interview, learn about the career path that's available to you at that company. Based on the response you receive, ask yourself where you'll be in five years if you accept the job you're applying for. If the employer tells you that there aren't going to be promotion opportunities, then you should reconsider working for that company, unless you think you'll be happy doing the same thing day after day for 5, 10, or 15 years. Make sure that the career path that will be available to you will allow you to eventually accomplish the long-term goals you've set for yourself."

How can applicants tell if they're going to enjoy a job before accepting it?

"Personalities are very important. Is the overall personality of the company compatible with your own personality? Have you met people working for the company you're applying to that you really like or know that you'll get along with? There's a lot to be said about having skills and the ability to do a job well, but if you don't like the people within

the organization, or you don't think you'll fit in because you have a different type of personality, then don't accept the job because you won't enjoy it."

If you had good grades in school, does that give you an advantage when entering the work force for the first time?

"I personally don't think so. I never ask about someone's grades. If you had top grades in school, your transcript will help you make a positive impression because it shows that you know how to work hard and can focus on accomplishing things, but grades are rarely a deciding factor when it comes to employment. A study was done by several Ivy League schools looking at why the top 10 percent of their graduating classes weren't in the top 10 percent in terms of on-the-job earnings. There are many people who are book smart. They always earned a 4.0 average in school, but they can't interact with people or they can't think for themselves to find solutions to various job-related tasks because they lack creativity. I have found there are many people like this, and there are some types of careers that these people simply should not pursue. Likewise, there are many jobs that this type of person is ideal for." As someone who is looking to start a career, you must begin by being totally honest with yourself. Pursue job opportunities that will allow you to focus on your strengths, while at the same time allow you to do things that you enjoy.

"If you don't like the people within the organization, or you don't think you'll fit in, then don't accept the job because you won't enjoy it."

Now that you've reached the top, what keeps you motivated?

"The higher you go in a corporate environment, the more people you'll have under you that look to you for guidance and that rely on you. For me, that's very motivating. I feel like I'm responsible for leading these people, and the company as a whole, in the right direction. That's always a challenge."

What is the biggest challenge you've faced in your career?

"The biggest challenge I have faced is one that I continue to struggle with almost every day, and that's balancing my professional life with my personal life. I've never been good at this, and it becomes an even bigger issue once you have children." One of the keys to success in life is finding your own balance between your career goals and your personal goals. During your lifetime, these goals will change, and it's your responsibility to juggle all the elements of your life and discover ways that work for you to successfully manage your career and personal goals without neglecting either. Developing good time management and organizational skills

"If you're a woman in business, you're not a business woman. You're a business person!"

will help you find the time for everything, but it's up to you to make the best use of the time you have.

What advice do you have for women working in a corporate environment?

"First of all, if you're a woman in business, you're not a business woman. You're a business person! Don't ever make an issue that you're a business woman. You are the same as everyone else. You have to play the game. You can't make an issue every time someone says something that you don't like. Some people are uncomfortable with women in management or executive-level positions, and, as a woman, that's something you have to be willing to deal with. Some industries allow women to excel more than others. Here at Paramount Parks, I have never felt that being a woman has held me back in any way. In our generation, employers are looking for the best people for the job, no matter what their sex is."

LAST WORD

"It is vital that you understand that nobody owes you anything. Whatever success you're going to achieve in your career has to be earned through hard work. Nobody is going to give you something that you haven't earned. Just because you have a college degree or you've been at a job for one year, don't start thinking you deserve to be a top-level executive. Working hard is what will bring you success."

DOUG LOGAN

COMPANY BACKGROUND

Even if you're not a sports fan, chances are you've heard of the NFL, NBA, NHL, and PGA, but what's MLS? Major League Soccer is an organized effort to bring the sport of soccer to America. The league began its inaugural 160-game season in April 1996. Major League Soccer consists of 10 teams, in two conferences, playing an April to September season. The teams include the Denver-based Colorado Rapids, Dallas Burn, Kansas City Wiz, Los Angeles Galaxy, San Jose Clash, New England Revolution, Columbus (Ohio) Crew, Tampa Bay Mutiny, New York-New Jersey Metro Stars, and Washington's D.C. United.

175

©1993 MLS™

Television broadcasts of games can be seen on ESPN, ESPN-2, ABC, and Univisión (Spanish Television). MLS was launched with over $75 million in capital, and each team consisted of newcomers as well as established world-class players. Major League Soccer has the team owners (investors), players, team names, logos, uniforms, stadiums, game schedules, and broadcast deals in place. If all goes well, the league will quickly build a following of fans from across America and around the world. Professional sports is a business, and launching a new professional and organized sport in America is a risky and ambitious endeavor that's been six years in the planning.

PERSONAL HISTORY

Working in construction, building concert halls and arenas, producing and promoting concerts, and launching a new sport in America are all on Doug Logan's résumé. Doug has completely switched careers several times successfully.

"I began my career in the construction business, working summers while I was still in school. I started working in this field full-time when I returned from Vietnam at the age of 23. Between that time and the age of 35, I worked my way to being a top-level executive in the heavy construction business. At the age of 35, I changed careers because I really wasn't satisfied with what I was doing." After leaving the construction business, Doug attended classes at a local college that dealt with career selection and changing careers. It was during this time that he examined his own personal and professional values and long-term objectives. Based on this personal analysis, he wrote down a generic and abstract job description that he wanted to pursue. With that written job description in hand, he set out to find a job that would closely resemble what he was looking for.

In 1978, Doug landed a job building and managing an arena. "My job consisted of supervising the design of the arena, putting together the financing, overseeing construction, and then managing the day-to-day operations of a 10,000-seat arena in Illinois. In 1986, I was hired by a large New York-

based company to establish a new division that would handle facilities management in the areas of sports and entertainment. Through this project, I became involved in some of the major sports and entertainment projects taking place in the world. At the same time, I started up a concert promotion company of my own that was ranked number 6 in the world the year that I left."

As 1993 came around, Doug became part owner of a Mexico-based entertainment and concert promotion company. When he accepted this job, he packed his bags and moved his family to Mexico. "I had just turned 50, and I told my wife and kids that I needed a new adventure. I spent three years at that job and then returned to America. At the time, I didn't exactly know what I was going to do with myself. I wound up working as a consultant. One of my jobs was finding a site for a hockey team and analyzing a new building for an NBA team. I also represented investors interested in sponsoring a rock 'n' roll tour.

In this latest stage of his career, Doug has determined that for him to prosper, he has to be at risk. He thrives on challenges and is motivated by the possibility of failure. "I don't fail, but knowing that I could keeps me working my hardest. Out of the blue, in September 1995 the opportunity at Major League Soccer came about. I started my job as the commissioner of Major League Soccer on December 1, 1995, and I've been having a ball ever since."

> *"My professional life takes on a real gamelike quality, and I don't consider victory or defeat as being absolute or terminal."*

You mentioned that you thrive on risk. How do you ensure that you don't fail?

"First of all, I'm not afraid to fail. My professional life takes on a real gamelike quality, and I don't consider victory or defeat as being absolute or terminal. I don't take my successes very seriously. I try to learn from my failures, but I don't take them as being fatal. What this philosophy allows me to do is weigh risk in a wholesome way instead of an emotional way. Sports and entertainment is a high-risk business. In the past, I have risked over $7 million of my own money on a concert tour, but by the same token I don't gamble during my leisure time.

you're going to take, think of it as something you want to do for 3, 5, or even 10 years, not for your entire life. Now, the decision about what type of job you take carries a lot less weight, because in your mind it's not something that you're going to be locked into for the rest of your life. I am a living example of someone who has changed careers several times. I've even changed industries, so I know that career transitions can be made successfully."

What other advice can you share for someone about to launch their career?

"Your first job isn't a merit badge. Don't just look at a position, job title, or salary when selecting a first job. Think of your first job as a continuation of your education. The last thing you should be looking at is salary or title. What you should be evaluating when selecting a first job is how much you'll be able to learn and how much responsibility

> *"I am a living example of someone who has changed careers several times."*

"When someone is setting out to get their first job, not being afraid to take a risk is very important in the selection of the first project. The first thing a young person has to do is come to grips with the fact that in today's society no decision you make will be a permanent one, especially when it comes to your career. Once you say this is the job

you will be given. When you take on responsibility and start making decisions, you're going to make a few mistakes. That's the very best way to learn. Viewing your first job as a learning experience may not sound appealing, but if you're not continuously learning you'll eventually reach a dead end in your career path."

"Think of your first job as a continuation of your education. The last thing you should be looking at is salary or title."

"Regarding the specifics of picking a job, the elements of a job are far more important than the job itself. You have to know about who you are and who you're not. If you're in a work environment with people who have low energy, you will find that job situation exhausting if you personally have a higher energy level. You'll spend too much of your time and effort trying to boost other people's energy at the same time you're trying to do your own work. When evaluating a job offer, try to determine if you'll be surrounded by people with an equal or higher energy level than your own. Something as trivial as whether or not you'll have a window in your work space becomes something that can impact your long-term happiness and be a success factor in a job. You have to sit down and determine what about a job is important to you. At the end of the day, the person that goes home whistling is the one that has reached a level of self-actualization.

"When I'm in the position of hiring people, I know there are certain things that I can't teach future employees. The first thing I can't provide is brains. Someone's basic intelligence is important, so when you're applying for a job make sure you can demonstrate your intelligence. The second thing I can't provide is character. During an interview, I try to determine an applicant's values and honesty. The third thing I can't teach or provide is a work ethic. I gravitate to people who say to me that they want to work, rather than they need a job. Finally, when hiring people, I always look for a quality that I call 'twinkle in the eye.' For me this has a connotation of creativity, and that's a quality that I look for. Someone's previous job experience, academic credentials, and personal references are all nice, but I am far less inclined to focus on them when evaluating an applicant for possible employment."

What are some of the biggest mistakes you've seen people make when applying for a job, and what qualities do you look for?

"I treat résumés as one of the two opportunities that society gives people in this world to write fiction. The other opportunity is a tax form on April 15th. Most résumés incorporate significant amounts of lying or exaggeration, so I tend to pay little attention to them. When I look at a résumé, length and verbosity don't impress me. Having a long and busy résumé is a drawback. Anything more than a single, one-sided sheet of paper is too much.

"From the standpoint of an interview, I look for poise and what an applicant's demeanor is. I will try to create points of tension during an interview to see how the applicant reacts to pressure. I look for people who are candid, open, and honest, and I can easily tell when people aren't being truthful. I also consider a command of the English language to be important. During an interview, I always provide opportunities for applicants to offer their own opinions. As they're speaking, I listen to how they speak as well as to what they're actually saying. You can tell how well-read people are by how they speak and what they say. Another quality I look for in an applicant is a good sense of humor."

During an interview, what types of questions should the applicant ask?

"Based on my own experience, an applicant should always walk into an interview already knowing the answers to most of the questions the interviewers are planning to ask. If someone walks through my door, knows my business, and has a fundamental knowledge of what I'm looking for in regards to the job opening, that applicant has a big leg up over a person who walks in having done no research about the company or job. Doing the necessary research before an interview is impressive. By doing research about a company, you will be able to get many of your questions answered before the actual interview."

If someone doesn't have connections with a company, how can he or she get an introduction into a company?

"Networking is always important. A huge percentage of job openings that are available are never posted or advertised. Entry-level jobs are a little different, but if you work hard to develop contacts and relationships, you can almost always get yourself an introduction that will go a long way toward getting you an entry-level position. The problem I see with today's young people is that their definition of entry level is very different from businesses' definition of an entry-level position. Because someone has a college degree or has spent four years studying a specific discipline, that doesn't mean that they're automatically entitled to an office, a secretary, and an expense account. It just doesn't happen that way. When you accept an entry-level job, you must be prepared to pay your dues. For a while, you have to be ready to get your hands dirty, work long hours, and maybe have your social life suffer."

How important are internships or summer jobs?

"I have offered full-time employment to many people who have held summer jobs with my company in the past because I know who they are and what they're capable of. Working during the summer or holding an internship while you're still in school is an opportunity to learn about the real world. That knowledge will prove to be extremely useful."

What skills should an applicant have that aren't necessarily taught in school?

"You must have a command of the English language and be able to communicate orally and in writing. You should be able to stand up in front of a group and make presentations. Writing skills are still important, even in this age of e-mail, where incomplete sentences are acceptable. In the next millennium, I think a working knowledge of a second language will also be very important.

"Because someone has a college degree or has spent four years studying a specific discipline, that doesn't mean that they're automatically entitled to an office, a secretary, and an expense account."

We are one of the last civilized cultures where having the ability to communicate in a second language isn't valued. Young people in Europe and South America are often bilingual. By the year 2008, statistics show that 27 percent of the American population will speak Spanish as their first language. Being bilingual and being qualified for the job you're applying for will give you a major advantage over other applicants."

LAST WORD

"You have to understand that there are sacrifices and trade-offs in life. Within your family unit, you have to evaluate the demands and requirements that your job will require and decide beforehand what you're willing to sacrifice in order to pursue a certain career track. Managing a personal and professional life can become one of the biggest obstacles you'll have to overcome. I have never received anything for nothing. I have had to earn every promotion and job that I have taken. This is how one becomes successful. It's not like winning the lottery. There are no free rides.

"Since I entered the work force in 1967, I have seen the world change dramatically. The only thing that I can guarantee people is that things are going to continue changing, so you must be willing to stay on top of these changes and adapt. Simply having a college degree is no longer a passport for success. These days, all a college degree is going to do is get you out on the playing field."

SCOTT FLANDERS PRESIDENT
Macmillan Publishing USA

COMPANY BACKGROUND

Macmillan Publishing USA, the umbrella identity of Simon & Schuster's reference publishing operations, is the industry leader in computer book publishing and a leader in home/library reference publishing. Among the company's lines are computer titles, including the best-selling *The Complete Idiot's Guide* series, reference works such as *Webster's New World Dictionary*, video game strategy guides from Brady, *Frommer's Travel Guides, Weight Watchers* and *Betty Crocker* cookbooks, ARCO test preparation titles, and the J.K. Lasser tax preparation publications.

These are just some of the hundreds of books that various divisions of Macmillan Publishing USA publish each year. Macmillan has main offices in New York City and Indianapolis. The company is a division of Simon & Schuster, which is the publishing operation of Viacom, Inc.

PERSONAL HISTORY

While there isn't a direct career path to executive of a publishing company, Scott Flanders, President of Macmillan Publishing, says, "I'm good at what I do because I love it so much." Scott graduated from the University of Colorado with a bachelor of arts degree in economics. He went on to get a law degree from Indiana University but wound up working as a business

and tax consultant, which necessitated Scott's becoming a certified public accountant.

"I attended law school after college in order to pursue my intellectual interests. I had a liberal arts undergraduate education, and I thought the additional knowledge that a law degree offers would provide me with skills that would be useful in whatever it was that I decided to do. I never planned on pursuing a career as a lawyer, but thought the disciplines required for someone to be successful in law school are extremely useful in all aspects of business. This additional graduate-level education really helped me to prepare for the rigors of the workplace."

Before getting his current position, Scott worked for Cooper's and Lybrand as a tax and business consultant. Although he was successful, the job did not inspire him. Scott's true passion was for reading and and when, in 1985, he was offered an opportunity to work in the publishing field, he took a career-related risk and jumped at the chance. He became Director of Business Development for Que Corporation, one of the world's first computer book publishers. In 1988, just prior to his 32nd birthday, Scott was named President of Que. Scott went on to become President of Macmillan Publishing USA in February of 1994. As

President, he is responsible for the company that gives Simon & Schuster an international leadership position in computer and reference publishing.

TOPICS COVERED IN THIS INTERVIEW
☞ **How taking risks can lead to success**
☞ **Setting career-related goals**
☞ **Getting your foot in the door at a company you want to work for**
☞ **Making the perfect impression during an interview**
☞ **The biggest mistakes applicants make when looking for a job**

You've discussed how pursuing an advanced degree helped you to focus on your career goals and become a more mature person. Should a college graduate immediately pursue a graduate-level education or first obtain some work experience?

"Ideally, I think it's a good idea to get a job and work for a year or two after graduating from college. The problem with this, however, is that many people find themselves having early success on the job, which results in them having a nice apartment or house, plus a car payment. Now, these people don't want to give up their high-paying job and go back to living on a strict budget in order to return to school. For long-term career success in the corporate

"The job you should ultimately accept should be the one that you have a passion for."

environment, I think it can be valuable for someone to get an advanced degree. Sure, there are plenty of highly successful people without advanced degrees, but for some types of jobs having the additional education will certainly be an advantage."

Did you consider it a risk to leave your position at Cooper's and Lybrand in order to pursue a career that you thought you'd enjoy more?

"The biggest career-related risk that I ever took was when I left my position at Cooper's and Lybrand in order to join a start-up computer book publishing company. This new job was neither in the financial or legal field, which was what I was trained in. The single biggest risk was leaving a secure career path for something that seemed a lot more interesting, challenging, and personally rewarding, but financially uncertain."

What advice can you offer someone who's evaluating a career-related opportunity that involves taking a risk?

"Don't accept a job just because it comes with the best compensation package or the best benefits. The job you should ultimately accept should be the one that you have a passion for. Discover within yourself what sets you apart from other people in the workplace, and then find a job in an industry that is appealing to you." For anyone who is young, taking a career-related

risk is something that should not be too intimidating. "When I changed industries I was much younger and I didn't have a family to support. I don't think I would take a similar risk today, but for someone who is young, the consequences of failure are all positive. From failure, a young person will gain valuable experience. Experience is often the accumulated wisdom that comes from failure."

If someone is offered a high-paying job doing something that they're good at but it's not the type of job that they are looking for, should they accept it?

"Only as a last resort. This whole theme of taking a risk is about believing in yourself and what you're capable of doing. You have to believe that you can be a successful contributor in an environment that is compatible with both your skill set and your interest. If you're not interested in a job, think twice about accepting it. The people who are the most excited about their work are the ones who ultimately become the most successful. Before accepting a job that you're not going to be 100 percent satisfied with, you should do everything you can to hold out for a job that really excites you. I believe it's worth taking a risk and passing on a job offer that's not what you're looking for, even if it means you'll have to borrow money to live until you discover the best opportunity for yourself."

compatibility

Scott Flanders ● 183 Macmillan Publishing USA

"Failure can be turned into an opportunity for growth and actually enhance your value—but not if you try to deny it."

Should someone be afraid of the possibility of failure when taking a career-related risk?

"As an employer, I am attracted to people who have experienced some failures in their career. By experiencing failure, people learn a lot about who they are and what their skills are. Failure can be an extremely useful learning experience. Failure can also be turned into an opportunity for growth and actually enhance your value— but not if you try to deny it. Anyone with a strong educational background and work-related skills should not be afraid of failure because they have something to fall back on. In my own case, if I failed in the publishing industry I knew that I could go back to the financial field, the tax field, or the legal field. A good education is something you can always fall back on, no matter what industry you work in."

Does it take a lot of courage and self-esteem to take a career-related risk?

"The most important thing that young people can do is be realistic about their strengths and weaknesses and focus on their strengths. Everyone has some talent that is of value in the right environment. I like to think of the career process as trying to find the best use of someone's talents. Approach the job search as a process. Don't take a risk for risk's sake. You should embrace change and be prepared to change your circumstances so that you end up with something that energizes you and makes you fulfilled professionally. Finding the right position, at

the right company, within the right industry may take some time and a lot of work, but you have to be tough and persistent. The ability to take risks is a trait that's within everyone. Being persistent and learning to analyze career opportunities are things that anyone can do.

"From an employer's point of view, there is nothing worse than having the wrong person in a job. They're miserable and the company suffers. People have to believe in themselves, find what's special about themselves, be objective, and understand that nobody is perfect. Everyone has special skills and talents that are valuable. The whole job-search process should be thought of as a puzzle or a treasure hunt. You're trying to find the right match between yourself and a job where you can contribute and you will be appreciated."

How can someone find out about the best job opportunities when they graduate from college or after they've earned an advanced degree?

"It's a marketing challenge. I would recommend that college students take a marketing class in school, because finding a job is just like marketing a product. When searching for a job, you'll have to deal with the classic marketing issues— product, price, packaging, placement, and promotion. You're the product in this case, and you're competing in the job market-place against many other people. You must choose the best packaging for your product [yourself] so that you can differentiate yourself in the marketplace. The potential

Don't take a risk for risk's sake.

> "When searching for a job, you'll have to deal with the classic marketing issues—product, price, packaging, placement, and promotion. You're the product in this case, and you're competing in the job marketplace against many other people."

employer must see the value in what sets you apart. That's the placement issue.

"At Macmillan Publishing, for example, many of the people who apply for editorial positions have a journalism degree or an English degree. All of their qualifications are pretty much the same. What we look for when hiring people are applicants with a passion in a specific area. For example, our company happens to be the world's largest publisher of books about dogs. If someone with a journalism or English degree is also an avid dog lover and knows all about dogs, that person has an important competitive advantage when they apply for a job at our imprint that publishes the dog-related books. This also applies to people with travel, cooking, or computer experience, because we also publish many books in these categories. I believe that the wisest strategy for applicants is to focus on the qualities and skills that they possess that differentiate them. Try to place yourself in front of as many companies where that difference will matter."

What tips can you offer someone who is working on a résumé?
"I am the least impressed with people who are very general in terms of the objective they list on their résumé. If someone states that they're looking for a senior management position where they'll have a broad impact, they won't capture the attention of the employer. The more specialized your résumé is, and the more customized it is for the specific job you're applying for, the better off you'll be.

"I look for candor in a résumé. I look for a hook that shows the applicant has a grounded sense of their capabilities. I think a résumé should demonstrate the applicant's ambition and desire to contribute. Making contributions to a company or organization is what causes you to move forward. It's not just having ambition that earns you a promotion; it's achieving results on the job. Those who get promotions are the people who achieve something that benefits the company that they're working for. Back in

"YOU DON'T GET PAID FOR BEING SMART. YOU GET PAID FOR RESULTS. YOU GET PAID FOR WHAT YOU DO, NOT FOR WHO YOU ARE."

1988, I was about to turn 32 years old and I became President of Que Corporation. The advice that was given to me then was, 'You don't get paid for being smart. You get paid for results. You get paid for what you do, not for who you are.' Based on this advice, these days, I examine people's résumés for evidence that they understand the importance of contributing to the company they work for. I'm not looking for applicants who are well educated but are simply looking for a job title and a compensation package. On your résumé, you should include information about relevant life experiences, especially if you don't have a lot of work experience."

How should someone go about setting their career-related goals?

"When I graduated from school, I went to work for the world's largest accounting firm. I held that job for three years and I performed well in it, but I really didn't enjoy it. Tax law really didn't interest me. I found it intellectually interesting, but it wasn't something that I loved doing. What I always had a true passion for was reading. One of my clients was the founder of Que Corporation, which at the time was a $4 million publisher of computer books. On one occasion, the founder of Que asked me if I'd be interested in doing something more interesting than tax law, and I jumped at the opportunity. What attracted me to Que was that it was a publishing

company, which meant that I could pursue my passion for reading. Thus, the advice I can share with young people about to launch their own career is that they should follow their passion.

"I believe in lifelong learning and wanting to have impact. That's what motivates me to wake up and go to work each day. Every day, I think about the most important things I can do to advance the causes of the business that I'm a part of. That has led me into higher and higher positions. At every stage in my career I have felt that what I was doing was important and rewarding. In a sense, I think the long term is a series of short terms, so by being successful at every step on the corporate ladder I kept earning promotions. For me, my promotions were a result of continuously working hard and doing the right things along the way. I didn't have a specific strategy that led me to the final destination of becoming the President of a major publishing company."

What's the best way for someone to get a foot in the door at a company?

"I believe you should use any technique imaginable to get yourself in the door. Begin by finding who the people are in the executive positions within the specific division of each company that you want to work for. Don't attempt to contact the President, CEO, or chairman of a company, unless you already have a personal connection with that

"Don't accept a job just because you think you can do it. Pursue a job that you really have a thirst for. Position yourself where that passion will bring value to the prospective employer."

person. If someone sends an unsolicited résumé to me, as the President of Macmillan Publishing, I forward that résumé to our Human Resources division. If someone has a strong interest in computers, for example, and wants to work in the publishing industry, he or she should target the publisher in one of our computer book divisions and send a résumé to that person. When you contact an executive within a company, you want to stress your relevant academic credentials, plus focus on what specific skills or knowledge you have that set you apart from the other applicants. What makes you the perfect person to fill a certain position? You want to stress the contributions you can make to a company.

"Simply sending your résumé to the human resources department at most large companies is probably not going to get you an interview. I think you have a better chance of winning the lottery than getting a job based on sending your résumé 'blindly' to a company's human resources department. If you're going to send résumés, send them to specific people, and include a cover letter that is powerfully written. You should succinctly and powerfully state why you should be considered for a specific position, and describe what you can offer to a company. State specifically why you want to work for a company. You only have about 30 seconds of someone's time to get their attention. Thus, your cover letter must differentiate you, be candid, and have a strong hook."

What's the best way for someone to make a perfect impression during an interview?

"Demonstrate humility. Emphasize that you

understand there's a lot that you don't know, but that you have a strong curiosity and that you have a desire to learn and contribute. I consider talented people to be the most useful asset that we have at this company. What impresses me are people who have a genuine interest in the company and in the job they're applying for. I think it's wonderful when an applicant asks me how someone coming into the company can most quickly make a difference. This is very different from asking how someone can be successful within the company. Asking how you can be successful within a company indicates a personal ambition instead of showing concern for helping the business. There's a subtle difference in these two statements, but the difference is extremely important in the mind of the employer."

What are the biggest mistakes you've seen applicants make during the job-search process?

"I think the biggest mistake is that young applicants just coming out of school fail to understand what their strengths and weaknesses are. As the applicant, you must have an objective understanding of yourself in order to know what types of positions to pursue. You can save a lot of time by not applying for positions that you're not qualified for. Making the right decision about the job you take is important. I think it's detrimental for someone to list four different jobs on their résumé in their first five years out of school. I won't hire someone with that kind of record. It's important that you, the applicant, find a job where you feel you'll fit in. Don't just throw your résumé out to every firm that lists a job opening."

When might you have to take a career-related risk?

According to Scott, the jobs that offer the best starting salary aren't always the best for your long-term success. "Don't necessarily go after the jobs that initially offer the most money. You should be thinking about where you'll fit in the best, not which company is offering a slightly higher starting salary. If you fit well within a company, you'll enjoy your work more, which means you'll last longer at the company and you'll advance faster. Choosing the right job will have a

much greater long-term impact on your paycheck than accepting a job that pays $1,000 more when you first join the company." Sometimes, taking a career-related risk means accepting a job with a lower starting salary, as long as it's a job you know you're going to love.

LAST WORD

"It's not what you know, it's what you do on the job that will be rewarded. Your education builds your knowledge base, but that's just your ticket for admission into the workplace. In school, you are rewarded with good grades based on what you know. In the workplace, you are rewarded based on what you actually accomplish."

TOM JACKSON
FOUNDER
The Career Development Team, Inc.
CHAIRMAN Equinox Corporation

COMPANY BACKGROUND

Tom works as a **consultant** to some of the largest corporations in the United States, and over the past **20 years** he has conducted **workshops** on career development that have been attended by more than **150,000** people. Tom has also lectured on career-related topics at over **400** colleges and universities.

PERSONAL HISTORY

Tom Jackson has made a career out of offering career counseling and résumé writing. Tom holds an MBA from the Wharton School of Economics and has studied at Georgetown Law School. He has written numerous books about finding a job and creating résumés, and has developed an interactive CD-ROM software package called *The Perfect Résumé*.

Tom began working as a career counselor after graduating from school and spending time in the military. He started by working part-time in personnel, which eventually led to him creating his own career counseling company.

TOPICS COVERED IN THIS INTERVIEW

☞ How specialized job-search computer software, such as *The Perfect Résumé*, can help you find a job

☞ Tips for developing direction for your professional life

☞ Creating a perfect résumé

☞ Making the best impression possible during the interview process

☞ What to do if your interview isn't going well (first, don't panic!)

You have spent over 20 years helping people find jobs. How did you develop the skills that you now teach to other people?

"It's not so much about getting a job as it is about getting anything you want in life. Early in my own life, I developed skills out of necessity that involved being productive and demonstrating initiative. I needed these skills growing up in an orphanage. Some people think that you have to be born with a silver spoon in your mouth in order to be successful and that's not true. I went from having a very difficult experience in my early life to finding ways to excel. I found different ways of achieving my goals and was proud of my own results. I learned the importance of being willing to take action, even if you don't know what the results will be, and also setting objectives for myself, rather than accepting what someone else tells me. I had to create my own sense of what I wanted my future to be, and then work toward making that a reality. These skills can all be applied to someone looking for a job."

What advice can you offer to someone who is graduating from school with no clear direction about what type of career they're interested in?

"Rather than saying that you don't have any direction, say to yourself that you haven't yet found a direction. Don't think that whatever job you wind up accepting is going to determine your entire future. If you don't know what type of career you want to pursue, begin by getting a variety of many different experiences and learning what you like and don't like from those work experiences. One way to do this is by working with a temp agency and accepting temporary work assignments at various types of companies.

"Eventually, based on what you learn about your likes and dislikes, you're going to have to answer the question, 'If I could have any job that I wanted, what would it be?' Based on your answer to this question, you should ask yourself, 'What should be the next job that I take that will help me to eventually be qualified for the position I ultimately

"Some people think that you have to be born with a silver spoon in your mouth in order to be successful and that's not true."

"If you don't know what type of career you want to pursue, begin by getting a variety of many different experiences and learning what you like and don't like from those work experiences."

want?' and 'What are the things that I like to do and that I can do well? How do these things combine?' Many people don't have any idea about how many different types of careers are available to them. Most people can only list 10 or so different jobs. By doing temp work or obtaining other types of work experience, you should be able to put together a list of 75 to 100 jobs that you'd be interested in pursuing. Don't operate based on limited knowledge. Operate from an abundance of knowledge regarding the types of careers that are out there.

"If you're still in school, be creative when you start looking for summer jobs or internships. Don't accept a job that pays minimum wage and has no future growth or learning potential. Look for a job that is less obvious for a student. Instead of working at an amusement park or at a fast-food restaurant, work for a company such as a law firm, an accounting firm, or a computer company."

How important is networking during the job search process?

"I think networking is extremely important, and it's something that you should begin doing when you're young. Identify people that you feel are leaders in their field or that can offer you good advice, and keep track of those people. When you begin looking for a job, start contacting those people and ask for their assistance and advice."

What tips can you offer for creating a first résumé?

"If you're creating your first résumé, the implication is that you don't yet have a lot of work-related experience. Thus, I would use a 'targeted' résumé format, which talks specifically about what you are capable of doing, not just what you have actually done. Deal with 'I can' statements, not just 'I have' statements when writing your résumé. Look to the future and identify your capabilities and state the types of things you can do. Using specialized software, such as *The Perfect Résumé* (available wherever computer software is sold), you can create your résumé and then easily shift it around to create a customized résumé for every job you apply for. This type of software offers a complete system for developing a résumé in a format that's been proven to work.

"I believe there are primarily three formats of résumés—chronological, functional, and targeted. A chronological résumé is more suitable for someone who already has previous work experience. A functional résumé focuses on the types of experiences and skills you have already mastered and have used in the workplace, while a targeted résumé focuses more on your capabilities and what skills you have that can be applied to future work experiences.

"Your actual résumé should not be flashy, but it shouldn't be plain vanilla either. You want to use an attractive font and a

"Deal with 'I can' statements, not just 'I have' statements when writing your résumé. Look to the future and identify your capabilities and state the types of things you can do."

visually appealing layout. Print your résumé on good-quality white paper. In terms of content, leave out of your résumé any information that won't contribute to you getting yourself an interview. For example, leave out your references. You can provide your references to the employer during the interview process. On your résumé, you don't have to state, 'References available upon request,' because that's obvious. Likewise, at the top of the page, you don't have to print the word 'Résumé,' nor do you have to include the addresses of the companies that you have worked for in the past. This information can be provided later."

What are the best references to have?

"The best references are from people who are professional and that know you personally. People with professional stature, such as teachers, professors, lawyers, bankers, company executives, and religious leaders, all make good references because their opinions about you will be valued by the potential employer."

What tips can you offer for making the best impression during an interview?

"The best thing you can do is to go into an interview being fully prepared. Do not, under any circumstances, go into an interview unless you know what the company does and you have already acquired some basic knowledge about the company's history, products, or services. If you go into an interview and say to the potential employer,

'I saw your ad in the newspaper; can you tell me what you do?,' then you will immediately be dismissed as someone not suitable for the job, because a question like that makes it obvious that you did absolutely nothing to prepare for the interview.

"Preparation and research are critical. When you go in for an interview, bring along an extra copy of your résumé and offer it to the person doing the interview. Be prepared to answer the difficult questions. If you're nervous about going into an interview, practice by doing role-playing exercises with a friend or family member." Practicing in a role-playing session is easy. Begin by thinking about the toughest questions the interviewer might ask you, and then practice answering those questions in a mock interview situation. Practice making eye contact with the interviewer, and determine how you plan to answer various questions. There are many books available, including some by Tom Jackson, that list many sample interview questions for various types of positions. Your college's career guidance office should also be able to provide you with a sample list of potential interview questions. The more practice you have before the interview, the more confident and prepared you will be during the actual interview process.

"During the first interview, do not ask about the company's benefits package, the medical plan, or the vacation schedule. These questions should be asked only after the employer has expressed a strong interest in hiring you. In the early stages of the inter-

"Do not, under any circumstances, go into an interview unless you know what the company does and you have already acquired some basic knowledge about the company's history, products, or services."

view process, ask questions about the company, about its training programs, and about the work environment. You can also ask questions about the type of people that they believe succeed within the company. Demonstrate to the interviewer that you're looking to the future and you're interested in moving your career forward.

"When the interviewer asks you a question, the best approach is to answer it as honestly and completely as possible. The biggest mistake I've seen people make is to go into an interview situation not knowing what they personally can offer to the company. You want to demonstrate that you will be a valuable asset to the company, but you don't want to exaggerate and make yourself appear more valuable than you actually are."

What can someone do if they feel that the interview is not going well?
"One mistake I've seen people make when they get the impression that an interview isn't going well is that they shut up and wait for their interview to end. Instead of doing this, take the initiative and talk to the interviewer about what you can offer to the company. Describe what work-related experience you have, and how that experience will help the company. Most importantly, talk about why you want to work for that company and why you believe you should be hired. If the interviewer doesn't

ask questions that will help to reveal important information about you, such as awards you won for various extracurricular activities in school, then it's your job to bring this information to light and work it into the conversation. You've got to be responsible and ensure that by the end of the interview the employer knows everything about you that you want them to know. Don't rely on the employer to ask you all of the right questions.

"If you leave the interview and truly feel that you didn't perform to the best of your potential because you were nervous, after the interview call up the employer and say, 'We just had an interview, but I was so nervous that I don't think that I demonstrated my full potential. Do you think I could come back for another meeting?' Before the interview, one way to avoid being nervous is to participate in role-playing exercises and to become totally prepared for the interview by doing extra research. At the start of an interview, if you are nervous, feel free to be honest and mention it to the interviewer."

How can someone get their foot in the door at a company?
"The first thing you should do is see if you have direct access to anyone who works for that company. Do your parents have a friend who works for that company? Have

"The biggest mistake I've seen people make is to go into an interview situation not knowing what they personally can offer to the company."

you asked your neighbors, your relatives, and all of your friends' parents if they have any contacts within that company? Take full advantage of your networking skills. Ask yourself, 'Who do I know that might know someone who works for the company?' The second thing you can do is find out the name of someone at that company, or someone who works in the industry you want to enter, and contact them directly. One way to do this is to read trade journals and track down the people who wrote the articles that were of interest to you. Even if the person is a top-level executive, if you tell their secretary that you read their article in whatever publication it was in, you'll almost always be allowed to talk with that person. Ask that person intelligent questions about their article, and try to discover who they know that might be able to make an introduction for you into a company.

"If you don't have any connections within a company, in addition to sending your résumé to the human resources department start by targeting a specific executive within the company that is in charge of the division you want to work in. Target the executive by name, and personalize all of your correspondence."

"TALK ABOUT WHY YOU WANT TO WORK FOR A COMPANY AND WHY YOU BELIEVE YOU SHOULD BE HIRED."

What are the skills that soon-to-be or recent college grads must have?

"Good communication skills are extremely important. You also must be able to express what you're good at and know how to speak up for yourself. Having at least a brief taste of what the real world is like before actually launching your career is helpful. You can get a preview by taking a summer job, an after-school job, or an internship before you graduate. Even if you have a superior education, what you will be lacking is real-world exposure, which is something you can only get through firsthand work experience. It's not something that can be taught in the classroom. Having good self-esteem and knowing how to perform research is also important." All of these skills can be learned by taking classes, reading books, and through real-world experience, although it will take time and practice to master them.

LAST WORD

"For someone who is still in school or who has recently graduated, I highly recommend making full use of the school's career placement office. If there are other colleges or universities in your area, you might also want to visit their career placement offices and check out what job opportunities they have listings for. As a backup or alternate resource, you can use an outside consulting or career counseling service, but you'll often have to pay to use these services."

THE TOP 10
THINGS YOU JUST GOTTA DO

NOW FOR SOME LAST WORDS
AND A FEW FINAL THOUGHTS...

Obviously, not all of the advice provided within this book pertains specifically to you. However, no matter what type of career you're planning to pursue, much of the advice should prove extremely useful. Remember, everyone featured within this book was once in exactly the same position as you are now. They managed to reach the top and achieve a high level of success, and now, by reading this book, you're in a position to benefit by learning from their mistakes and experiences. Not only do the people featured within this book discuss their own experiences, they also know firsthand what employers are looking for in today's job market.

Unfortunately, there is no surefire, guaranteed way to get yourself a job. Understanding the process, however, and being prepared for what you encounter in the real world are your best tools for success. Ultimately, whether or not your receive a job is entirely up to you and how you present yourself through your résumé and during your job interviews. If you managed to graduate from college, then you have the basic skills and knowledge you'll need to enter the work force. The experience will come with time.

Now that you've read the wisdom of some of the hottest business leaders in America, here's a quick summary of some of the key points you should keep in mind when preparing your résumé, preparing for an interview, choosing whether or not to accept a job offer, and managing your time during the whole job-search process.

WHEN PREPARING A RÉSUMÉ...

1. Keep it short and to the point. If your résumé is more then one side of an 8.5" x 11" piece of paper, shorten it.

2. Your résumé MUST be typed, but don't use fancy fonts or typestyles.

3. Print your résumé on good-quality white paper.

4. Customize your résumé to match the job you're applying for.

5. Don't include your hobbies on a résumé, unless they relate directly to the job you're applying for, or help to portray you as a well-rounded person. Be sure to list your accomplishments and skills, along with your goals.

6. If applicable, do *not* include you current salary or earning history in your résumé.

7. If the company you'll be submitting your résumé to uses a computerized résumé management system, and will be scanning your résumé into their system, use as many key words and phrases as you can in order to describe your work experience and goals. Also, keep the format of your résumé simple.

8. Reread your résumé CAREFULLY, and fix any "speling" mistakes and typos.

Now, reread it two or three more times, and really fix all of the spelling mistakes and typos. Finally, have someone else read your résumé to make sure that it's perfect—*before* you send it out.

9. Never send a photocopy of your résumé. Don't just send your résumé to the human resources or personnel department of a company. Also, target an executive within the company that's in charge of the division you're hoping to work in. If you're applying for a job in the marketing department, for example, send a copy of your résumé to the vice president of marketing at the company.

10. Write a personalized and custom-written cover letter to accompany each résumé you submit to a company. Keep the cover letter short, but make it upbeat and attention-getting. Be sure to highlight your skills and/or experiences that might not be featured on your résumé. Don't repeat information. Also, within the cover letter, show that you have a general knowledge about the company you're applying to. After sending your résumé, wait a few days and follow it up with a telephone call to ensure that it was received. At this point, try to schedule an interview.

BEFORE AND DURING THE JOB INTERVIEW...

1. Dress professionally! Sorry, no jeans, T-shirts, or sneakers. Remove nose rings, tongue posts, and any other forms of personal expression that don't fit in in the work environment. (There are exceptions to this rule—for example, if you're applying for a job in the entertainment industry where the dress code is often casual.)

2. Do research about the company you're about to interview with.

3. Create a list of questions that you plan to ask the employer during the interview. Don't ask about salary, benefits, or vacations until late in the interview process. If possible, try waiting until the employer brings up these topics.

4. Practice doing mock interviews with a friend or parent. Try to determine the types of questions you're going to be asked, and think about how you plan to answer those questions. Visualize yourself during the interview making a good impression.

5. Show up early for the interview. Whatever you do, don't be even one minute late!

6. From the moment you step through the door of the company you're interviewing with, act professionally.

7. Be polite to EVERYONE you meet at the company.

8. Never lie or stretch the truth about anything. Be open and honest about yourself, your skills, and your work experience.

9. Don't babble, but answer all questions in complete sentences, not just with a "yes" or "no" response.

10. When you get home after the interview, immediately write and send a personalized thank you note to the person or people who interviewed you. Make reference to something specific that you discussed during the interview to refresh the interviewer's mind about who you are.

TO DETERMINE IF YOU'LL REALLY ENJOY THE JOB YOU'RE APPLYING FOR...

1. On a piece of paper, write down what you believe are your biggest strengths and most useful skills. What do you think your weaknesses are? Be honest with yourself. Nobody else has to see this list.

2. Now, write down what your interests are. What type of work do you think you'll enjoy doing?

3. Write a fictitious job description that would represent what you feel is the ideal job for you. As you ultimately apply for each job, compare the job you're applying for with the job description you wrote. In an ideal situation, you want both descriptions to be similar.

4. Think about, and then write down, your professional/career goal(s) for the upcoming year. The next 3 years. The next 5 years. The next 10 years. Try to be specific.

5. Do research and determine several industries that require people with your skills and interests. Visit your local or school library, or use your computer to access on-line databases and reference materials. Read newspaper and magazine articles that relate to the industries you select. Talk to as many people as you can that are currently working in the industries you choose.

6. Within the industries you select, pinpoint several specific companies that you think you might want to work for.

7. Do the jobs you're applying for involve doing work that you enjoy and that interests you? Do the jobs you're applying for offer the opportunity for you to learn new skills and challenge yourself? What type of career path (promotion opportunities) do the jobs offer?

8. What are the people like that you'll be working with? Is your personality similar to theirs?

9. Are the work environments within the companies you're applying to places where you think you'll be productive and happy?

10. Will the job you're applying for allow you to work your way closer to achieving your long-term goals?

PUTTING DAY-TIMERS' 4-DIMENSIONAL TIME MANAGEMENT SYSTEM TO WORK FOR YOU WHEN APPLYING FOR JOBS

During his interview for this book, Day-Timers' President, Loren Hulber, talked about what his company calls its 4-Dimensional Time Management System. Using some of the concepts that make up this system, you can take what seems like a monumental task of finding and applying for a job and transform it into something that's very manageable.

In general, if you consider yourself to be a totally unorganized person who gets easily distracted, or you somehow never find the time to work toward accomplishing your goals, then you should consider learning more about the Day-Timers' 4-Dimensional Time Management System. The skills you will learn will help you achieve success once you launch your career.

The key elements of the 4-Dimensional Time Management System are:

☞ **Focus**

☞ **Plan**

☞ **Act**

☞ **Team Up**

FOCUS

Okay, what's your ultimate goal for the immediate future? To get yourself a job...right? That's your "Mission Statement." Well, to get that job, there are many tasks you're going to have to accomplish first.

Whatever you do, don't make the mistake of trying to accomplish everything at once.

Off the top of your head, list some of the tasks that you must accomplish that will lead to your getting a job. Right now, don't worry about the order or the importance of each task as you list them. Begin simply by getting this list down on paper. Here are some ideas to get you started:

☞ **Define your capabilities and skills**

☞ **Determine who your references will be**

☞ **Select industries that you're interested in working in**

☞ **Define your personal goals**

☞ **Find specific job openings at companies you want to work for**

☞ **Network to find additional job opportunities or to make introductions into companies that you want to work for**

☞ **Create a résumé**

☞ **Research the industries and companies you're interested in**

☞ **Draft a cover letter to accompany your résumé**

☞ **Put together a list of the jobs you're going to apply for. Select the person/department you're**

continues

going to send your résumé/cover letter to.

☞ **Develop a personalized address book that contains the names, phone numbers, addresses, e-mail addresses, and other pertinent information about each company. You can use a traditional address book, a pad of paper, or contact management software for your computer.**

☞ **Customize your résumé and cover letter for each job you're going to apply to.**

☞ **Send your résumé/cover letter**

☞ **Follow up your résumé with a phone call.**

☞ **Schedule job interviews**

☞ **Prepare for interviews**

☞ **Follow up interviews with a thank you note**

Looking at this list, the whole job search thing may seem totally overwhelming. The truth is, this is a big job, but if you plan carefully, and divide your ultimate goal into a series of many smaller, easier-to-attain goals, then your chances of success just improve dramatically. During this Focus phase of your job search, you must define a purpose or mission—get yourself a job.

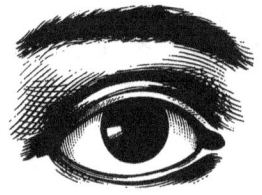

PLAN

The trick to accomplishing each of the tasks listed in the Focus section is to organize them, prioritize them, and then develop an organized plan of action. Let's begin by taking the list of tasks we created a moment ago, establishing it, and putting each item in the order in which you'll have to accomplish it. Under each task, you should also list relevant subtasks.

☞ **Define your personal goals and objectives. What you do want out of your job in both the short and long term?**

☞ **Define your capabilities and skills— what are you really good at?**

☞ **Define your weaknesses—what skills or knowledge do you think you currently lack? What can you do in the short or long term to overcome these weaknesses?**

☞ **Based on your personal interests, strengths, and weaknesses, what industries have jobs that you are most suited for?**

☞ **Perform research on the industries you select, and learn more about them. What companies within those industries would you be interested in working for? Perform additional research on those specific companies. Keep a list of potential company names, phone numbers, and addresses.**

- ☞ Find out about the job openings available at the companies you're interested in. Do this by networking, reading "Help Wanted" ads, attending job fairs, visiting the career placement office at your school, visiting each company's World Wide Web site, and/or by calling up each company's human resources department.

- ☞ Draft a general résumé for yourself

- ☞ Draft a general cover letter that can accompany your résumé

- ☞ Put together a list of references you plan to include on your résumé or in your cover letter. Contact those people directly, and get their permission to use them as a reference before you include them.

- ☞ Put together a list of the job openings at the companies you want to apply for.

- ☞ Customize your résumé to match each job opening and then customize your cover letter to the person you're sending it to at that company.

- ☞ Develop your personalized address/phone book of companies and contacts. As you proceed, keep detailed notes about all contacts you have with each company. You can do this on paper, or by using specialized contact management software on your computer.

A few of the contact management software packages that you can purchase from your local computer or office supply superstore include: Day-Timer Organizer®, Lotus Organizer®, ACT!®, and Microsoft Schedule+®. Most of these software packages cost under $100, and can be used to manage all of your contacts and scheduling information. Specialized CD-ROM software packages designed to help applicants create their résumé and find a job, such as *Tom Jackson Presents The Perfect Résumé* (Davison & Associations), also feature contact management programs.

- ☞ Send out your résumé/cover letter to the people you decide to target within the companies you want to work for.

- ☞ Wait several days after sending your résumé/cover letter. If you don't hear from the company, follow up with a telephone call.

- ☞ Set up job interviews with companies that are interested in you.

- ☞ Prepare for the interview. Do additional research about the companies you're about to interview with. Decide what you're going to wear and how you're going to present yourself. Put together a list of questions you plan to ask during the interview. Practice answering interview questions with a friend or relative.

continues

☞ **Go for the job interviews—show up on time, dressed appropriately, and be totally prepared. Remember, attitude is everything.**

☞ **Immediately follow up each interview with a personalized thank you note. Make sure you spell the name of the person/ people you met with correctly.**

ACT

The next step is to take your plans and put them into action—one step at a time. Get your hands on a calendar or date book, such as a Day-Timer. On today's date, write "Start Job Search." Now, go through the above list, and based on your personal schedule, determine realistically how long each task will take you to accomplish. Next, add up the total number of days you think it will take you to complete all of these tasks, and mark that date on your calendar. This is the date (your deadline) for accomplishing your ultimate goal—getting a job.

Based on the timetable you create for each task, add each task to your calendar/ planner. You now have a complete set of small goals which you have to complete by specific dates in order to stay on schedule.

Now, look at today's goal and forget about everything else for the moment. Today's goal is to focus all of your energy on defining your personal goals and objectives. If you allocated one day for this task, sit down with a pen and a pad and start thinking about what you want out of your life and what you want out of your job.

Define your family, career, financial, social, leisure, health, and self-development goals.

Right now, if your current full-time activity is to get yourself a job, then that's what you should be doing. If you can't concentrate on this work at home or in your dorm room, find someplace quiet, where you can think and work productively. Pay careful attention to the small goals you have set and have written down on your calendar/planner, and do your best to stay on target.

At the start of each day, refer to your calendar to determine what your goal for that day is, then spend a few minutes to write down the specific tasks you must accomplish that day in order to achieve that goal. Prioritize this list based on order of importance, placing the most important tasks at the top of the list.

So, let's say today's task is putting together your list of references. For example, your goals for the day might include: making a list of the references you'd like to use, tracking down old bosses from summer jobs and internships, and calling each reference personally to ask them for permission to list them as a job reference. Also, think about whether you'd benefit from having your references write letters of recommendation, or if you'd be better off having potential employers call your references.

As you work your way through each task, put forth your very best effort and maintain a positive attitude. You WILL get yourself the job that you want and that you'll enjoy, but you must do the necessary work to get it. Visualize yourself working in the perfect job, and keep thinking about what it'll take for you to actually land that dream job.

TEAM UP

The final portion of the 4-Dimensional Time Management System involves teamwork. When you're finding yourself a job, this is primarily something you have to do on your own, because it's ultimately you that must sell yourself to a company. You can, however, use your networking skills to find job leads and make introductions for you into companies. If you have close friends or relatives who have been through this whole experience, perhaps they can assist you in accomplishing some of the tasks that you'll need to complete in order to get yourself a job. Don't be afraid to use every resource that's at your disposal, including the career placement office at your school.

ONE FINAL THOUGHT...

This book has allowed you to benefit from the work-related experience of some very successful people in many different types of industries. Now you should consider taking advantage of the people around you (friends, friends' parents, relatives, neighbors, etc.) and try to learn from their experiences. Don't pursue jobs or opportunities because your parents want you to, or because that's what your friends are doing. You're the person who must show up for work each day once you land a job, so find opportunities that *you* want to pursue. It's no coincidence that virtually every business leader interviewed within this book stated how important it is that you love the work you do!

INDEX

A&M Records, 151
ACCO World Corporation, 39
Adion Human Resource Communications, 130
Alexis de Tocqueville Society of the United Way of Southeastern New England, 98
Alexis, Kim, 65
Alumni, contacting, 100
America Online, ix, 103, 121, 130. *See also* Internet; World Wide Web.
American Brands, 39
Arakawa, Minoru, 12
ARCO test preparation titles, 181
Armani, Giorgio, 89
AT&T, 105
A.T. Cross Company. *See also* Boss, Russell A.
    company background, 97
Audi, 111

Berenger, Tom, 65
Bergin, Michael, 65
Berman, Rick, 143, 145
Betty Crocker cookbooks, 181
BLIMPIE International, 26, 29, 30, 31. *See also* Conza, Anthony P.
    company background, 25
    web site address, xi
Bose, Amar, Dr., 111–16
    background of Bose Corporation, 111
    on choosing a career, 113–14
    on how to think and solve problems, 113

on internships, 116
on making a good first impression during interview, 116
on networking, 116
on paying attention to the human aspect of the business, 115
personal history, 112
questions applicant should ask company's employees outside interview situation, 114–15
questions applicants should ask during interview process, 114
on surviving the job interview, 115
Bose Corporation, 112, 113. *See also* Bose, Amar, Dr.
    company background, 111
Boss, Russell A., 97–109
    advice to recent graduates setting career-related goals, 99
    background of A.T. Cross Company, 97
    finding the best job opportunities, 100
    importance of career guidance and alumni offices, 100
    importance of having an advanced degree, 99–100
    importance of work experience outside family business, 99
    on interviews, 100, 101–2

on networking, 100, 101
personal history, 98
personal pressure in joining family business, 98–99
taking tests to determine career choice, 99
Boy Scouts of America, 98
Boys & Girls Clubs of America, 26
Bradbury, Edward W., 97
Business Week, 27, 73, 139

Career Center, web site address, 123
Career Development Team, Inc., The. *See also* Jackson, Tom
    company background, 189
Career goals, setting, 3–4, 13, 22, 91, 99, 135, 136, 145–46, 152–53, 161–62, 168–69
Career Magazine, web site address, 123
CareerMosaic, web site address, xi, 123
CareerNET, web site address, 123
Career placement office, 100, 192, 194
CareerWEB, web site address, 123
Casio, Inc., 82, 87. *See also* McDonald, John J.
    company background, 81
    web site address, xi
CBS, 137
CEO Exchange, The, 130
Chadsey, Jack, 89–95
    background of Sunglass Hut International, Inc., 89
    developing long-term strategies, 95

205

Chadsey, Jack, *continued*
    on follow-up, 93
    on importance of network-
        ing, 92
    on importance of résumé, 92
    on job satisfaction, 94
    making a good impression
        during an interview, 93
    on owning and operating your
        own store, 95
    personal history, 89–90
    personal obstacles that had to
        be overcome 94–95
    on preparing a résumé, 92–93
    questions applicant should ask
        during interview, 93–94
    on setting job-related goals, 91
    on skills needed to be successful
        in retail, 94
    on best way to find opportuni-
        ties in retail, 90
    on what it takes to be successful
        working in a retail
        environment, 91
Champs Sports, 59–60
Charlie Brown's, 19
City Year, 73–74
College Grad Job Hunter, web site
    address, 123
Communication skills, 127, 170,
    179, 194. *See also* Interper-
    sonal skills
    definition of, 127
Complete Idiot's Guide, The, 181
CompUSA, 39
Compuserve, ix, 130
Computer City, 39
Computerized résumé scanning
    programs, 163
Conza, Anthony P., 25–31
    A.C.T. (Attitude/Communica-
        tion/Tolerance/Think)
        guideline, 29–30
    background of BLIMPIE
        International, 25
    on cover letters, 28
    on having a mentor, 31
    on having a positive attitude, 27
    on job satisfaction, 30–31
    on interviews, 28–29
    on launching a career, 27

    on lessons learned from starting
        his own business, 26–27
    personal history, 25–26
    personal philosophy toward
        success, 29
    on personal obstacles that had
        to be overcome, 31
    questions applicant should ask
        during interview, 29
    on résumés, 28
    on personal motivation, 31
Cooper, Jane, 167–73
    on advantages of good grades, 172
    advice for women working in
        a corporate environ-
        ment, 173
    background of Paramount
        Parks, 167
    biggest challenge faced, 173
    difference between larger and
        small companies, 170
    finding the best job opportuni-
        ties, 169–70
    importance of communication
        between employees and
        employers, 171–72
    importance of communication
        skills, 170
    on interviews, 171
    on networking, 169–70
    personal history, 168
    personal motivation, 173
    questions applicant should ask
        during interview, 172
    on reading the personality of a
        company, 172
    on résumés, 171
    setting career-related goals,
        168–69
Cooper's and Lybrand, 182, 183
Costner, Kevin, 65
Cover letter, 92, 155, 156, 199–
    200, 201
    custom written, 28, 44–45, 105,
        187, 200
    difference from résumé, 37
    what to include, 45, 85, 106
Crain's New York Business, 52
Cross, Alonzo Townsend, 97
Cross, Benjamin, 97
Cross, Richard, 97

Davis, Michael, 137–41
    background of Motown
        Animation, 137
    dressing appropriately for
        interviews, 140
    maintaining sense of
        humor, 141
    making a good impression at
        interviews, 138–39
    on networking, 140
    on personal business cards, 139
    personal history, 137–38
    questions applicant should
        ask during inter-
        view, 139
    on résumés, 139, 140
    on setting goals, 139
Day-Timers, Inc. *See also* Hulber,
    Loren J.
    company background, 39
    4-Dimensional Time Manage-
        ment System, 199
    web site address, xi
Dayton Hudson Corporation, 89
Definitive Internet Career Guide,
    The (Oakland University),
    web site address, 123
DeVries, Bill
    advice on getting started, 60–61
    background of Foot Locker, 59
    dressing appropriately for
        interviews, 62
    how to choose companies to
        apply to in retail, on 60
    on importance of network-
        ing, 61
    mistakes people make when
        applying for a job,
        62–63
    on-the-job training, 61
    overcoming obstacles, 63
    personal history, 59
    personal qualities that have
        allowed for success, 63
    on résumés, 62
    questions applicants should ask
        on interviews, on 62
    on setting career goals, 63
Diesel Shades, 89
Downsizing, 17, 83

Egghead Software, 39
Eisner, Michael, 139
Electronic résumé databases, 135
E-mail, x
  computerized scanning of
      résumé, 131–32
  follow-up with company, 133
  format for résumé, 133
  using to submit résumé, 120, 132
Employment agencies, 107
Esch, Natasha, 65–71
  background of Wilhelmina
      Models, 65
  biggest mistakes young people
      make, 68
  breaking into the modeling
      industry, 67–68
  importance of grades in
      school, 70
  making a good impression
      during an interview, 69
  personal history, 66
  questions applicant should ask
      during interview, 69–70
  on résumés, 68–69
Entry level jobs, 5, 14, 15, 21, 34,
      35, 54, 58, 60, 68, 77–78, 85,
      90, 131, 136, 147, 160, 167,
      177, 188
Equinox Corporation. See also
      Jackson, Tom
  company background, 189

Family business
  acquiring outside work
      experience, 99
  challenges women face, 38
  preparing to enter into, 74–75
  proving yourself, 75
Fendi, 89
Fields, Debbi, 1–9
  advice for young people setting
      career goals, 3–4
  advice for women, 8–9
  advice on finding a job you'll
      love, 4
  background of Mrs. Fields
      Cookies, 1
  dressing appropriately for
      interviews, 5
  on interviews, 3–4, 6–7

  mistakes people make when
      applying for a job, 6
  personal history, 1–3
  personal qualities that allowed
      for success, 7–8;
  questions applicant should ask
      during interview, 5
  on résumés, 6
  selecting the place to work for,
      on, 5
  skills not taught in school, on, 6
  transforming a dream into an
      international business,
      on, 2
Filo, David, 118, 119
First Job, Great Job, web site
      address, xi, 123
Flanders, Scott, 181–88
  background of Macmillan
      Publishing USA, 181
  on believing in yourself,
      183, 184
  biggest personal career-related
      risk, 183
  failure as a learning experience,
      184
  on flexibility, 184
  on getting foot in the door at a
      company, 186–87
  having passion for a job, 183, 186
  importance of advanced degree,
      182–83
  making a good impression
      during interview, 187
  passing on a job offer, 183
  personal history, 181–82
  personal motivation, 186
  on résumés, 185–86, 187
  setting career-related goals, 186,
      188
  taking marketing class in school,
      184–85
  on taking risks, 183, 184
  as tax and business consultant,
      182, 186
  understanding your strengths
      and weaknesses, 187
Foot Locker, x, 60. See also Bill
      DeVries
  company background, 59
Forbes, 27, 139
Ford Motor Company, 137

Four Dimensional Time Manage-
      ment System (Focus/Plan/
      Act/Team Up), 41, 199–203
Franchises. See BLIMPIE
      International; Mrs. Fields
      Cookies
Frommer's, 181

Gaultier, Jean Paul, 89
General Motors, 111
Graphics Arts Association of
      Michigan, 40, 41
Greenblatt, Sherwin, 112
Guess, 89

Hall of Fame at Frank Hawkins
      Institute of Private
      Enterprise, 26
Head-hunting firms, 107
Honda, 111
Hotel/resort industry
  career track for management
      in, 35
  experience need for, 34
  finding best positions in, 35
  importance of networking
      in, 36
  job satisfaction, 38
Houston, Whitney, 65
Hulber, Loren J., 39–49, 199
  background of Day-Timers, 39
  on being organized and stress-
      free, 42–43
  on cover letters, 44–45
  difference between a job and
      career, 43
  dressing appropriately for
      interviews, 49
  4-Dimensional Time Manage-
      ment System, 199–203
  on getting a good job even if
      you earned poor grades
      in school, 47
  how to master organizational
      skills and time
      management, 42
  on internships, 46
  key to personal success, 40–41
  on networking, 41–42
  organizing job search, 48–49

Hulber, Loren J., *continued*
   overcoming anxiety before and
      during a job interview, 48
   personal history, 40
   on qualities sought in a
      potential employee,
      43–44
   questions applicant should ask
      during interview, 45–46
   questions applicants should
      avoid asking during
      interview, 47
   on résumés, 44–45
   on showing skills to a
      prospective employer, 42
Human resources, 17, 35, 37, 76, 77,
   84, 92, 101, 120, 162, 187

IBM, 159
Image Comics, 137
Inc., 104, 139
Insight, 151
Institute of American Entrepre-
   neurs, 26
Intermec Corporation, 124
International Francise Associa-
   tion, 26
Internet advertising, 117–18
Internet, ix, x, 66, 90, 117, 118, 119,
   121, 129, 130. *See* Career
   Development Team, Inc.;
   Lotus Development Corp.;
   Monster Board, The; World
   Wide Web; Yahoo! Inc.,
   using to find a job, 120
Internships, 45, 191, 194
   importance of, 46, 47, 57, 68,
      93, 116, 179
Interpersonal skills
   describing within a résumé for
      computer scanning, 132
   how to acquire, 7, 22–23, 94,
      126–27
   importance of, 94, 101, 126
Interview(s), 115, 171, 178
   acting professional during, 15,
      29, 37–38, 93, 101, 197
   advice about the process, 54,
      57, 101
   avoiding slang words
      during, 141

being punctual, 6, 70, 156–57,
   164, 197
follow-up, 93, 102, 197, 202
importance of recommenda-
   tions, 101, 106
making a good impression, 15,
   49, 54–55, 69, 76–77, 93,
   106–7, 116, 138–39, 148,
   163, 187, 192–93
mistakes to avoid during, 23,
   62–63, 93, 115, 126,
   131, 140
overcoming anxiety and
   nervousness, 6–7, 48,
   107, 192
preparing for, 107, 125–26, 192,
   197, 201
qualities employers look for, 44
questions applicant should ask,
   5, 16–17, 29, 38, 45–46,
   55–56, 62, 69–70, 78,
   84–85, 93, 101, 107, 114,
   126, 139, 148, 172, 179,
   187, 193, 197
questions applicant should be
   prepared to answer, 3–4,
   70, 85–86, 101, 164
researching company prior
   to, 197
sending personalized thank you
   note, 139, 197
showing understanding of
   company, 29
techniques for, 15, 16, 28–29
ten tips for before and
   during, 197
topics to avoid asking during, 47,
   56, 69, 84–85, 94, 107, 192
what to wear to, 6, 15, 49, 55,
   62, 69, 77, 84, 106, 134,
   140, 164, 197, 202

Jackson, Reggie, 3
Jackson, Tom, 189–94
   deciding what type of career to
      pursue, 190–91
   importance of communication
      skills, 194
   making a good impression
      during interviews,
      192–93

on internships, 191, 194
on networking, 191, 193–94
personal history, 189, 190
on references, 192
on résumés, 191–92, 193
J.K. Lasser tax guides, 181
Job hopping, 53, 71, 105, 109, 169
Job interviews. *See* Interviews
Job satisfaction, 4, 30, 38, 78, 79, 94,
   135–36, 165
   ten tips for determining level
      of, 198
Job search
   applying to several compa-
      nies, 63
   Day-Timers' 4-Dimensional
      Time Management
      System, 199–203
   importance of networking, 101
   organizing for, 48–49, 199–203
   questions to ask prior to start
      of, 53, 99, 135, 198, 199
JobSource, web site address, 123
Job training programs for
   restaurants, 21, 22–23
JobTrack, web site address, xi
JobTrak, 121–22
JobWeb, web site address, 123
Johnson, Beverly, 65
Jose Limon Dance Company, 26

Kaleidoscope, 151
Kaplan On-Line Career Center, web
   site address, 123
Karan, Donna, 89
Kashio Manufacturing, 81
Kashio, Kazuo, 81
Kashio, Tadao, 81, 82
Kashio, Yukio, 81
Kids Foot Locker, 59, 60
Kinney, 59, 60
Klein, Calvin, 89
Konheim, Bud, 51–58
   advice for achieving long-term
      success, 57–58
   background for Nicole Miller,
      Inc., 51
   finding stimulating work
      experiences, on 56–57
   how to approach career search
      and choice, 52

on importance of internships, 57
on importance of loving your work, 53
on interview process, 54, 55
personal history, 52
questions applicant should ask during interview, 54–55
questions to ask yourself prior to beginning job search, 53
starting out at a low paying entry-level job, 58
Koogle, Tim, 124–27
background of Yahoo! Inc., 117
on interpersonal skills, 126–27
mistakes applicants make when applying for a job, 126
personal history, 124–25
preparing for a job interview, 125–26
questions applicant should ask during interview, 126
on résumés, 126

Lady Foot Locker, 59, 60
Language, second, importance of, 179–80
Lange, Jessica, 65
Leach, Robin, 52
Lee, Pamela Anderson, 65
Lincoln, Howard, 11–17
background of Nintendo of America, Inc., 11
dressing appropriately for job interviews, 15
how to find best job opportunities, 14–15
on interviews, 16–17
on joining the military, 12
lessons learned from parents, 13
on networking, 17
personal history, 11–12
qualities sought in potential employee, 15
questions applicant should ask during interview, on, 16–17
on résumés, 15
on setting personal career goals, 13

Logan, Doug, 175–80
adapting to change, 180
background of Major League Soccer, 175
importance of communication skills, 179
importance of internships, 179
on interviews, 178
on networking, 179
not being afraid of taking risks, 177
personal history, 176
questions applicant should ask during interview, 179
on résumés, 178
viewing first job as a learning experience, 177
Long hours, working, 14, 145, 171
Lotus Development Corp., See also Zisman, Michael D.
company background, 159
web site address, xi, 163

Macmillan Publishing USA, xi, 181, 182, 185. See also Flanders, Scott
company background, 181
web site address, xi
Magnavox, 151
Major League Soccer, xi, 175, 176. See also Logan, Doug
company background, 175
web site address, xi
Marantz, 151
Margaret Riley's Job Guide, web site address, 123
Marshall Field's, 89
Marvyn's, 89
May Department Stores, 89
McCann, Jim, 103–9
background of 1-800-FLOWERS, 103
on cover letter, 105–6
on developing financial security, 108–9
on developing new skills and experiences, 105
importance of daydreams and fantasies, 108
importance of familiarity with technology, 105

importance of having early work exposures, 104
importance of working in different types of jobs, 109
making a good first impression during an interview, 106–7
on networking, 106
overcoming nervousness before and during an interview, 107
personal history, 103–4
personal qualities that allowed for success, 107–8
on postponing marriage and family life, 108
questions applicant should ask during interview, 107
on résumés, 105–6
working with a head-hunting firm or an employment agency, 107
McDonald, John J., 81–87
background of Casio, Inc., 81
on common sense, 87
on consistency, 86
finding job opportunities, 83–84
on interviews, 84, 85–86
mistakes applicants make, 82–83
on networking, 83–84
opinion of current business world, 83
personal history, 81
personal skills that led to success, 86
pros and cons of working at a non-American-owned corporation, 87
questions that the applicant should ask, 84–85
on résumés, 84, 85
selecting a company to work for, 83
McDonald's, 124
Microsoft Network, The, ix
Milestone Media, 138
Miller, Nicole
background of Nicole Miller, Inc., 51
dressing appropriately for interviews, 55

Miller, Nicole, *continued*
   finding stimulating work
      experiences, 56–57
   how to approach career search
      and choice, 52
   on importance of intern-
      ships, 57
   on interviews, 54–55
   on leaving a job if you hate it,
      53–54
   personal history, 52
   questions applicant should
      ask during interview,
      54–55
Modeling industry
   breaking into, 67–68
   difference between large and
      small agencies, 68
   importance of internships, 68
   networking, 68
   what to wear for interviews, 69
Monster Board, The, 133–34. *See*
   also Taylor, Jeff
   company background, 129–30
   using to find job openings,
      136
   web site address, xi, 123, 136
Motorola, 124
Motown, 151
Motown Animation. *See also* Davis,
   Michael
   company background, 137
Motown Records, 137
Mrs. Fields Cookies, 1–2, 7, 8. *See*
   also Fields, Debbi.
   company background, 1

National Restaurant Association, 26
NBC, 137
Nervousness during interviews,
   overcoming, 6–7, 48, 107
Networking
   definition of, 42
   how to begin, 42, 100
   importance of, 17, 22, 36, 41–
      42, 61, 68, 76, 92, 101,
      106, 116, 140, 146–47,
      155, 179, 191, 193–94
New York State Restaurant
   Association, 26

Nicole Miller, Inc., ix, 54, 55, 57. *See*
   also Miller, Nicole;
   Konheim, Bud
   company history, 51
   web site address, xi
Nintendo of America, Inc., 12. *See*
   also Lincoln, Howard
   company background, 11
   web site address, xi
Nintendo Power, 11

Oakland A's, 3
Oakley, 89
Office Depot, 39
Office Max, 39
Olive Garden, 21
On-campus recruiting, 162
1-800-FLOWERS, x. *See also*
   McCann, Jim
   company background, 103
   web site address, xi
Outback Steakhouse, 5

P.J. Walsh, 51, 52
Paramount Parks, 171, 173. *See also*
   Cooper, Jane
   company background, 167
   web site addresses, xi
Perfect Résumé, The, 189, 191, 201
Philips Electronics, 151
Philips Media Home and Family
   Entertainment, 153, 155. *See*
   also Simon, Sarina
   company background,
      151, 152
   web site address, xi
Philips, Gerard, 151
Pillar, Michael, 143, 145
PolyGram, 151
PolyGram Home Video, 151
Positive attitude, 5, 7, 27
Prodigy, 130

Que Corporation, 182, 183, 186

Ray-Ban, 89
Recruitment office, 116
References, 6, 37, 76, 192

Research, importance of, 16, 27–28,
   69, 71, 76, 93, 100, 154–55,
   179, 192
Restaurant Associates Corp., 20. *See*
   also Valenti, Nick
   company background, 19
   web site address, xi
Restaurant industry
   difference between working for
      a large chain and
      individual business, 21
   obtaining practical experi-
      ence, 20
   résumé-writing for jobs in, 23
   training program, 21, 22, 23
Résumé City, 129
Résumé(s)
   computerized scanning of,
      132, 163
   customizing, 106, 196, 200
   format for submitting via e-
      mail, 133
   importance of cover letter, 28,
      44, 85, 105, 187
   references in, 6
   sending with personal referral,
      17, 36, 92
   software packages, 189, 191
   spelling in, 37, 38, 156, 163, 196
   submitting electronically, 120,
      132–33
   techniques to avoid, 15–16, 23,
      36, 77, 84, 92, 131, 163,
      178, 196
   ten tips for preparing, 196
   what to include in, 6, 15–16, 23,
      36–37, 44–45, 53, 62,
      68–69, 85, 92–93, 105–6,
      126, 131–32, 139, 140,
      147–48, 155, 156, 162,
      171, 178, 185–86, 187,
      191–92, 193, 196, 199–
      200, 201
   where to send, 17, 27, 28, 69,
      92, 101, 120, 156, 162,
      187, 196
   writing for computer
      scanning, 132
Retail business
   being flexible in, 63, 91
   choosing companies to apply to,
      60, 91

getting started for management
  position, 60–61, 90, 91
importance of customer
  service, 91
importance of personal
  interview, 62
networking in, 92
Revo, 89
Risk taking, importance of, 6, 95,
  157, 177, 183, 184
ROAR, 129–30
Roddenberry, Gene, 143

Search, Inc. 130
Seattle Mariners, 12
Sidewalk Studio, 151
Simon & Schuster, 181, 182
Simon, Sarina, 151–57
  background of Philips Media
    Home and Family
    Entertainment, 151
  on cover letters, 155, 156
  importance of researching about
    a company, 154–55
  mistakes applicants make in
    interviews, 156–57
  on networking, 155
  personal history, 152–54
  on résumés, 155, 156
  setting her own career-related
    goals, 152–53
  on taking risks, 157
  on what it takes to be
    successful in a large
    company, 154
Soft-Switch, Inc., 159–60
Sonesta Hotels, 34. See also
    Sonnabend, Stephanie
  company background, 33
  web site address, xi
Sonnabend, Stephanie
  as big-picture thinker, 38
  background of Sonesta Hotels, 33
  best career track to manage a
    hotel or resort, 35
  challenges faced by women in
    the workplace, on 38
  finding the best positions at
    hotels and resorts, 35
  on getting a foot in the door of
    a company, 36

on having letters or recommen-
  dations, 36
on importance of cover letter, 37
on importance of networking, 36
on job satisfaction, 38
making a good impression
  during an interview, on
  37–38
personal history, 33
personality needed to work at
  hotel or resort, 35
personality traits that have
  allowed for success, 38
on résumés, 36, 37
on taking summer positions as
  interim jobs, 36
type of experience needed to
  break into hotel/resort
  business, 34
Sperry Rand Corporation, 81, 82
Staples, 39
Star Trek: Voyager, x, 144, 145, 147.
  See also Taylor, Jeri
  company background, 143
  web site address, xi
Success, 139
Success, achieving long-term, 57–58
Summer jobs, 23, 46, 94, 191, 194
  importance of, 179
Sunglass Hut International, Inc., 90,
  93, 94. See also Chadsey, Jack
  company background, 89
  web site address, xi
Swartz, Nathan, 74
Swartz, Sidney, 73–79
  advice for entering the
    workplace, 79
  background of The Timberland
    Company, 73
  on getting a job within a
    specific company, 77–78
  on getting noticed at a
    company, 76
  on hiring employees, 75–76
  importance of patience, 79
  making a good impression
    during an interview,
    76–77
  mistakes applicants make, 77
  personal history, 74
  personal qualities that allowed
    for success, 78–79

on preparing to enter a family
  business, 74–75
questions applicant should ask
  during interviews, 78

Target, 89
Taylor, Jeff, 129–36
  background of The Monster
    Board, 129–30
  dressing appropriately for
    interviews, 134
  electronic résumé databases, 135
  follow-up by phone, 133
  how the job market is changing,
    134–35
  on jobs with short-term
    payoffs, 136
  personal history, 130
  on résumés, 131, 132, 133
  setting job-related goals, 135, 136
  using e-mail to get a job, 132, 133
  using The Monster Board, 133–
    34, 136
  value of job-search firms for
    entry-level workers, 131
  writing résumés that will be
    scanned by computers,
    131–32, 133
Taylor, Jeri, 143–50
  advice for women, 149–50
  background of Star Trek:
    Voyager, 143
  goal-setting strategy, 146
  making a good impression at
    interviews, 148
  on networking, 146–47
  on not giving up, 150
  personal history, 143–45
  personal motivation, 149
  qualities sought in potential
    employees, 147
  questions applicant should ask
    during interview, 148
  on résumés, 147–48
  selling yourself too hard, on
    148–49
  setting career-related goals, on
    145–46
Temporary agencies, 76, 107
Tests that help determine career-
  suitability, 99

Thank you notes, sending, 139, 197
Timberland Company, The, 74, 75, 76, 77. *See also* Swartz, Sidney
  company background, 73
Time management skills, 41, 42–43, 199–203
TMP Worldwide, 129, 130
Toast Masters, 7

Unisys Corporation, 81
United Paramount Network, 145
USA Today, 27

Valenti, Nick, 19–23
  background of Restaurant Associates, Corp., 19
  getting a head start in the restaurant industry, 22
  how to set career-related goals, 22
  importance of restaurant's training program, 21
  on interviews, 23
  on networking, 22
  personal history, 19–20
  personal qualities that allowed for success, 23
  on résumés, 22
  on what applicant should look for when applying for a job, 22
  on what it takes to be successful in restaurant industy, 20–21
  on working for large restaurant chains or individual restaurants, 21
Versace, Gianni, 89
Viacom, Inc., 167

Wall Street Journal, 27, 73, 139
Walt Disney Company, 139, 153, 155
Webster's New World Dictionary, 181
Western Atlas, Inc. 124
Wilhelmina, 65
Wilhelmina Guide to Modeling, The, 66
Wilhelmina Models, 69. *See also* Esch, Natasha
  company background, 65
  web site address, xi, 66
Williams, William T., 138
Women
  advice for entering workplace, 8, 52
  advice working in a corporate environment, 173
  challenges faced, 8, 38, 71, 149–50
  managing career and family life, 8–9
Woolworth Corporation, 59, 60
World Wide Web, 90, 117, 119, 121, 122, 129
  illustrations of sample menus, 121, 122
  job postings, 163
  list of job/career-related sites, xi, 123

Yahoo! Inc., x, 117–18, 119, 120, 121, 124. *See also* Koogle, Tim; Yang, Jerry
  company background, 117
  web site address, xi
Yang, Jerry, 117–23
  advice to would-be entrepreneurs, 120–21
  background of Yahoo! Inc., 117–19
  goal of company, 119

personal history, 118–20
using Yahoo! and Internet to help find a job, 120
using Yahoo! to help launch a career, 121–22

Zisman, Michael D., 159–65
  advice on setting career goals, 161–62
  background of Lotus Development Corp., 159
  dressing appropriately in an interview, 164
  importance of a graduate degree, 160–61
  importance of staying flexible, 160
  making a good impression in an interview, 163–64
  on-campus recruiting, 162
  personal history, 159–60
  questions applicants will be asked in interviews, 164–65
  on résumés, 162–63
  on tenacity, 165

www.ingramcontent.com/pod-product-compliance
Lightning Source LLC
Chambersburg PA
CBHW081144180526
45170CB00006B/1918